GIGOLO

GIGOLO

BEN FOSTER WITH CLIFFORD THURLOW

THISTLE
PUBLISHING

This first edition published in 2018 by:

Thistle Publishing
36 Great Smith Street
London
SW1P 3BU

www.thistlepublishing.co.uk

PREFACE

The man was watching over half-moon glasses as I slipped my oiled hands over her narrow back, through the cheeks of her bottom and down her long slender legs.

He was wearing a white linen suit with a striped tie from some school or club. On the table in front of him was a single line of cocaine and a pair of gold earrings like two miniature wind chimes.

The plane banked and I almost toppled over.

'Don't stop now,' the woman said, her voice deep, commanding.

I grabbed the side of the table to regain balance and started again, working out the knot clusters in the area between her shoulder blades, releasing the pressure as she breathed in, applying it again as she breathed out.

'Yes, there, that's better.'

'Ten minutes to landing.' It was the pilot's voice over the speakers.

'Five more minutes,' she said firmly.

I continued making thumb circles over her shoulders, my legs braced during the descent. We were in an 8-seater Learjet, the interior pale cream with polished oak trim.

The man watching the massage removed his glasses and tucked them into a circular silver case that he slipped into his jacket pocket.

'Time to put some clothes on, darling,' he said.

She took a long breath through her nose and rolled over. She swung her legs around, sat on the edge of the table and fluttered her hand towards the closet at the rear.

'Get a dress for me, the white one,' she said, and I did so.

As I turned back, she was leaning over the table, trim and girlish in the amber lighting. She removed one of the thin tubes attached to the earrings, snorted the line of cocaine, reattached the tube and hooked the earrings in place. She dabbed her fingertips in the white dust left on the table and ran it over her gums. I held the dress as she stepped into it and ran the zip up her back. She went up on her toes as she swivelled round to face me.

'What would we do without you, Ben?' she said, and kissed me twice on the corners of my mouth. 'Now, what have you done with my shoes?'

I reached for them under the seat, white toeless pumps with red soles. She slipped them on, sat beside the man and took his hand.

'Two minutes to landing.'

I buckled up. I could see the Thames below snaking its way through the warren of steel and glass buildings. We landed at London City Airport and taxied into the zone marked for private jets. The exit door opened. The woman fluffed up her hair. The man straightened his tie, then pointed at the ministerial red box on the floor next to where he had been sitting.

'Bring the box for me, there's a good chap, it weighs a ton.'

We were waved through immigration and I followed them to the car park where a man with cropped greying hair and muscles bulging from a black tee-shirt stepped from a Range Rover with tinted windows.

'I'll take that, mate,' he said, and took the red box.

The driver opened the door for the woman, placed the box on the passenger seat and they purred quickly and silently into the distance.

I made my way back through the airport and got a ticket on the Docklands Light Railway. In my pack, I carried a present for Kelly, a box of Baci Italian chocolates wrapped in love notes.

1
TWO JOBS

It all began in 2006.

England was knocked out of the World Cup on penalties by Portugal. No surprise there. X-Factor winner Shayne Ward was top of the charts with *That's My Goal*. The *Daily Mirror* reported that chocolate was good for you; now I wouldn't have to feel guilty buying it for the kids. The temperature that summer hit 36° C (that's 97° F), and Warren Buffet, one of the richest men in the world, had given away $44 billion to health charities.

If I had that kind of money, I'd probably do the same. Don't they say what goes round comes round? I'd buy a new car first, though, mine was a piece of junk, a ten year old ex-postal van that had already done 127,000 miles when I bought it from a mate for a hundred quid. It ran more on prayer than petrol.

The radio was all right though and I sang along with Shayne Ward as I drove the 15 miles along the A 305 from our council house in Twickenham to Egham, where I began the evening shift at six at a place we called The Lodge, a gloomy grey building remodelled as a secure unit for young adults with learning disabilities.

I was a support worker on minimum wage. Kelly, my wife, did three afternoons a week in a laundry, and we had three little-ones aged two, four and five who broke my heart when I thought about all the things I wanted to do for them. It was hard enough trying to make a living now. What was it going to be like for them when they grew up?

You can't get by with only one job and I had spent the small inheritance from my Gran completing the Level 3 Diploma in Body Massage. I was a qualified masseur with a certificate, insurance and one client I had met in a gym when I was given six months' temporary membership to provide free massages, which worked out very well for the owners of the gym.

Massage was a strange profession for someone from my background, but when I read about the course in the brochure from St Mary's University, the thing that jumped out at me was that the qualification was recognised in Canada. I had a sort of daydream, not a plan, just a vague idea that one day we might emigrate. I had never been to Canada, I didn't know anyone in Canada. But I knew it had lots of space and seemed like a great country to bring up kids.

As a teenager, I'd worked out of Lowestoft on a beam trawler catching herring, cod and plaice. It's a good job for a youngster and I thought I'd probably be going out to sea for the rest of my life. Then the fish dried up, the laws on fishing permits changed and most of the boats went into dry dock. That was in 1996. I was twenty, and there was still plenty of work if you went out and looked for it. After forty years laying tarmacadam, my grandfather had just died at sixty-eight, of exhaustion, my mum said, and I moved to Twickenham to look after my Gran.

After being a fisherman, I wanted to work outdoors and got a temporary post with the council planting trees. Then the council ran out of trees, or money, or both, and I started with a contractor laying paving stones. When that came to an end, I found work as a labourer, a job with good money until the developers started using gang bosses who only employed East Europeans. You hate the foreigners when they take your job. Then you find out they're paying inflated rents to live in old caravans so they can send home twenty quid a week to feed their families. That's when you realise it's the system that's wrong and you don't hate them anymore.

But you still have to go and find another job.

I had always used my muscles to earn a living. Massage is physical, you have to be strong, but also gentle, intuitive. It is a form of meditation, not only for the person receiving the massage, but also for the one giving it. The movements are rhythmic, repetitive, calming. It had certainly calmed me down. I'd always had a tendency to leap before I looked, I'd jump into anything. But when you have a family, you start to be more cautious. I'd left my twenties behind me. I was thirty now. I jogged ten miles a day, avoided the drink, and was as fit as I had ever been.

That was probably why they had taken a chance at The Lodge and employed me without the relevant qualifications. The work was mentally gruelling. Few blokes lasted three months. I'd already done six. I had no other prospects and needed that regular wage packet. We got by. But one little thing, like the fridge giving up or the van breaking down, and I'd have to take on extra shifts until we'd paid off the bill.

The lads in the unit were generally nice boys, but had psychological problems and would fly off the handle at the least provocation, often for no reason at all. You had to use gentle force so that they didn't feel they had to take you on. I didn't mind getting the odd punch, it came with the job, but it upset me if the boys got hurt. Their lives were difficult enough as it was.

I would be seeing my massage client Friday, then the weekend off. I just had to get through two long days of double shifts, six till midnight, midnight till six, when at least the boys would be drugged out of their heads and I could put my feet up with a mug of tea.

The drive from Twickenham to Egham took about thirty minutes. But I was afraid of the van overheating and limped along in the inside lane with the sun burning my arm as it rested on the open window. Trucks blasted their horns as they shot by, the whole world was in a hurry, and I was a couple of minutes late by the time I rattled over the potholes and parked below the trees surrounding The Lodge.

Vinnie Castro, the night manager, had an office with bay windows overlooking the entrance. He tapped the face of his watch as I ran up the stairs and met me in the hall.

'About bloody time,' he said. 'Go and help Marley, will you, he's in the day room. They're pissing on Little Billy again.'

I rushed down the corridor and burst in. Marley held two lads by their collars. They looked sheepish and pleased with themselves at the same time.

'Need any help?' I said.

'It's all over 'cept for the cleaning, man.'

Marley had long dreads held in a beanie in the colours of the Jamaican flag and a strong accent, although he had grown up in South London. He was a Rasta, a gentle giant with a nice way with the lads.

I gazed around the room – the ping-pong table, flat screen TV angled against the wall, shelves of books and board games, windows with bars. Troy was doing his usual thing, sitting on his hands in a blue armchair rocking back and forth. Alex had command of the TV remote and was switching channels as fast as he could. The babel of cut off words and changing colours made it feel as if you really were in a mad house. A couple of lads stood with their faces pressed against the windows and Little Billy was in the corner soaked in urine.

Chris was the ring leader. I threw up my hands as I approached him.

'Chris, why do you keep doing that?'

'Doing what?'

'You know what. Why do you keep pissing on Billy?'

'He asked for it.'

'I don't think that's true.'

'You calling me a liar?'

'No, Chris, I am not calling you a liar. I just don't think it's true.'

I glanced at Little Billy. He was grinning, nodding his head up and down, and I thought, oh no, perhaps it is true! 'Come on, Billy,' I said. 'Let's go and take a shower, shall we? And, Chris, help Marley clean this mess up.'

'Not my job.'

'I know it's not your job. Just do it to be nice.'

'Not my job.'

'What is your job?'

'What?' He looked back at me as if I had spoken in a foreign language and had no idea what I was talking about.

'Just help Marley and be nice.'

'Not my job.'

These kinds of conversations could go on forever. I led Billy down the corridor and upstairs to the bathroom.

The lads at The Lodge developed fads and fetishes that would last a few weeks, then stop again. Chris and his henchmen, Del and Jordan, had peed on Billy half a dozen times in the last two weeks. I assumed it had a few more weeks to run, then something else would start.

Several lads had obsessions with bodily waste. I'd had excrement as well as pee thrown at me. Occasionally I would have to change two or three times during the course of a shift and still drive home with my clothes reeking. I wore loose white trousers and a white polo shirt, oddly the same uniform as I wore as a masseur, and one of the big expenses on our weekly budget was buying economy-sized bottles of 'Shout,' the stain remover.

What the boys lacked was personal attention. When I did have time to be alone with one of them, they quickly responded and became almost normal. Most had learning difficulties. Some, on the other hand, were extremely intelligent, they just saw the world in their own special way. If they were reading a book, they could concentrate no matter how much racket was going on and remember everything they had read. What they needed was programmes to fit their individual problems, not to be lumped together as 'special needs.' I had mentioned this to Vinnie and he'd promised to pass it on up the chain of command.

Another thing I had noticed was that the lads had less sense of right and wrong than Ollie, my five year old. They appeared to have no conscience and, almost without exception, were unable to understand or share another person's feelings. When I'd asked Chris to help Marley clean up the mess he'd made, his expression remained blank and the concept of doing something 'just to be nice' was totally beyond his grasp.

While Billy was in the shower, I found some clean clothes. When he was dressed again, I asked him why Chris and the others kept pissing on him. He just grinned and shrugged his thin shoulders.

'Don't let it happen again, all right?'

'It's too hot.'

'You're telling me. Hottest day of the year.'

'Why?'

'Search me, Billy, I've got no idea.'

'Must be the weather.'

Billy was grinning. I wasn't sure if he'd made a joke or not, and that was another thing: the boys could always surprise you.

We made our way back downstairs.

'Now, go and watch the telly and stay away from Chris.'

Marley had already mopped up and I walked down the corridor with him to the entrance.

'Sorry I was late, mate, I owe you one.'

'Don't worry, Bro. Time is a banana.'

'What's that?'

'It bends like the universe.'

That was Marley wisdom. I was never exactly sure what he meant and would spend the rest of the night thinking about it.

There was one other worker on the six o'clock shift, Andel Svoboda, a Czech male nurse, a quiet, serious man with a severe expression and a wife and children back in Prague. Our job for the next hour was to keep the peace until dinner time, when as much food got thrown about as eaten. I'd clean up while Andel arranged the medicines and we'd have 'quiet time' in the day room watching TV before they went to bed; usually the drugs had taken effect and there was no complaint.

When one of the lads had a night trauma, we'd spend hours changing sheets and cleaning a boy up. On the worst occasions, we had to strap them into a straight-jacket, then lock them in a padded room where they would wail like a hurt animal until a doctor arrived and gave them an antipsychotic drug that left them like zombies for days after. It was heart-breaking and I'd drive back to Twickenham feeling depressed.

There were times when I was screamed at, spat on, punched and scratched. I would run out of clothes to change into and arrive home with poo on my shirt and my feet yellow with urine. I'd hurry upstairs, take a bath and go straight to bed. Kelly would wake up and she knew me well enough to know I just wanted to close my eyes and not talk about anything. The job wasn't only hard on me, it was hard on Kelly as well.

That Thursday, one of the hottest days of the year, was a good day. The heat had exhausted the lads. I read the paper with a cup of tea and the road home was empty except for the crows that hopped indignantly out of the way as the van approached. The sun painted orange stripes across the horizon. I filled up at the service station and bought some chocolate bars.

The children were already awake and Kelly was like a circus performer feeding Claire, dressing George, my strapping four year old, and overseeing Ollie, busy pouring cereal into a bowl. They all had blue eyes, but only Ollie had my inky dark hair. Claire and George were fair like their mum.

The moment I opened the door, Ollie spilled half the packet of cereal over the counter and ran up to me.

'Daddy, daddy,' he cried and grabbed for the bag I was carrying.

This may have been inspired by great love, but it was more likely that he was after the Crunchie bar he knew I'd bought. I held the bag out of reach.

'Please, dad.'

'Ollie, no. Not before breakfast,' I said, and placed a Crunchie and two Milky Ways on the high shelf.

'I said please.'

'And I said no, not before breakfast.'

'Not hungry, dad.'

'If you're not hungry, you don't want a Crunchie.'

'He got you there, Ollie,' Kelly chipped in.

Ollie thought about that for half a second and decided to give in gracefully.

I helped put the cereal back in the box and emptied my pockets. I had a £5 note and a handful of change.

'Just under a tenner, babe,' I said. 'Hope that's enough.'

'It's never enough.'

'I'm sorry …'

'I'm not complaining. Just commenting. The prices go up and the wages stay the same.'

'It'll get better.'

'Can't get any worse.'

She turned. The light was behind her. She wasn't angry or irritated. She was smiling. It was going to be another hot day. The kitchen door was open. The sun was pouring in and she looked like an angel with the light in her hair. I gave her a hug.

'Love you,' I whispered.

It was coming up to seven and I was drained. I kissed the kids, climbed the stairs, stepped over the safety gate and fell into the warm bed Kelly had vacated. Ollie went to a playgroup run by Carly, a neighbour who had a little girl the same age. It was Kelly's task to keep the little-ones quiet so I could get some kip.

I'd got through another Thursday double shift. It was Friday. My appointment was at three that afternoon.

2
BETTER NEVER LATE

The sun was baking, hotter than ever. I must have lost a couple of kilos jogging in Crane Park with my shirt off and getting a suntan. I was back in time for lunch with the family – scrambled eggs on toast, and I scoffed down every crust and crumb the children left on their plates, the yogurt sticking to the sides of the plastic pots, the bits of orange Claire had spat out.

'You're not hungry by any chance?' Kelly said.

'Better in me than in the bin.'

'You are the bin, Ben,' she remarked and George laughed.

'Bin Ben, Bin Ben, Bin Ben,' he repeated.

Claire giggled. Her first words had been Ma Ma. She had quickly mastered Da Da, and was now fixated on No no, No no, like a mantra she sang in her sweet little voice as she moved around the kitchen.

I scooped her up on my knee.

'Da Da. No no. No no.'

She kicked and wriggled until I put her back down and she continued on her way. Claire already had a strong independent streak; she was going to need it with two older brothers and the big bad world out there.

I cleaned my teeth, kissed the kids and set off in pressed whites just after two. I had given myself more than enough time unless there was a major problem and, needless to say, that day, of all days, there was a major problem. There had been an accident. I counted six police cars and an ambulance with flashing blue lights. A lane was closed and I sat in the heat for twenty minutes watching the seconds tick by knowing I was going to be late for my Friday massage. Rufus Bradley was thirty something, thin with fine, pale yellow hair and, at six foot, the same height as me. He lived with his mum at home – who wouldn't, given the choice? Home was a Georgian mansion close to Kempton Park Race Course with stables and rolling meadows as far as the eye could see. He paid me £20 plus £5 expenses for a 45-minute back rub, the persistent pain caused, as far as I could tell, by lying about on the goose down couches, or sofas, I should say, chatting on the phone with his girlfriend, the English actress Annabel Lee Hartley, who had just got some big role in an American TV series.

The money certainly came in handy and I enjoyed my weekly journey into this world so alien to my own. The roads were chock-a-block. Fumes in a haze obscured the sky, but the moment I turned off the main road, I entered a quiet country lane shaded by trees. The house was the same style as the public library in Twickenham, but ten times as big. The rooms were vast with high-ceilings, portraits of men in uniform and, on one wall, a display of swords and old guns. Everything sparkled, the windows, the porcelain in polished dressers, the faces of the clocks that all showed different times and chimed out of sequence as if in this house time had a different significance.

There was a rose garden with statues covered in moss and the horses in the open field stopped at the fence to watch as the van crunched over the white gravel drive. Every time I entered the tall gates I thought to myself: how can some people have so much when there are so many people who have so little? This was not political or philosophical, even envy, just a fleeting thought that vanished from my head immediately I pulled up at the entrance.

I unloaded my folding table from the van and heaved my bag of candles and oils onto my shoulder. The main doors were open and a girl on a platform ladder was cleaning the chandelier when I walked in. She was pretty in a pink gingham uniform and had a long face as she pointed upwards as if to heaven.

'Thanks,' I said.

She used the same finger to mime cutting her throat.

'You're welcome,' she replied, and I climbed the stairs.

Rufus had a suite of rooms with a view over the paddock at the front of the house. He was, as usual, lying on a sofa, reading with a towel around his waist. He didn't look up when I clattered in with my table.

'Afternoon,' I said, and stared at the cover of a book that hid his face. It was *Kate Moss: Model of Imperfection*.

'I didn't think you were coming.'

'Sorry I'm a bit late. You wouldn't believe the traffic.'

He lowered the book. 'I don't think you are privy to my beliefs, or lack of them.' He took a long breath and waved his hand towards the shady area between the two sets of open windows. 'Now you're here, I suppose.'

I laid the table face down to extend and fix the legs in place, then flipped it over. We had already established that he didn't like the smell of the aromatherapy candles or the flowing rivers and wind chimes of my massage music. I left them in the bag and went through to his bathroom to wash my hands. The room was massive with a bath on legs like animal claws and a shower bigger than my entire bathroom. I dried my hands.

'Ready when you are.'

He got up slowly like a cat and sidled across the room towards me.

'I suppose no one ever thought to tell you: You don't get ahead by getting behind. Every moment lost is never recovered.'

'It won't happen again.'

'I know.'

'Sorry…'

'I love that. People think by saying that trite little word that their actions don't have consequences. Here.'

He gave me his towel, which I spread over the surface of the table. I was going to say time is a banana, quoting Marley, but he wouldn't have appreciated it. I held the side of the table steady and Rufus climbed up in his boxers. He made his head comfortable in the face hole, stretched out and tucked his arms into his sides. I ran some drops of almond oil down his spine and added a dab to my palm. I rubbed my hands together, warming them, and began to work the muscles and soft tissues, each slow steady stroke reducing tension and stiffness.

I'd felt a stab of anxiety being late. I thought I was going to lose my only client, but the anxiety faded the moment I started the massage. As I relaxed, the feeling transferred to Rufus. I applied pressure to his lower lumber region, digging in with the heels of my hands, and his breathing became steady, slower and deeper. In a few minutes, he was sighing contentedly.

Massage develops and restores the muscular, circulatory, lymphatic and nervous systems, assisting the body to heal itself of disorders while increasing general health and well-being. Each patient is different. It is vital to establish the optimum amount of pressure: too much and the muscles grow tense, too little and there is no benefit. With experience, you grow to know through your fingertips where there are areas of pain and soft tissue problems. He wriggled.

'Yes, right there,' he said, pointing at a spot just above his waist on the right side of his body. 'What is that?'

'It looks like a bite to me, probably a mosquito.'

'Mosquito,' he repeated. 'I doubt that very much.'

'It's nothing serious, Rufus. Try not to tense up.'

He settled down. I added more oil; it was pale yellow, the same colour as his hair, and had the sweet smell of almonds.

As you find the rhythm, your mind drifts off. My view through the open window was of trees lining fields, a turquoise sky without a cloud. I was joined to Rufus by my fingers rubbing oil into his shoulders and back, but that was the extent of our connection. While he inhabited a world I couldn't even begin to imagine, my reality was a relentless struggle just to survive. I had a feeling that massage was going to be my future, I'd felt that from the day I started taking courses, but finding regular clients in the circles I moved in had been impossible.

I had fixed up my own spa at home. Ollie and George shared a bedroom and, while Claire was still in a cot in our room, I used the box room as a massage centre. Carly, who ran the playgroup, had a herniated disc. It is not something you can cure, but she came for treatments twice a week and it certainly relieved the pain. Pete Taylor, the postman, another neighbour, had a fine ear for tuning cars. He pounded the pavement every day. I'd give him the occasional foot rub and he'd kept the Red Beast, my van, running long after it was ready for the breakers. No one I knew had spare cash to pay for a massage. I did a lot of skill swaps, but when someone was in need, I was happy to treat them for free.

We were all working families on the estate. Everyone was hard up, but there was a sense of community. Some people said it was dying out, but it wasn't, it was there, just below the surface.

There are spiritual, psychological, even mystical aspects to massage, qualities I had not thought about when I began taking courses, but it is those qualities that become important, even central. Massage is the oldest form of healing. The word in English comes from the French *massage*, but exists as *massa* in Greek, Latin and Arabic.

In Saqqara, close to the famous Step Pyramid in Egypt, stands Tomb Akmanthor, also called the Tomb of the Physician, built more than 4000 years ago and containing beautifully preserved murals that show men having their feet massaged. Hippocrates – the Father of Western Medicine – wrote: 'The physician must be experienced in many things, but assuredly in rubbing.'

I had barely finished a book since I left school, but I'd read everything there was to read about massage. It is a way of life, a vocation. Massage creates a sense of care and communication. After treating a client, your connection becomes intimate. Yet, although I'd known Rufus since my time giving free massages at the gym, we had never gone beyond the relationship of employer and employee. I did my 45 minute treatment – more often than not it was closer to an hour – and picked up the £25 that he never actually gave me, but left on one of the side tables.

The same thing happened that day. Not even a thank you. Rufus wrapped the towel around himself, fluttered his fingers across the room and I zipped the money in my back pocket – new shoes for Claire and groceries for the weekend.

I was packing up the table, when I heard voices like tinkling tea cups rise up the stone walls and through the window. I glanced out and saw several ladies followed by three men enter the main doors below. Parked in a semi-circle were four cars that I had not heard pull up while I was finishing the massage: a black Rolls Royce Phantom, two black Range Rovers and a yellow open-top Ferrari with white leather seats. It was like a display at a motor show made ridiculous by the sight of my battered old van with the post office insignia painted out.

I turned back to Rufus

'Me and my big mouth,' he said.

'What's happened?'

'You, that's what's happened. Mother wants to meet you.'

As he was speaking, there was a double tap and the door swung open to admit a tall, marble-skinned woman who was obviously in her fifties and could have passed as Rufus's sister. She wore a fitted white dress with a pattern of red and blue roses, high heels on slender feet and carried a hat with a red and white polka dot ribbon. Her perfume reminded me of strawberries and cream, summery and fresh.

'Ah, how wonderful!' she exclaimed, her voice soft, refined, but with an accent I couldn't place. 'You must be the amazing masseur we've been hearing about.'

She turned, wide-eyed to Rufus.

'Yes, this is Benjamin Foster. Benjamin, my mother, Lady Catherine.'

'Ben,' I said.

'Catherine,' she responded. 'Among friends.'

Our eyes met for just a second and the way she then looked me up and down reminded me of the wholesalers inspecting the catch when I was on the trawlers. She held out her hand, which I wasn't sure whether to shake or kiss. I did the latter, bending forward to plant my lips on her soft skin.

'I'm pleased to meet you.'

'You are such a gentleman,' she said, and I gathered by the way she said the word 'gentleman' that she was American. 'I have some friends downstairs who would love to meet *you.*'

'I'm sure Benjamin has better things to do,' said Rufus.

He looked embarrassed for some reason and all the tension I'd spent an hour working out was back in his narrow face.

'Nonsense,' she said and turned to me. 'He wants to keep you all to himself and that's not fair, is it?'

'No, I suppose not.'

She glanced briefly at Rufus. 'You see,' she added, dropping her hat over a table lamp and wrapping her arm through mine. 'Come, this is going to be such fun.'

'What about the massage table?' I said as we were leaving the room, and she threw out her free hand.

'Someone will bring it.'

We walked arm in arm down the wide curving staircase. It felt as if we were being filmed for a movie.

'Now, do tell me, before you get lynched by the mob, how is Rufus's back?'

'I'd say it was in pretty good shape. His spine's straight and most of the knots have gone now.'

'That is such good news. Maybe you could treat one to a massage?'

I wasn't sure if 'treat one,' meant she wanted a free massage, or whether she wanted a treatment. Not that I gave it much thought.

'I'd be honoured,' I replied.

We reached the bottom of the stairs. The girl must have finished cleaning the chandeliers and the ladder had been removed. Shafts of intense light pierced the windows and shimmered from every surface, making it difficult to see. We entered what they called the Great Hall and my life spun like a flipped coin and changed forever.

3
THE COMMITTEE

Numerous chairs and sofas were arranged around a walk in fireplace where a group of ladies in pastel outfits sat with legs elegantly crossed as if waiting to be photographed.

Including Lady Catherine, there were ten women of various ages. I would have said they were foxy. But that would have been inappropriate. They were beautiful, by far the most attractive and best-dressed women I had ever seen in one place all at the same time.

At the far end of the Great Hall were three men, two in shorts and casual shirts, the third in a white linen suit with a white straw hat. They were too far away for me to hear what they were saying, but when they laughed their big voices boomed and echoed over the high ceiling.

The moment we entered, one of the women approached with her hands pressed against her chest as if in shock. She was thin, but shapely in a pale lemon dress with masses of chestnut hair and green eyes – the sort of woman once seen is not easily forgotten. She took my free arm.

'Now who do we have here, Kate? Have you been keeping secrets?'

'What is a woman without secrets?'

'Do tell. You know what they say about a secret shared …'

'Yes, it's no longer a secret.' She smiled. 'This is Ben Foster, darling. He's the one who's been rubbing the knots out of Rufus's back.'

'Lucky Rufus.'

The woman smiled at me.

'This is Lady Margaret,' Lady Catherine continued. 'But *you*,' she said, stressing the you, 'can call her Maggs.'

'He can call me any time he wants,' Lady Margaret said, and the other women laughed. She squeezed the muscles on my right arm. 'You seem terribly strong. Is it from all that massage?'

'I run every day, and work out.'

'That's marvellous.' She quivered and looked around at the seated audience. 'I'm tingling all over.'

'That's too much champagne on an empty stomach,' said a woman sitting on a high-backed antique chair.

Lady Margaret threw up both hands.

'Is there any other way to drink champagne?' she replied, and turned back to me. 'Let's ask Ben what he thinks?'

'I'm not much of a drinker, to be honest,' I replied, and again she gave a little shudder.

'That's so praiseworthy,' she said and I blushed as she rose up on her toes and kissed the corner of my mouth. 'You are obviously not Irish?'

I shook my head. 'No…'

'You have that wild Irish look, blue eyes and dark hair. It is something I have always found attractive.' She paused. 'Now, come and sit down and tell us what sort of massage you do.'

I sat on a grey sofa with red tassels. The women leaned forward with surprised expressions and big eyes as if I were a rare breed of dog or a Roman coin dug up in the garden. I felt awkward, self-conscious, out of my depth. But, at the same time, I had a sense that I wasn't gazing through a window into another world that excluded me, I was on the inside, the centre of attention.

Nothing like this had ever happened before. I had never spoken to a 'Lady' in my life, and here I was speaking to two on the same day. It was like being at an interview and I would come to realise that that was exactly what it was.

'Now, do tell?'

I took a breath. 'Mostly I do Swedish massage with what I call an Oriental twist,' I said, and the women erupted in laughter.

My cheeks burned and they were still laughing when the three men made their way through the hall towards us. While the other two continued, the man in white stopped and slipped his hands into his jacket pockets. He looked familiar. I wasn't sure from where. He studied me over half-moon glasses and our eyes met.

'How wonderful to hear the sound of women's laughter,' he remarked.

I wasn't sure what to say and it was just as well that Lady Margaret came to the rescue, although what was said was puzzling.

'One hundred pounds, James?' she suggested, and he looked back at me with an expression that was impossible to read.

'If you insist. Two days?'

'Make it five hundred guineas, then?'

'Whatever you say,' he replied, and left the Great Hall.

Lady Margaret moved closer on the sofa and lowered her voice to a whisper. 'Now, how much do you charge for a massage?'

'With a twist?' added the woman in the antique chair.

There was another ripple of laughter. I could feel a flush rise up my neck and was thinking: 'Play it cool, don't be an idiot, don't undersell yourself' – something Kelly said I always did. I gritted my teeth and tried to look casual.

'Fifty pounds for a forty-five minute session,' I blurted out.

'Fifty pounds,' one of the women repeated.

'And how much for the night?' said Lady Margaret.

I was unable to speak. My throat had tightened and I was saved from making a complete fool of myself by Kate, Lady Catherine.

'Leave the poor boy alone, Maggs. You'll scare him off.'

Maggs stroked the back of my hair. 'You're not scared of me, are you?'

'No, not at all,' I managed.

That's what I said, but it wasn't what I felt. I wasn't exactly frightened, but had that feeling working blokes have when they come face to face with what my Gran would have called 'their betters.' We feel clumsy. We're not sure what to say and know whatever we say will sound ignorant. We may know deep down no one is better than anyone else, but people with posh voices who always say the right thing at the right time make you feel awkward and uncouth. My brow was damp. There was nervous sweat under my arms. But there was a nagging little voice that kept saying 'Play it cool, this could be your lucky break'.

Maggs was still stroking my hair when the maid I had seen cleaning the chandeliers appeared as if by magic.

'Bring some Perrier, dear,' Lady Catherine said, and the girl left again.

The sun was bright through the open windows, but my eyes had adjusted to the light and now it occurred to me why the women gathered around the fireplace had at first appeared to be posing for a photograph. That was where I had seen several of them before, on television and the newspapers.

One was an actress, better known for being in the papers than for her film roles. Another was a model whose face with high cheekbones and an unnerving expression appeared in magazine ads and on hoardings all over London. The woman sitting on the high-back chair like she ruled the world was often on television, a Conservative MP with a strident voice who talked over everyone and didn't listen to the questions when she was being interviewed. Her brow was faintly lined and she watched me like someone watching a cat waiting for it to do something funny.

These people were famous, important, titled, rich. I charged Rufus £25 for a massage and felt guilty asking for twice as much, but I had no doubt they could afford it. I glanced down at my trainers. They were scuffed and scruffy. I'd been meaning to get a new pair and fifty quid was what they cost these days.

I glanced up as the maid returned pushing a trolley with bottles of Perrier. She added ice and lemon slices to tall glasses, served everyone and slipped away again. The women continued to study me, they looked at each other and then one of them, younger than the rest, all in white like a bride with white flowers in her hair, held up her Perrier as if making a toast.

'He is like a glass of clear water,' she said, not looking at me, but Maggs, who softly clapped.

'You always say the perfect thing, Vivienne,' she remarked.

I swigged down the Perrier like a man who had just crossed the desert and Lady Catherine refilled my glass. As she did so, Rufus arrived in riding clothes and brown leather boots.

'What a pleasure. How's the back?' Maggs asked and he shrugged as if bored.

'It's getting there.'

Before Maggs could continue, the politician spoke over her. 'Have you been in touch with Annabel, by any chance?' she asked him.

'Every day.'

'She's avoiding me. I don't know why. Tell her to give me a call, will you?'

'If I remember,' he replied. He brushed his hand over his combed back hair and turned to me. 'Do let me save you from the committee of over-excited hormones.'

'He doesn't need saving, darling, he's perfectly happy where he is,' his mother responded.

'Yes, I am,' I said, coming to my feet. 'But I really should go. There's always so much to do.'

'And never enough time to do it,' Rufus said sharply.

Maggs took my arm. 'Do you have a card?' she asked, and I thought: Oh, no, I've blown it. My shoulders sagged.

'No, I don't, I'm sorry.'

'Never complain, never explain and never apologise,' said Lady Catherine. 'A gentleman *never* carries a card. He writes his number down on a slip of paper.'

As Lady Catherine spoke, the politician reached for her bag and that instant I remembered her name. Angela Hartley was bursting with repressed energy, small, tense, fine-boned, a woman who really needed a massage. She gave me a pen and a spiral notebook in which I wrote my mobile number.

Rufus walked me out to the van. My table and bag were leaning against the back and I opened the doors to slide them in.

'Do you ride?' he asked.

'No, never tried it.'

'Oh, well, see you next week,' he said and strode off towards the stables.

As I fired the motor, the woman in white floated out from the main doors like an angel in a nativity play. I switched off the engine and got out. She stopped, feet together, head to one side, a look of concern in her blue eyes.

'It must have been awful being grilled like a sardine, poor thing,' she said and held out her hand. 'Vivienne Raynott.'

'Nice to meet you.'

'You were very brave in there. Like a soldier in the trenches.'

She stood motionless beside the van, quiet for a moment. There was something serious and sad about her, which made her all the more attractive.

I wasn't sure what to say and said stupidly: 'This is my old banger. I should take it to the dump, really.'

'It's just an A to B machine. It got you here.'

'But it might not get me home again.'

She took a breath and thought about that. 'Then it will be an adventure,' she said and put her hand on my arm. 'It's like meeting a stranger. It's always exciting when something happens that you don't expect.'

'As long as it's not the car breaking down,' I replied and she smiled.

'You know something, Ben, I have a feeling we are going to be friends for the rest of our lives.'

She turned and wafted along the line of black cars to the yellow Ferrari. She shot down the drive and I remained where I stood watching the dust settle. In the field alongside the house, I saw Rufus moving in a slow trot. He was bent to one side as if to avoid falling from the horse. The air was hot and still. I stepped into the Red Beast and set off, the gravel drumming under the wheel arches. I'd only had two glasses of Perrier, but my head was spinning. My heart thumped in my chest. The smell of Vivienne's perfume was in my nose like a narcotic. Like an aphrodisiac.

The women I had met in the Great Hall were refined, striking, each beautiful in her own way, chic and sexy with tanned slender legs and their breasts popping over the tops of their dresses. They didn't hide their sexuality, they exploited it, exposed it. They had acted as if they found me attractive, but they could have been making fun of me. I'd felt like a clown with my red cheeks and big scruffy shoes.

'I have a feeling we are going to be friends for the rest of our lives.'

That's what Vivienne Raynott had said, but what did it mean? People didn't say that sort of thing, not the people I knew. Was I reading more into the encounter than was really there? It wouldn't be the first time. Kelly said I was naïve, that people took advantage of me. It was probably true, but better that than taking advantage of other people.

I had been turned on by Vivienne, what normal man wouldn't? But relations with a woman like her was a fantasy, a daydream. If I could earn some cash for the occasional massage that would be great. More than great. It would be life changing. Beyond that, I loved Kelly and my kids and had no intention of jeopardising what we had.

I glanced at my watch, a plastic Casio, £5 from Mr Singh at the Indian stall in the market. It had just gone five. I drove straight to my six o'clock shift. The van rattled along. The Beast was like a drum kit, I knew every beat and jangle. The traffic was building up. Road rage was in the air. Horns blasted. City boys in Porsches raced by. The sun through the windscreen was like a laser beam.

The van bounced over the ruts as I swung into The Lodge, the trees bedraggled, the paint fading on the grey building with its iron bars, a sight that suddenly seemed unreal, or surreal, the contrast between life back in the Great Hall and life for those sad lads was so immense it was like I'd passed through a time warp in *Doctor Who* and arrived among people on a different planet.

Vinnie Castro was watching from the window and gave me the thumbs up. I was ten minutes early. Little Billy was piss free, the readers were reading and Marley was working up a sweat playing table tennis with three of the lads, the ball flying about the day room. I wasn't sure why, but I'd felt depressed on the drive from the Great Hall, but it passed immediately.

I went and talked to Troy, sitting on his hands as always.

'Don't you want to play ping-pong, Troy?'

He paused from nodding his head. 'Not today, thank you.'

'You let me know when you do.'

He stared at me for a second and carried on nodding.

Marley gave another boy his bat and strolled towards me drying his face with a handkerchief.

'Hot as the fires of Hades,' he said. 'How's your day been, Bro?'

'Same old, same old. I got stuck all afternoon in this big house with ten beautiful women,' I said and he nodded thoughtfully.

'Don't forget, man, in the dark they all look the same.'

Marley left to catch the bus home. The two lads who always stared out of the window were staring out of the window. I went to join them. The sun had gone behind some tall buildings and the light filtering through the trees made the same pastel shades as the dresses the women wore in the Great Hall.

4
NAUGHTY MONKEY

The text woke me from a restless sleep at half past eleven on Saturday morning:

Dear Ben, what a pleasure to meet you the other day. May I request your services as a massage therapist tonight at 7.30 at Frowley Manor? Lady Margaret

My throat went dry. Adrenaline pumped through my heart. I was exhausted after three double shifts in a row. I'd felt weary. Suddenly I was buzzing.

Lady Margaret was texting me!

Play it cool, man, play it cool.

Dear Lady Margaret, Very grateful for your request. Please can you text the postcode. Ben

Dear Ben. Frowley doesn't have a postcode. See you at 7.30. Must fly. Lady M

Dear Lady Margaret, OK, many thanks, Ben.

I sat on the edge of the bed. I felt dizzy. I'd had plenty of time to reflect on meeting the ladies of the so-called Committee and had come to the conclusion that they had been making fun of me. They had no intention of allowing my working man hands to stroke their flawless white bodies and the text from Lady Margaret was another joke, egging the pudding. After all, she had not even told me where Frowley Manor was.

Now what?

I dragged on some clothes and went downstairs. Kelly and the kids were in the garden – old bikes, rusty tools, a wheelbarrow with the wheel falling off. Kelly was filling a Tesco's bag with weeds she'd pulled up from around the rose bushes, the white blooms almost as big as cauliflowers. Getting the garden fixed up was on my 'to do' list but there was never enough time to get it sorted.

'Morning,' I called.

'Hello sleepy head, you're up early.'

'I just got a text. I'm going to see if Pete's home. I might have something on.'

'Some work?'

'Fingers crossed.'

'Dad, dad, bring back a Crunchie,' Ollie called.

'You're going to look like a Crunchie at this rate,' I told him. 'Another thing, I don't think I heard a please.'

'Please ...'

'Too late, Big Guy.'

Pete's house was identical to my own. Pete and Carol's children were grown up, so it was remarkably tidy and arranged in a way that made it look twice as big. Carol worked as a receptionist at the hospital, Jamie was doing his A-levels and Lynne was at university. Since my old Toshiba had succumbed to a virus, Pete had let me use his to check my emails.

We looked up Lady Margaret and Frowley Manor. It was a real place not far from St Mary's Church in Sudbury built in mediaeval times.

'One famous visitor was Oliver Cromwell – and listen to this,' he read. 'He died in 1658 and when the Royalists came back to power in 1660, they dug up his corpse and cut his head off. That's charming that is.' He looked back at me. 'So who's this Lady Margaret, then? Have you met her?'

'I give that toff out by the race track a massage every Friday. Maggs is a friend of his mother.'

'Maggs?'

'That's what she told me to call her.'

'Going up in the world? Won't be able to speak to you at this rate.'

'Come on, I haven't even done it yet.'

He grinned and sat back in his swivel chair. 'I like the idea of you giving me a foot massage, then giving Lady Muck a neck rub.'

'You're disgusting, you know that?'

'It'd make a change from them having their heels on our necks.'

'They're just people. They're all right.'

'You think so?' He raised his finger as he stared back. 'Be careful, Ben, that's all I'm going to say.'

He looked up the route to Frowley Manor and I wrote down the directions.

'While you're about it, look up Vivienne Raynott, will you?'

'Another mate of yours?'

'Oh, yeah, best of friends.'

He tapped in the name, Google amended Vivian to Vivienne, and up came the Hon. Vivienne Agnes Sinclair Raynott: born 1978, which made her 28, Wycombe Abbey School, philosophy at St Hilda's College, Oxford, author, whisky heiress. He clicked on images.

'Is that her?'

I nodded.

'With the bloody Queen. I'll tell you this, be careful, rub her up the wrong way and you'll end up in the Tower.'

I thought: these people aren't just rich, they're what my old granddad used to call the Big Nobs, the gentry.

When I got home, I told Kelly I had a booking for seven-thirty. Her head dropped to one side as she slipped her hands over her hips.

'What time?' she said.

'Tonight, half past seven.'

'Half past seven on a Saturday night? Bit odd isn't it?'

'I don't know, is it? These people keep different times to us.'

'What people?'

'I met Rufus's mum out at Kempton, you know, my regular. It's one of her friends, a rich lady.'

'And she wants you to give her a massage tonight?'

'She's probably going out somewhere special, I don't know. I'm getting fifty quid, babe. That's a bloody fortune.'

She took a breath. The money had taken the wind out of her sails. 'Just make sure you get paid before you do the massage. You know what these people are like?'

'I will, promise.'

Kelly looped her arms around my waist and pulled me close. 'I'm so proud of you, Ben. Really proud.'

'Don't know why. I haven't done anything.'

'Don't think I don't know how many hours you've worked this week.' She leaned forward and whispered in my ear. 'I love you, Ben Foster.'

'I love you, Kelly Foster.'

We kissed while Ollie and George hooted and whistled.

Yuck. That's horrible. They're kissing.

We went to the park so the kids could run around and burn off some energy. I watched Ollie help Claire climb the steps on the slide. She whizzed down, hands in the air, her little face beaming. It goes without saying, once was not enough. Ollie knew his sister was prone to tantrums when she didn't get her own way and patiently joined the line so she could have another go. As I watched Kelly push George on the swings, my eyes grew misty. Our children were tanned and healthy, bright and smart. There wasn't anything I wouldn't do for them.

'Where do you want to have lunch, Big Guy?' I asked Ollie when we were ready to leave.

'McDonald's,' he said, and punched the air with his fist.

I drew out some cash at the ATM machine and the kids were zonked out on burgers and fries by the time we got home. I managed to have a nap, then read my course notes. I hadn't forgotten anything, but I'd had very little hands-on practice since I started work at The Lodge and, like a pianist, you have to keep honing your skills. I jogged for an hour, took a long shower, two squirts of Paco Rabanne Pour Homme, and I was ready in my best whites. The engine fired, the road was clear and Oasis was on the radio.

Twenty-four hours had passed since I had met the women in the Great Hall. I had thought about little else in that time. It was like a dream come true that Lady Margaret had actually booked an appointment. I kept telling myself to be cool, be confident, think before you speak. It doesn't matter that she's Lady Margaret. She's just a person, a client.

If I could do a good job, perhaps she would recommend me to the other women – the Hon. Vivienne Raynott, Maddy Page, the model with one of the best-known faces in the country, the amazingly gorgeous Zara Swift, film star, celebrity, chat show regular. How did they know each other? What were they doing there that day in the Great Hall?

It made a change to have a mystery in my life when normally it was just the same old, same old, long hours with the special needs lads, the daily battle to keep our heads above water. It's best not to tempt fate with high hopes, but as the Red Beast rattled along the road to Sudbury, I couldn't help thinking my luck had finally changed.

High walls and steel gates guarded the entrance to Frowley Manor. I pressed the call button.

'You are expected, sir,' said a male voice that wasn't posh but clipped, assertive.

The gates opened and I drove through a tunnel of trees to a courtyard paved in York stone – one thing I do know about is paving stones. A black Range Rover, one of the cars I had seen the previous day, stood below an overhanging bush filled with purple flowers. The house was a miniature castle with turrets and arched windows. I could smell horses and assumed there were stables out back. I grabbed my table and crossed the courtyard.

For some reason, I expected to find a butler in an old-fashioned costume, but the man at the door was casual in black trousers and a polo shirt; my height, wiry and strong with cropped grey hair.

'My van all right there?' I asked and he nodded.

'That'll do just fine, sir. This way.'

I entered a dark panelled hall containing a suit of armour and pewter vases with displays of flowers and ferns. I followed the man along an arched corridor lined with paintings until we reached a room with a high ceiling supported by polished beams. A balcony carved with a coat of arms perched on the bare stone wall like a box at the theatre.

Maggs, Lady Margaret, was standing on the balcony wearing a shiny floor-length white gown.

'Thank you, Douglas, that will be all,' she said.

He indicated an alcove beyond a low stone arch. 'You can place your table over there, sir,' he said, and about-turned like a soldier on his black Nike trainers.

Lady Margaret appeared beside me as I was setting up.

'You found us. It's like we're in darkest Africa, everyone gets lost,' she said, and kissed me on both cheeks. 'How are you, Ben?

'Very well, actually, Lady Margaret.'

'Maggs. Maggs. Maggs,' she repeated.

She smiled. I smiled. This was the moment to ask for my money, as I'd promised Kelly. But the moment passed.

'Where do you want me?'

As she spoke, she dropped her silk gown over the arm of a chair. She remained with her back to me for a moment longer than was natural, time enough for me to admire her slender back and bottom, then turned, arms outstretched. I must have looked at her for less than a second but took in every contour and curve. She had a girlish body, not an ounce of fat, firm small breasts and her pubic hair was clipped in a landing strip.

My throat went dry when I was embarrassed. Now it had closed over completely. I tapped the top of the table, then took a grip on the sides to steady myself. Lady Margaret climbed nimbly up and sat on the edge swinging her legs. She made a beckoning motion and stared into my eyes as I drew closer.

'I have so many knots, Ben. So many. Knots and nodules and aches and pains. It's going to be jolly hard work getting them all out.'

'I'll do my best,' I replied.

She relaxed with her face in the table aperture and her coppery-coloured hair like a ring of fire around her shoulders. I would normally have chosen some ambient music from my iPod and lit some aromatherapy candles, but it went clean out of my head. I coughed and my voice came out in a whisper.

'Stretch your spine and hold it for ten seconds,' I said. 'Relax. Don't think. Go with the flow.'

'Oh, I intend to.'

She took deep breaths as I spread oil over her back.

Swedish massage consists of five basic motions: effleurage, petrissage, friction, vibration and tapotement. Effleurage requires long sweeping strokes with open palms, fists and forearms. Beginning at the top of the spine with spread fingers like the branches of a tree, you initiate a treatment with reverse effleurage, running your hands lightly down either side of the spine, over the buttocks, up the sides of body, then back to the top before applying more pressure for the second sweep.

After ten full sweeps, you commence continuous figure of 8 movements over the shoulder blades. You follow this with thumb circles to work out the tension in the triangular area between the shoulders. You apply pressure while your patient is breathing out, you release pressure as they breathe in.

In one of my courses, I had been taught that the mind is like an elephant being led by a monkey. Through massage, you learn how to shoo the monkey away and become an elephant: noble, dignified, in control of your own thoughts and passions. At that moment, I wasn't an elephant. I was a monkey. I was reciting the massage steps in my head. I knew the sequence by heart, it's like saying the alphabet, but I was finding it hard to concentrate on anything other than the fact that I was sliding my oiled hands over the buttocks of a beautiful titled woman in an ancient manor house while she moaned and sighed and started to grow wet beneath my fingertips. The monkey liked it and the elephant felt ashamed. I moved away.

'Don't stop, Ben. Not now.' Her voice was deep, rich, sexy, commanding.

'I'm not,' I said. My voice, by contrast, was a whisper. 'Can you turn over?'

As she did so, she parted her legs. Her vagina was moist and she did something hard to believe. She ran her finger between her legs and then licked it.

'Mmm,' she said, and stretched out with the back of her head in the aperture.

I was in robot mode. I massaged her feet, calf muscles and inner thighs with alternate diagonal stroking from the inside of her leg across to the outside. She started to moan and it was a relief to get to the end of the sequence and massage her head.

The air in the room was muggy and still. My brow burned. I had an erection. I had massaged women in sensitive areas before, but I had never lost self-control. I was a healer, proud of my skills. I wanted to help people, not take advantage of them. It's not very nice, but men are men and mates in pubs would size up women and rate them as they passed: she's a 7, she's a 5, she's a 2. She's a slag. Lady Margaret was a 10 and she knew it.

I had finished. I was exhausted. I wanted to go home.

'Thank you,' I said.

'It is me who should be thanking you.' She smiled. 'Now, how much do I owe you?'

'Fifty pounds, please.'

She slipped down from the table and stepped into her robe. She crossed to the far wall, pressed a call button and Douglas entered with a silver tray containing a red £50 note. Lady Margaret murmured something I couldn't quite hear and Douglas about turned. As I was folding my table, he strode back into the room with a bottle of champagne in an ice bucket and two glasses. He placed them on a table carved with flowers and leaping deer, then left again.

'You did say you didn't drink,' Maggs said. 'By that do you mean you don't touch alcohol, or not very often?'

'I probably drank too much when I was younger. I sort of stopped…'

As I was speaking, she passed me the bottle.

'Can you open this for me?'

I don't think I had ever opened a bottle of champagne before. First I struggled to remove the gold foil, then came a wire mechanism that was awkward to unscrew. As I was trying to pull out the cork, she put her hand on my arm.

'You have to turn the bottle one way and the cork the other.'

I did so and the cork exploded with a satisfying pop. She took the bottle from me and filled two glasses.

'When you say no to champagne, you say no to life.' We touched the rims of our glasses. 'To you, Ben Foster.'

'To you, Lady Margaret.'

'Maggs,' she replied sternly.

I drank the champagne, the bubbles went up my nose and I immediately felt light-headed.

'You must open more bottles for me. It's important to know certain things.'

She smiled and her lips made perfect bows as she sipped her drink. She was glowing, hair lush and shiny, big eyes like green jewels gazing at me in the half light as if she had known me all her life. I wanted to reach out and grab her like we were in a movie, like it was a special moment that I shouldn't let pass. At the same time, I felt stupid thinking such thoughts and stood there with my throat dry in spite of the champagne. I was sure my knees were trembling.

'I'll call you next week,' she said.

'That would be great,' I replied.

She pointed at the silver tray. I put the £50 into my back pocket and did up the zip. I made my way with the table under my arm back along the corridor with its landscapes and sea-scapes, back across the hall and Douglas opened the door for me. I was floating.

'Goodbye, sir,' he said, and closed the door.

It was dark, warm still. A slice of moon was rising. At sea without light pollution you can pick out the constellations and old sailors would guide the trawlers by the stars. I was confused, contented, unsure if what had just happened had actually happened. I pushed the table into the back of the van, climbed in and turned the key.

Nothing. Not even a spark. I tried again.

Nothing.

I hit the steering wheel and tried one more time.

Nothing.

I got out of the car and popped the hood. While I was staring into the mass of greasy cables and pistons, Douglas appeared with a torch.

'Have you got a problem, sir?'

'Bloody thing won't start.'

'Try again.'

I did so and he shook his head. 'Dead as a door nail,' he said, and lowered the bonnet for me. 'Wait a moment.'

He marched back into the house, I assumed to call a breakdown service. He was gone for a couple of minutes and returned with a reassuring smile.

'Lady Margaret has asked me to make up one of the guest rooms, sir. She would like to invite you to dinner.'

I remained motionless with my mouth hanging open. If I had a comfort zone, this was so far out I was afraid I would never find my way back again. I thought for half a second about getting a taxi, but it would have cost the best part of the fifty quid I had just earned and there were a lot of needy places for that money. I could have asked Douglas to drive me home in the Range Rover, but it didn't occur to me at the time.

'Well, that's great, thank you,' I heard myself saying, and crossed the courtyard back to the house. I paused in the hall.

'This way, sir.'

'Just a moment, I should text my wife,' I said, and he stood there waiting while I did so.

Maggs rose from her chair as I entered the room. She must have taken a shower, her hair was combed but wet. She had changed into a green dress that shimmered like fish scales and matched her eyes.

'I do love surprises,' she said.

We finished the rest of the champagne and I had a glass of red wine with a dinner of cold chicken, a tomato salad and wedges of brown bread with olive oil served by Douglas. The cook was off for the weekend. I thought about asking where her husband was, but didn't.

Classical music played through hidden speakers.

'Do you like Bach?' she asked.

'If this is Bach, I like it,' I replied.

'The Brandenburg Concertos. They make me feel sad and happy to be alive. Do you know what I mean?'

'Yes, sort of, I suppose.'

'People live their lives without ever knowing who they really are. I have a feeling Bach knew exactly who he was and where he was going.' She paused. 'Do you?' she then asked.

'Absolutely. I want to make a go of the massage business so I've got enough money to give my three kids a decent start.'

'That's commendable. I like that,' she said. 'The secret of success isn't knowing what you want – that will come. It is knowing what you don't want.'

'There are a lot of things people don't want, they just have to put up with them.'

She thought about that but didn't reply. We moved away from the table and sat in armchairs set either side of a low coffee table stacked with books that looked as if they had never been opened.

'There was something I meant to ask you: what exactly is an Oriental twist? Does it come from the Kama Sutra?'

I shook my head. 'No, nothing like that. Massage in the East is centred more on meditation. It's about healing the mind as well as the body. That's what I try to do.'

'And you do it very well, I must say. I feel almost totally healed.' She laughed. 'The ladies of the Committee thought it meant something far more – esoteric.'

'The Committee?' I asked her and she churned the air with her fingers to dismiss the question.

'It doesn't mean anything,' she said.

We carried on chatting. I realised that I had never really talked like this before. The nearest I ever got to what you might call intelligent conversation was with Pete.

As she went to pour more wine, I placed my hand over the glass.

'Always say yes and try before you say no.'

'I've already tried.'

'Then try some more.'

She was lively, persuasive, as if everything in life were a pleasure and should be ignored if it weren't. The wine tasted better the more I drank. I felt unsteady as the music reached a crescendo and watched Maggs cross the room to gaze out at the sky.

'I adore the moon,' she said. 'I am one of those flowers that only bloom at night.'

Douglas appeared that second and Maggs waved over her shoulder as she left the room.

'I'll show you to your quarters, sir,' Douglas said, and the way he said it made me smile. I was less self-conscious after that last glass of wine.

'You weren't in the army, by any chance?'

He pulled back his shoulders. 'Man and boy. Twenty years in the Paras. If it moves, I've shot it. If it don't, I've jumped on it.'

'Bit of a change doing this?'

'If you don't change, you're dead. I'm going to give it two more years and open a little boutique hotel down on the Adriatic. Can't beat Italian women.' He smiled. 'Although I'd like to.'

'Sounds like a plan.'

'Plan for the worst. Hope for the best. Do that, son, and you can't go far wrong.'

He led me up a rickety staircase to a bedroom with a slanted roof. There was a big four-poster bed and I wondered if Oliver Cromwell had spent the night there when his coach broke down.

Douglas pointed to the adjoining room. 'Your bathroom. You'll find everything you need.'

He was right. There was shampoo from Fortnum & Mason, shower gel, bars of soap still in their packaging. I stood under the hot needles of the shower trying to get my head back on straight. I was exhausted – mentally, physically, whichever way you could be exhausted, that's how I felt. It had been a long hard week at the care home. Meeting ten beautiful women sounds like every man's dream, but when it happens, it shakes the foundations of who you are. As for giving Lady Margaret a massage, it was something I didn't even want to think about. My mind was racing. And I was thrilled to have fifty quid in my back pocket.

I curled up naked in the huge bed. I fell asleep instantly and thought I was seeing things when I suddenly woke up. The curtains were open. Starlight lit the room and Maggs was standing at the end of the bed like a ghost in her white silk gown. She let it fall to the floor. She pulled back the sheet, rubbed her nose against my nose then leaned back with her finger sealing her lips.

She kissed me, a real full-lipped, deep-tongued kiss that drove out any feelings of fatigue and lit my senses until they burned like fire. My cock was instantly hard and she wriggled down over my body to take me into her mouth. She licked my cock, plunged it into her throat, then flicked the tip of her tongue over the groove. She slipped one of my balls into her mouth, then the other. She sucked me until I was on the point of coming and stopped. She looked up.

'You're big, Ben,' she whispered. She smiled. 'Big Ben.'

As she spoke, she pulled towards me and I slipped up inside her. She rocked back and forth. I could feel the muscles of her sex tightening and releasing. Again I was on the point of orgasm when she slowed and stopped. She turned, lowered her vagina over my face and took my cock back down her throat. We came at the same time, long and hard and noisy. She sucked me dry, held my sperm in her mouth and let it trickle down my throat when we kissed.

She slipped over on her back, shuddering and sighing. 'Big Ben,' she murmured in a small voice and dipped down to take my softening cock back in her mouth. She sucked me until I was hard again, and we made love without hurry, slowly, gently, savouring every second.

5
IT'S ONLY SEX

The sun made patterns of brilliant light on the bed. I was unsure where I was until I spotted the portrait of Lady Margaret staring down from her position straddling a horse with a coat the same shade of chestnut as her hair. The room was stuffy and I opened the window. I was at the front of the house and could see a church spire over the trees.

How did I feel that morning?

I felt electric. Rewired. Fully charged. I felt as if I had grown two inches taller. I felt pleased with myself. I felt ashamed of myself. But, to be honest, more pleased than ashamed.

Sex with Kelly was natural, uncomplicated. She was a missionary position girl, trusting and inexperienced. She was an only child with elderly parents she had taken care of from the age of twelve. They'd gone quickly three weeks apart the year she turned eighteen. We had met shortly after when I was laying paving stones in the street where she lived. She had walked into a puddle of cement and looked really sad when she realised her shoes were ruined.

'I'll have to buy you a new pair,' I said.

'I'll keep you to that.'

'I'll come round Saturday, half past ten.'

She shrugged. 'That's what they all say.'

'They might say it, but I mean it. Saturday. You live near here.'
She paused for a moment, then pointed. 'Number 22.'

I grinned. 'I'm Ben. Pleased to meet you.'

'Kelly.'

'Half past ten Saturday.'

She knew I was serious and was deciding whether she actually wanted to meet up with a stranger she'd never laid eyes on before.

'All right,' she said, and skipped off down the road to number 22.

It was love at first sight and our first date has a sad as well as a happy ending. I did buy her a new pair of shoes, the best in the shop, and she was still wearing them. We married in Lowestoft where my family lived and the crew from our old trawler made an arch of fishing rods outside St Margaret's Church. The kids popped out one after the other and we struggled from week to week to make ends meet.

Kelly had lost a lot of schooling, she was unworldly, but strong and determined. She was five years younger than me and the way we met had seemed like destiny. We both needed someone to love, to build a life with, a family. She called me naïve and gullible. But we tend to see the faults in others we have in ourselves. She was just the same, an innocent. Our lovemaking followed a familiar pattern. She bit her bottom lip at the magic moment and I treasured the hazy look in her eyes. Oral sex had never entered the bedroom. She had been a virgin when we met and I loved her more than anything in the world.

Sex with Maggs was multi-faceted, colourful, feverish, like sex in a porn movie.

That movie ran in a loop through my head as I took a shower and I only realised as I was dressing that I still had the same problem with the van I'd had the night before. I made my way downstairs and outside. The courtyard was cool, shadowed by tall trees. I got in the van, said a quick prayer, and turned the ignition key.

Nothing.

When I looked under the bonnet, I saw in the daylight that both cables had been disconnected from the battery. Not one. Both.

I had no idea how this could have happened and looked in vain in the back of the van to see if I had a spanner. I was wondering what to do next when a flat-bed truck pulled into the drive carrying a VW Golf Hatchback GTI – gleaming, white as a new fridge, scratch free, rust free, the very car I would have chosen if I'd had the money. A mechanic in blue overalls lowered the hydraulics, reversed the Golf from the truck and parked behind the Range Rover.

At that point, Douglas appeared in the doorway.

'Someone disconnected my battery last night, that's why it wouldn't start,' I told him.

He threw up his big shoulders. 'Wouldn't know anything about that, sir. Lady Margaret is waiting in the morning room.'

'Have you got a spanner so I can reconnect the battery?'

'While you're having breakfast, I'll sort everything out.'

'I've got to get home,' I said.

'Always best to face the music on a full stomach.'

As we were speaking, the mechanic approached with a folder and I noticed he was carrying two sets of keys.

'Best not to keep a lady waiting,' Douglas added. 'If you take the door on the right from the hall, you'll find your way through the house to the morning room.'

I followed his instructions and found Maggs in a domed conservatory with about a million panes of glass. She was dressed in grey silk pyjamas and a grey dressing gown with her feet pushed into slippers with shields decorating the tops.

She smiled. 'There you are. Are you hungry?'

'Not really,' I replied. 'Someone disconnected my battery last night.'

'That is so naughty,' she said. 'Have some coffee and toast. I hate eating alone.'

There was toast in a rack. She poured coffee from a silver pot. There were various jams and marmalades, each with their own spoon. She buttered and spread jam on a half slice of toast.

'Try the plum, it's delicious.'

I did and it was.

'And how are you this lovely morning?'

'I feel a bit guilty, to be honest.'

'Guilty?' She looked surprised.

'Yes, well, you know ...'

'Actually, no, I have no idea. Guilt has always seemed a particularly odd thing to me. People,' she said, 'take sex far too seriously. It's only sex.'

'But you know, I have a wife ...'

'That's lovely. I have a husband.'

'Was he the man in the white suit I saw yesterday?'

She obviously didn't like being asked direct questions and thought for several moments before she answered.

'I suppose you're going to ask me next what our bet was about?'

'I don't understand.'

'Of course you don't. I had a bet with James that you would be sleeping under my roof before the end of the weekend. And here you are.'

'It had all been planned?'

'Are you unhappy, Ben? Think before you answer.'

I did think. I thought carefully. I'd been trapped, manipulated, used. But I wasn't unhappy.

'No,' I said, and she smiled.

'I believe in marriage, Ben, I really do. But it's not a prison, is it?'

'I suppose not.'

'What's your wife's name?'

This seemed like a strange question. 'Kelly,' I answered.

'That's pretty.' She buttered and spread a different jam on another piece of toast. 'Apricot,' she said, placing it on my plate and leaning forward. 'Don't feel guilty. It is too silly. May I be so bold as to offer you some advice?'

I nodded. 'I guess so.'

She ran her tongue over her lips before continuing. 'Whatever you do, don't confess to Kelly. When husbands tell their wives they are having an affair, they are just bragging. They want to show their wife they are still desirable. *You* don't need to do that.'

As I ate another half slice of toast, it occurred to me that Lady Margaret wasn't that dissimilar to Chris at The Lodge. She had no sense of right and wrong. It also occurred to me that she had instructed someone, probably Douglas, to disable my van. He looked like the kind of man who could disable anything.

I ate the toast and buttered some more. My stomach was empty and my head was full of conflicts. While Kelly was at home with the children making their modest breakfast, I was with a beautiful woman with whom I'd had the best sex ever sitting at a table with a snow-white linen cloth in the most incredible room I'd ever been in. The conservatory with its exotic palms and reflected light looked out over rolling fields bordered by mature trees. The chinaware tinkled. The cutlery was silver. I had an initialled linen napkin on my knees and the coffee was the best I had ever tasted.

'It's a nice house,' I said.

'Yes, we are so lucky. It's been in Jasper's family for generations. My husband,' she added, and leaned forward. 'May I ask you a personal question, Ben? Don't be offended.' She paused. 'You don't play around, you don't cheat on Kelly?'

'No.'

She smiled. 'None of those nasty STDs.'

'Sexually transmitted diseases? Absolutely not, no way.'

She sipped her coffee then dried her lips. 'For one so young, Vivienne is a very good judge of character. You really are a glass of clear water.'

I should have asked her if she had any STDs. She was the one who believed people took sex too seriously. But I didn't have the confidence to say anything like that. I ate all the toast in the rack and was drinking a second cup of coffee when my phone buzzed with a text.

It was from Kelly: was I all right? Is the van going?

'Excuse me,' I said.

I messaged back that I'd be home soon and everything was fine. I never lied to Kelly, but these were special circumstances.

'I really ought to get going,' I said.

Lady Margaret glanced at her watch and stood. 'You were hungry. I'm so pleased,' she replied. 'Let's go and see what's happening.'

We made our way back through the house. When we reached the door, I saw the tail end of the flat-bed truck vanish through the avenue of trees with my van on the back. I ran out into the courtyard.

'Oi, hang on a minute,' I shouted.

I was too slow, it had gone. I looked back. Lady Margaret was standing in the wide porch, Douglas at her side. He threw me a set of keys.

'Catch,' he said. 'Press the button.'

I did so and the lights on the VW flashed as the doors locks clicked open.

'We thought white was the most suitable, given your profession,' Lady Margaret said and my mouth fell open. 'It's for you,' she added.

'Me? What? Are you joking?'

'It's too early for jokes.'

'It's for me?'

'It is.'

'You can't be serious. You can't just give someone a car.'

'Why not?'

'You just don't. The expense for one thing.'

'It's a tax write off. The Chancellor of the Exchequer paid for it.'

'What?' I shook my head. 'I can't accept it, Lady Margaret ...'

'Maggs,' she said impatiently. 'Now, speak to Douglas, will you? I really must fly.'

She turned and disappeared back into the house.

'Best not to fight it, sir. Things are the way they are.'

'You mean it's really mine?'

He gave me the second set of keys and folder he was holding. He pointed. 'There's a phone number. Give it a ring and they'll sort it all out for you. Goodbye, sir.'

'What about the insurance? I can't drive without insurance.'

'You call that number. I'm sure it's all taken care of.'

He closed the door behind him and I climbed warily into the white VW Golf as if it might be a car bomb or, more likely, a Time Machine that was going to take me back to reality. I turned the key. The engine hummed as I eased the gear shift into first. I touched the accelerator, circled the courtyard and slipped into second as I drove through the tunnel of trees.

I was driving home, wondering how the hell I was going to explain this to Kelly, when my phone vibrated with a text. I didn't read it until I arrived and parked outside the house.

I just heard from Maggs that she feels completely invigorated after your massage. Please may I make an appointment for 2.00 this afternoon? Vivienne Raynott

6
THE £50 NOTE

After texting Vivienne for her address, I strolled up the path and gave the knocker a good hard tap. I walked back to the car and leaned on the side with my arms folded. I felt like I'd won the lottery and almost certainly had that 'cat that got the canary' look, as Gran would have said.

Kelly opened the door. She had Claire in her arms and the boys were peeking out from behind her legs. She wasn't smiling.

'Hello, darling,' I called. 'Look up, not a cloud in sight. Fancy going for a drive?'

'Why didn't you let yourself in? Forgot your key?'

'No.'

'Well, come on in then, I'm busy.'

'Got something to show you, Kells.'

'You can show me inside.' She looked cross. 'What you doing leaning against that car? You know what people are like.'

'Yeah, you can run over their kids as long as you don't touch their car.' My jaw ached. I was grinning from ear to ear. 'Come on. Come and take a look.'

Kelly shook her head. 'Three kids are enough, Ben, I don't need another one.'

They trooped up the path. Ollie opened the gate and I bent low with a flourish like Sir Walter Raleigh.

'Your carriage awaits.'

Kelly wasn't amused. Her job made a break from looking after the children, but moving wet laundry from washers to dryers was heavy work and by Sunday she had usually run out of patience. She readjusted Claire on her hip and stared back at me.

'What's going on, Ben? You on something?'

'Yeah, a winning streak for a change.'

'Is that your car, dad?'

I brushed my hand over Ollie's crew cut. 'It's our car, Big Guy. Why don't you take her for a spin?'

Ollie climbed in the driver's seat and started pulling at the steering wheel. I opened the passenger door for George.

'Me. Me,' Claire cried.

'She's learned a new word,' I said and Kelly frowned.

'Don't know who she takes after. That's all she says now.'

I put Claire in the back. She was wearing a red pom-pom hat and a red dress from the Oxfam shop. She looked like a puppet on a string as she jumped up and down on the seat. Kelly had taken on her customary pose, hands on hips, head cocked to one side, a sceptical cast to her blue eyes.

'Where were you last night?'

'You know where I was. The van gave up the ghost and Lady Margaret had a room made up for me at her place.'

'Lady Margaret,' she repeated. 'You said it was some rich lady.'

'Lady Margaret is a rich lady.'

'Her husband was there, I suppose?'

'No, he wasn't, as a matter of fact. But her butler was.'

'Her butler! You'd think this was two hundred years ago.'

'I'll tell you this, Kells, we think it's all changed. Nothing's changed.'

'So the van's given up and you've come home in a new car. I suppose it belongs to her?'

'No, it's mine. It's ours.'

'They're having a laugh, Ben. You don't give someone a massage and then they give you a car. Life doesn't work like that.'

'It does if you're rich.'

'They must have more money than sense. That's all I can say.'

'It's not like that. It's a tax adjustment, that's what she said. She didn't pay for it, the Chancellor of the Exchequer did.'

'And who do you think the Chancellor of the Exchequer is? That's you and me. It's all the ordinary people who pay their taxes. Pete. Your mates at The Lodge.'

'I didn't think of that.'

'Of course you didn't.'

'Here,' I said.

I took out the £50 note and when I gave it to her, she studied it as if it were a photograph.

'You know something, it's the first time I've ever held one of these in my own hands.' She looked up. 'Did you ask for the money in advance?'

'I didn't to be honest.'

'Be careful, Ben. People don't give you a car, even if the taxpayers paid for it, not unless they want something.'

'They just want a massage. I happen to be good at it.'

'Nobody said you weren't.'

'Look, I've got another booking at two o'clock.'

I showed her my phone and she read the text.

I just heard from Maggs that she feels completely invigorated after your massage. Please may I make an appointment for 2.00 this afternoon? Vivienne Raynott

'Who's this one?'

'Another friend of Rufus's mum. She was with Maggs and some other women last time I gave Rufus his weekly rub down.'

'You call her Maggs?'

'She told me to. You know what it's like when I treat someone. It's like you're their new best friend.'

Kelly stared into my eyes. She was nodding her head slowly up and down. The world around us was silent and I could almost hear the cogs clicking over in her head. She had a red £50 note in her hand, a new car outside the house, a look of concern in her blue eyes.

'We're all right, Ben. We get by. We've got what we need. Don't do anything bad, anything dishonest.'

'I haven't, Kelly, and I won't. Nothing like this has ever happened before and it's not going to happen again. Let's just enjoy it.'

She bent down and looked inside the car.

'No. No,' Claire shouted.

'Come on, jump in,' I said. 'Let's go for a ride.'

I opened the driver's door and spoke to Ollie.

'Where do you want to go, sunshine?'

'I know, dad, let's go and buy a Crunchie.'

'Yeah, why not. We'll go down to the park.'

It's shallow, it's sad even, but when you drive in a stream of new cars and you're in a broken down old van, you feel like a loser, like everyone is going somewhere and you're still at the starting line. We judge ourselves, and each other, on things which I knew from learning yoga massage are insignificant, even irrelevant. But it appears to be the human condition to see the gloss, the outside of things, and not look any deeper.

Yoga massage originated in India 2,500 years ago and is little changed to this day. The master takes the patient through a sequence of yoga postures while massaging along the body's energy lines and pressure points. The goal is to put the body's energy back in balance. That morning in the park watching the children play under the trees, I thought that's just what I need: rebalancing.

Kelly had asked me if I was on something and I was. I was high on adrenaline, the hormone that directs a surge of blood to specific areas of the body – my mind that was buzzing and my cock in its permanent state of semi-arousal. I couldn't stop picturing myself in that four-poster bed with the moonlight turning the room silver. I had done things with Maggs I had never done before and every little detail went round and round in my head. Just saying to myself the words 'Lady Margaret' was a thrill.

She had been right, of course. It would have made no sense blurting out a confession to Kelly. What had happened wasn't my fault. Maggs had made sure my van didn't start. She stripped naked for the massage and plied me with champagne. I can't imagine any man under those circumstances getting all huffy and kicking her out of bed. I shook my head to still the movie. That night with Lady Margaret was a one off. It was a sweet memory, but I had too much to lose and resolved not to let anything like that happen again.

I watched the red pom-poms on Claire's hat bobbing up and down as she ran through the dappled sunlight behind a barking brown Staffie. She fell over and I could see by her expression that she wasn't sure whether to cry or not. I picked her up.

'No. No,' she said.

I rubbed her nose with my nose. 'Yes, yes,' I replied and she laughed. 'Let's go and have a pizza, shall we?'

Claire struggled to get down. 'Me. Me,' she said.

Kelly grabbed my arm. 'What did I tell you?'

I called the boys. 'Come on you two, lunch time,' and George chased Ollie across the grass.

We broke into the £50 note – we had to at some time. I felt proud letting the kids have whatever they wanted and went a bit crazy for once in my life and ordered a beer.

7
VIVIENNE

The walls were hung with the strangest pictures I had ever seen:
a man with his fist jammed in the rectum of another man, a
naked man pointing a gun, his arm level to his penis like it was
another gun; men in masks, women in chains, pierced penises, the
images in matching frames beneath spotlights that ran on rails on
the ceiling. I felt instantly embarrassed and unsure of myself.

'Do you like them?'

Vivienne was standing behind me dressed for ballet in a
white tutu and pumps, a costume that was so unexpected it had
thrown me off balance when she opened the door to her apartment, a penthouse close to Kensington Palace. I turned. Her
brow was tight and she had a searching look on her long narrow
face. I was about to lie but stopped myself. It was a habit I didn't
want to get into.

'Not exactly,' I answered. 'But I don't dislike them.'

We moved on and stopped before a shot of a naked white
woman wreathed in cigarette smoke watching a black man mas-
turbating. I assumed it meant something but had no idea what.
Vivienne spoke as if working out what she wanted to say. She
grabbed at the air with her long fingers.

'Photographs capture a moment in time. They're like memories. This is different. It makes us wonder what has already

happened and what is going to happen next. We become a part of the story.' She looked into my eyes. 'Robert Mapplethorpe was a true genius.'

I assumed that was the photographer, but didn't ask.

We moved along the display.

'Do you recognise anyone?'

There were various women in various states of undress, none smiling. I shook my head. She pointed at a woman in black leather motorbike gear, then another, naked.

'Marianne Faithful, Brooke Shields, Sigourney Weaver, Debbie Harry, Yoko Ono. They were all icons in their day. But it's not their day anymore.' Her voice dropped to a whisper. 'It's our day.'

Her moods changed quickly. Her silvery blonde hair was bright as chrome in the spotlights. I could smell her perfume. It was light and airy, a scent I didn't know, and seemed personal to her. She was so beautiful, I couldn't bear to look at her.

We turned from the photographs. Along the centre of the room on plinths were carvings and twisted loops of steel. She stroked a white marble nude with oversized legs and small breasts.

'Henry Moore. I love him. Touch, it's so sensuous.'

The marble was cool beneath my fingertips.

'Isn't it luscious?' she said.

'Yes, luscious,' I repeated.

I watched her glide along the wall of pictures and turn off the overhead lights. The sun through the tall windows was warm, my hands were damp and I felt a desire to reach out and touch her, hold her, to feel her skin. The resolve I'd made eating pizza with my kids had vanished like a puff of smoke.

'It's such a pleasure to have you here, Ben. I never entertain.'

'It's a privilege,' I said and meant it. 'I've never been any-where like this before.'

'Do you know Amsterdam?'

'No.'

'When I saw the Van Gogh's, I cried. We'll go one day.'

She span in a pirouette, danced across the open space and out through the door at the end of the gallery. I glanced again at the photographs and it struck me that everything in the room was in shades of black and white, the images, the grey slate floor, me in my white costume like a character on stage. I set up the massage table in the space between the white Henry Moore sculpture and a black stone figure of a mother and child. The shadowy faces staring from the walls was like an audience waiting for the play to begin.

My heart was pounding in my chest. Something had happened to me and it may have been as pathetic as driving a new car. All my life I had been weighed down by that working-class feeling of not being quite good enough. Massage had helped me to overcome that to a certain extent, but it's like a birthmark, you never completely lose that sense of inferiority. I had felt ill at ease in the Great Hall with those fine ladies. That feeling hadn't gone, but it had weakened. Vivienne had made me feel welcome. This was her secret world and she had invited me to be a part of it.

Most days I was mopping up pee and buckling lads into strait jackets to stop them harming themselves. My life had turned upside down. Vivienne Raynott was a society lady, a friend of the Queen. It was heady stuff. When I jogged, I usually sprinted the last two hundred metres and it made me buzz with energy. That was the feeling I had that July afternoon, like I'd run faster than I had ever run before and jumped over a vast yawning chasm.

As I stroked the marble sculpture, Vivienne's appearance in the doorway was like a scene from an unfolding story created by the photographer whose work lined the walls. The images portrayed the dark parts of our humanity. I couldn't work out why Vivienne liked them so much, unless it was the attraction of opposites. She was pure and delicate in a gallery of the crude and obscene. She was wrapped in a towel, the beginnings of a smile on her lips.

'Are you ready for me?'

'I should wash my hands,' I said.

'Come.'

I entered the bedroom. Everything was white, as was the bathroom with its marble sinks and shiny silver fittings. Vivienne, Maggs, Lady Catherine, they lived such different lives from me, from ordinary people. Kelly had said 'they must have more money than sense.' But that was untrue, a cliché. They were not lacking in common sense at all. On the contrary. They were smart, aware, chosen people. Vivienne with her art, Maggs with Bach. The comments they made and the things they talked about made me realise there was so much to know about so many things and how little I knew about anything.

As I dried my hands, I gazed into the mirror. I was a traveller at the beginning of a journey, destination unknown, and really wasn't sure who it was looking back at me in the reflection.

Vivienne was waiting, naked, stretched out on the table, the towel on the floor.

'I'm surprisingly strong, Ben,' she said. 'Don't be afraid to press hard.'

I didn't want to look at her and made myself busy. My shoulder bag was under the table with some aromatherapy candles, the iPod with music, a variety of oils, jojoba, almond, apricot kernel, Kukui nut oil, arnica for sports injuries. Oils help you get the best balance between grip and slip, their perfume heightening the sense of smell, the most neglected of the senses. Some oils make patients sparkle with new life; others help them fall into a deep sleep. I would never have told anyone, but I secretly thought of myself as an alchemist choosing and blending oils in a quest to find the gold in the soul of every person.

'Would you like me to light some candles and play some music?' I asked.

'No, nothing. Let's enjoy the silence?'

Everything Kelly said about me was true. I lacked confidence. I was unsure of myself. I was naive. But the moment I warmed some jojoba in my palms I became a different person, the me inside me, the me I was supposed to be. Massage is a performance. You play the role of the healer and become a projection of yourself when the show begins. Everyone is born with one skill. I felt blessed to have found mine.

The room was bright with blocks of shadow as the sun moved across the windows. When I had first looked at the Henry Moore sculpture, I'd thought the proportions were wrong. Now it appeared delicate, feminine, fragile. I ran a few drops of oil over Vivienne's spine. I saw now that her back, the cheeks of her bottom and the tops of her legs were criss-crossed with a mesh of fine shiny lines.

'You have a lot of scars,' I said and her reply was a whisper.

'I think they're beautiful.'

I wanted to ask more, how and why, but it would have been inappropriate. I was a stranger in the strange land of the rich and was coming to see that they do things differently there.

'Take a deep breath, hold it for a count of ten and relax.'

The nervous system is like a seesaw. You can't be relaxed and nervous at the same time. As Vivienne held her breath, so did I and my nerves grew still. I began by running my spread fingers down either side of her spine. She sighed. Her body was like porcelain with fine cracks. But the feel of her skin was soft like dipping your hands into warm milk. She had told me to press hard, but I was afraid she would shatter under pressure.

I carried on over her damaged bottom and up the sides of her body, repeating the initial effleurage ten times before moving on to her shoulders, where I found a ball of knots. Vivienne didn't have the financial anxiety most of us have, but anxiety comes in many forms – perhaps she had lost her boyfriend to a rival, or her mother didn't love her, or her father loved her too much. There had to be a reason why her back was covered in scars.

Applying figure of 8 movements over her shoulder blades, I was able to isolate the knot clusters. We all have stress and react to it in different ways; we drink, take drugs, get violent, and it depressed me that so few people turn to yoga or massage to cure their problems and pains. As I worked on the knots, they began to loosen. The body stores mental tension that remains buried until long after the causes have passed. Massage eases the tightness in the muscles that arise from that built-up tension and I could feel it prickling my fingertips as it rose to the surface and vanished from Vivienne's long slender back.

She turned over. Her eyes were bright like blue neon. She had wide shoulders with deep wells shaded blue beneath her collarbones. Her breasts were symmetrical and sat firmly above a frame of protruding ribs, a narrow waist and jutting hipbones. Her shaved pussy was as white as a seashell and gave her a vulnerable, child-like appearance that created in me opposing sensations. I wanted to take her in my arms, protect her, hold her tightly, while my body's reaction ran contrary to that emotion. The blood was racing through my veins and I had an erection that was growing painful.

I massaged her ballerina feet and wanted to kiss her toes. I ran my hands up her legs and over her ribcage, avoiding her breasts. As I began to work my thumbs into the top of the shoulders above her collarbones, she placed her palms around the back of my head.

'You can kiss me now,' she said.

I loved her voice, it was deep and sweet like a musical instrument. We kissed, a lover's kiss, long and sensual. I was standing at the side of the massage table. She reached down to stroke my penis.

'Poor Ben. He's been neglected.'

She swung her legs from the table, slipped down on her knees and pulled my white jogging pants down to my feet.

'There you are, poor baby,' she said and took me into her mouth.

My eyes closed. Stars glimmered behind my eyelids. The Hon. Vivienne Raynott, author and heiress, was sucking my cock. It was unbelievable. Me. A care worker. A nobody from nowhere. I wanted this. I had wanted it from the moment she left the Great Hall and came to tell me 'how brave I was,' how 'we were going to be friends for the rest of our lives.'

Through massage and yoga, I had learned that every person is a blend of *yin* and *yang*, of opposing traits and qualities. Good and bad. Kind and hard-hearted. Generous and mean. I was proud of myself. I was disappointed with myself, and I wouldn't have wanted to be anywhere in the world other than where I was at that moment. Men dream of sleeping with beautiful women. I was living the dream.

Vivienne pulled my jogging pants and boxers over my grubby trainers, stood and led me by my cock from the gallery to her bedroom with its white bed and downy pillows. I kicked off my shoes, my shirt, and lay back like a king as she continued to lick and suck and nibble my cock and balls.

'Mmm, beautiful,' she said.

She ran her lips down the shaft as if she were playing a harmonica. She moved her tongue in circles around the head. She made sighing sounds like a cat with a bowl of cream. As my body tensed, she moved away and pressed herself against the white metal bars of the headboard, eyes glassy, her voice a whisper.

'My face,' she moaned.

She jerked the skin up and down the length of my cock and sprayed her face, my load coating her eyes and rolling down her cheeks into her mouth. I was panting like I'd just jogged around the park. I watched as she scooped up a dollop of sperm on the end of her finger and slid it between her lips. She kissed me and I tasted my own semen.

'Hit me,' she then said and turned to take hold of the bed frame.

She pushed out her bottom.

My cock softened. I was unsure of myself. She turned and smiled.

'Have you never spanked a girl before, Ben?'

I shook my head. She stared into my eyes. Her voice was harder, demanding, authoritative.

'It isn't difficult. Just a little tap. It won't hurt.'

I gently spanked her bum cheeks with my open palm.

'There, you see. And again. Harder.'

I spanked her again. Harder. And again, harder still. And she was right. It wasn't difficult.

'Harder. Don't stop until I tell you to.'

The sound of my hand striking her skin echoed over the ceiling. Her bottom turned pink, each slap leaving a white hand print. My cock grew hard again. Perhaps she sensed that. It was all new to me. She didn't tell me to stop. I didn't stop. My hand was beginning to sting. My heart beat faster. New unknown sensations ran through me like bursts of electricity. I was sheathed in a film of sweat and my flesh felt as if it were peeling from my body like a snake shedding its skin. Whoever I was when I had arrived at that apartment had faded into the past. I was a different person now.

Suddenly, she grew tense. She took a firmer grip on the metal bars of the headboard and her body began to shake. She turned and pulled me on top of her and we moved together like two dancers who had spent a lifetime learning a set of intricate steps. The heat expanded between us as our bodies moved closer then eased apart. She sucked air through her teeth and held her breath.

We weren't fucking. We were making love. It was a performance. Her back arched. Her body went stiff and we erupted in orgasm, our duet creating something greater than ourselves.

We fell back into the down pillows. I felt drained yet recharged and more alive than I had ever felt in my life.

'Now,' she gasped. 'That's better?' She nursed my cock in her hand, squeezing gently. 'Your *cazzo* is a sculpture. It's a Henry Moore.'

I didn't know what *cazzo* meant and didn't ask. She looked back into my eyes and a wave of excitement crossed her features.

'We are going to make a mould and cast it in bronze. Would you like that?'

'I don't know. Will it hurt?'

She laughed. 'A little pain can lead to a lot of pleasure.'

'Is that why ...' I stopped and she shook my penis.

'When innocence ends, pleasure begins.' She paused. Her expression changed. 'Jealousy is only hurt ego. Revenge is meaningless. Life is abstract. If there is any point other than pleasure, I haven't found it.'

She snuggled up beside me. Her words were like poetry and I repeated them to myself as I closed my eyes. I may have dozed off and woke with Vivienne sucking my penis again. She stopped and I watched as she extracted a pubic hair from between her teeth.

'Do you trust me, Ben?'

'Yes, of course.'

'Cross your heart and hope to die?'

I smiled. 'Yes.'

'Thank you,' she said.

She stepped from the bed and stretched, going up on her toes and holding her palms together above her head. She then crossed the room to a chest of drawers and removed a black silk scarf. She covered my eyes and tied the scarf at the back of my head. I heard her cross the room to the bathroom and return again.

'Roll to one side for a moment.'

I did so and she stretched a towel beneath me.

'Put your knees up and *don't* move.' She stressed the word don't. 'Are you ready?'

'As ready as I'll ever be.'

I listened to the snip, snip, snip of a pair of scissors as she cut away tufts of my pubic hair. I heard the hiss of foam being sprayed from a container and she began to shave my lower stomach and balls. She held my penis in her long fingers. As she ran the razor down the shaft, I held my breath and thought for one unbearable second that she was going to castrate me, that she was an angel and I was the devil being punished for all the bad things I had done.

'You're shaking,' she said and I let out my breath.

'This is worse than going to the dentist.'

'You are such a baby.'

She was slow, careful, methodical. She returned to the places where the hair was stubborn, added fresh foam and ran the razor over the area again. She washed and dried the shaved parts, then popped my cock back in her mouth, her saliva like balm, and I became hard again. When she peeled away the scarf, my cock looked oddly naked and much bigger.

'Do you like it?'

'I'm not sure.'

'It's much better. Girls hate it when they get smelly pubes between their teeth?'

'I've never thought about that to be honest.'

She was smiling, joyful, totally at ease with her nudity, with mine. It was hard to believe she was older than Kelly. She looked like a teenager. It was strange and confusing. I felt as if I had fallen in love and kept having to tell myself it's only sex. She sucked my cock again, slowly, like the last dance at the end of a long evening.

'He really is rather beautiful,' she said and skipped from the bed.

It was time to go. We drank glasses of water. I dressed. She sat at a bureau, still naked, removed her cheque book and reached for a pen.

'Ben Foster, or Benjamin.'

'It doesn't matter.'

I stood over as she wrote the number 50 in the appropriate box. She paused, then added another 0. She wrote 'Five Hundred Pounds Only,' signed the cheque and gave it to me.

'That's too much, Vivienne.'

'No it's not. Not for a work of art in progress,' she replied.

8
DEEP BREATHING

Claire fell asleep laying on top of me as I read *Charlie and the Chocolate Factory* for about the twentieth time. Ollie and George identified with Charlie Bucket. I suppose I did as well. Charlie is a poor boy who has a stroke of luck finding a golden ticket in a chocolate wrapping that allows him to enter the secret world of Willie Wonka's chocolate factory.

'Why can't we have Wonka chocolate, dad?' Ollie asked.

'It's only a story. It's probably the same as a Crunchie.'

'What, with honeycomb?'

'Can't see why not.'

'I wanna Wonka,' George intoned in his deep little voice and Ollie groaned.

'It's only a story,' he said.

'Right, you two, back to your own room. I'm going to put Claire in her cot.'

'Can we have another story, dad?' Ollie asked.

'If you get into bed and be quiet.'

The boys ran out, George copying Ollie by pressing his finger to his lips. Ollie gave George the occasional shove, it's what older brothers do, but he watched out for him crossing the road and was always protective. I was sure they would be friends for the rest of their lives and I was sorry not having a brother to share my secrets with.

Claire was sighing, deep in sleep. She was a non-stop ball of activity from the moment she opened her eyes in the morning and snuggled straight down sucking the corner of her blanket when she went to bed at night. It made my eyes grow misty just looking at her sleeping.

We'd learned from all the bringing-up-baby guides that getting children used to books was the best start in life and helped them adjust to school when they started. No one thought of those things when Kelly and I were growing up and we knew how important education was because we didn't have any. I read another story to the boys and went downstairs to join Kelly.

We had the new *Doctor Who* series on video recorded for us by Pete. I watched David Tennant, the Time Lord in a pin-stripe suit, leap through space and time with Billie Piper, his companion, blonde with bright eyes and teeth like a shark.

'Here we go, saving the world again.'

'Shush. I'm watching.'

'No wonder he's got bags under his eyes.'

'Is that the green-eyed monster talking? He's gorgeous.'

'He looks gay to me,' I said and she turned with an irritated expression.

'You can tell by the way Billie Piper looks at him he's not gay.'

'Billie Piper, now that's another story. She's…' I paused. 'She's luscious.'

Kelly sniffed the air. 'Luscious,' she repeated. 'That's a new one.'

'Only word for Billie Piper.'

'Dream on,' she said, and I didn't say sometimes dreams do come true.

In two days, I had slept with two of the most beautiful women in the world. I had a new Volkswagen Golf and a cheque for £500.

I had a satiated if slightly tender penis and I was living in a parallel galaxy. Millions of ghosts had emerged through a time warp in the universe. Four Daleks in a void ship were following Doctor Who and I had no doubt he would save the world before I found a way to explain to Kelly how my private parts came to be denuded of pubic hair.

I kept picturing the fine silvery lines meshed across Vivienne's back, her bottom turning pink as I spanked her, the way it felt as if the world had been reborn as we erupted in orgasm. Why had she been wearing ballet clothes when I arrived? Why did she want to make a mould of my penis? What did *cazzo* mean? It was obvious, but nothing with Vivienne was obvious.

When innocence ends, pleasure begins.

Had I lost my innocence along with my pubic hair?

The only reason men shave their pubes is when they get crabs, and that gave me an idea. I would tell Kelly there was an outbreak at The Lodge and the staff had been advised to shave as a precaution. That's what I was thinking about while the characters in *Doctor Who* flickered across the screen. Then it struck me: I don't have to tell her anything at all. Kelly was uncomfortable with nudity. She rarely saw me naked, unless I was stepping from the bath. I just had to be careful and save the explanation in case I needed it.

I squeezed the dimples above Kelly's knee and she almost jumped off the couch.

'Ouch. I hate it when you do that.'

'I'm going to read, Jelly Belly,' I said and kissed her cheek.

When I was broke or bored or feeling down, I chose one of the books from the shelf in the bedroom and reading always put me in a better mood. Not that I was in a bad mood. I was confused. I wanted to feel ashamed, remorseful, angry with myself. But I didn't. I wasn't. What had happened with Vivienne that day was beautiful, natural, life-affirming. It was going to happen again. We were at the beginning of something, not the end, and I had no intention or desire to stop it.

I picked up Martin Kirk's *Hatha Yoga* and settled down on the bed with my head against the pillow.

It always comes as a shock when I tell people that you can relieve stress simply by breathing properly. *Pranayama,* the Sanskrit word, means breath control, a force when mastered that intensifies the body's energy levels and aids the heart in its job of pumping blood through our veins. Shallow breathing, customary for most people, doesn't oxygenate the blood. The result is a build-up of toxins. It is those toxins that make us feel sluggish, restless, despondent. Deep breathing nourishes and repairs body cells. It washes out toxins and makes us feel content and balanced. I had learned a simple technique easy for anyone to practise:

Inhale for the count of two
Exhale for the count of TWO
Inhale for the count of two
Exhale for the count of THREE
Inhale for the count of two
Exhale for the count of FOUR
Inhale for the count of two
Exhale for the count of FIVE

By repeating this several times, when you breathe normally, you feel more alert. You can stay in focus longer if you need to concentrate, and still the mind if you want to meditate. The secret of meditation, its very purpose, isn't to think about something, to ponder some puzzle or mystery, but to think about nothing at all. I exhaled and took another breath, but it wasn't the void that I entered, it was Vivienne Raynott's gallery of sadomasochistic images with Vivienne stretched out between the Henry Moore sculpture and the black stone woman and child.

I had never lied to Kelly. Now each lie was compounded by another lie – Maggs, Vivienne, I didn't even have the courage to tell my wife I had a £500 cheque in my pocket, money we so desperately needed. It was hardly the worst thing that could have happened. It was the best thing that had ever happened, and that made it all the more confusing. I was like one of those lottery winners who suddenly had a fortune and wanted to blow it all so I could get back to normality. Or the drunk with a hangover who swears in the morning he will never drink again and can't wait till the pubs open so he can have a pint at lunchtime.

I cleaned my teeth, stepped over the safety gate and went back downstairs. Kelly was watching another episode of *Doctor Who* and I snuggled up close on the couch.

'Don't say anything,' she said.

'Love you,' I replied.

First thing Monday morning, I repaired the wheelbarrow and cleaned out the rest of the weeds from the garden with Ollie and George. I drove to the bank to deposit the cheque and used the credit card to buy new trainers for the three of us knowing the money would be there to cover it when the bill came in.

The boys knew better than me what Kelly bought in the supermarket and filled the trolley with their favourite things. Ollie must have had an addictive personality – I wasn't sure who he took after – and his eyes lit up when we stumbled upon a special offer on five-packs of Crunchies. He jumped up and down he was so excited.

'Get five dad, go on, get five.'

The supermarkets had convinced us it was cheaper buying economy packs and that's how they made their money, making us spend more to save more.

'I will this time. But they have to last a week. All your teeth are going to fall out if you keep eating chocolate.'

'Thanks, dad,' he said, and gently laid the Crunchies in the bottom of the trolley.

By the time we went through the checkout, we had enough packets of biscuits and crisps to last till Christmas.

'Don't go mad, Ben, you've only done two extra massages,' Kelly said as she unloaded the bags. 'New trainers as well...'

'It's called positive thinking,' I replied. 'When you stop worrying about money, the universe opens up and it comes pouring in.'

'I suppose all your rich friends have been telling you that.'

'No, they don't think about that sort of thing.'

'What do they think about?'

'I don't know, art and music, you know, like Bach, Van Gogh. When you don't have to worry about money, you can think about other things.'

'Still makes me wonder how someone can just give you a new car.'

'Like you said, Kells, we paid for it out of our taxes.'

She had taken my new trainers out of the bag; white Nike's with red lightning stripes down each side. 'They don't look cheap.'

'They cost what they cost,' I said. 'Honestly, don't worry. I have to look my best if I'm going to get more work. Five massages a week and I'll be earning the same as what I'm getting at The Lodge.'

I gave her a hug, the boys howled in protest – as usual, and there was a knock on the door.

Carly, our kind neighbour, had arrived for her massage. Lily, her little girl, was Ollie's girlfriend and I was sure there would be tears before lunch if George and Claire intruded on the private world of big boys and girls.

With Carly stripped to her knickers and bra, I oiled my hands with the last of the arnica and told her to count to ten as she held her breath. She had shooting pains along the sciatic nerve and down the back of each leg. I massaged her lower back, concentrating on one area. Working out the tightness in the lumbar muscles reduces the stress on the intervertebral disc, relieving the discomfort, though not its cause.

'Ah, that's so much better. You have magic hands, Ben.'

'I know, I should be a conjuror.'

'You'd earn more money, like that, whatshisname, you know, Darren something or other?'

'Derren Brown.'

'That's him. You could do that. You've got a face for the telly.'

'Someone once told me I had a face for radio,' I said and she laughed.

'Aw Aw. Ouch. It hurts when I laugh.'

It was warm with the morning sun lighting the room. I opened the window as wide as it would go and glanced out at the garden. The roses still had their blooms and a pair of blackbirds were pecking over the fresh earth where I'd cleared the weeds. Like the garden, everything that had been muddled in my mind the previous night was clearer in the daylight.

I worked my way over Carly's thighs. There was no stirring between my legs. I was a professional again, not that Carly was anything like Vivienne. She was about the same age, under thirty, and getting heavy with big hips and a wide backside. A bottle of Lucozade stood on the side table. People thought it was an energy drink, but it is full of empty calories and the sugar doesn't give you more drive, it gives you a momentary boost and then you feel more weary.

'Hope you drink plenty of water, Carly, you have to hydrate. It's good for the sciatica. It's good for everything.'

'I don't like water, it leaves a nasty taste in your mouth.'

'It's better for you than all those fizzy drinks.'

'I know, but a little bit of what you fancy does you good.'

'As long as it's not too much of what you fancy,' I said.

She laughed and said ouch again.

We really are our own worst enemy. Old people were dying that summer from dehydration, and still they wouldn't drink water. Another thing that struck me as a bit strange, most of the poor women on the estate were fat and all the rich women I'd met in the Great Hall were thin. Was there a secret diet only rich people knew about?

Before lunch, I went for my jog. I called at Pete Taylor's house, but he was still at work. He started in the dark at four, spent four hours with his unit sorting the mail into the different 'walks,' then spent another five hours hiking five miles to deliver 600 letters a day. A five mile walk is good for you, but better when you're not stopping and starting. I glanced across the road at the white Golf sparkling in the sunshine and carried on through the estate to the park.

I ran fast, it was hot, and I sweated out all the toxins and doubt. Boys raced each other on skateboards. Girls sunbathed in their underwear. I saw a mother duck snapping at little dogs as she herded her five ducklings back to the lake. Families were eating pizza. Everything today was the same as yesterday. You can't change the past or the inevitable. I had read that in one of my books and it's true. I had set out on a path and there was no turning back.

After lunch I went back to give Pete a foot massage. I wanted to tell him about those last couple of days. I needed to tell someone, but it was so unlikely that I'd got with two classy women in two days it would have sounded like a great big boast at best, a gigantic lie more likely. I couldn't avoid telling him I had a new car, he was going to see it soon enough, so I worked out a more feasible story while I stirred some foaming gel into a bowl of hot water. While his feet softened in the bowl, I told him the Red Beast had finally died and Lady Margaret had arranged for me to have a new car on a lease through some tax fiddle.

'Must have been a bloody good massage,' he said.

'The best,' I replied.

'So what's she like?'

'You know, money to burn. Big house, butler who used to be a Para, more like a bodyguard. Nice though…'

'The butler?'

I laughed. 'Actually, not a bad bloke. He wants to open a hotel in Italy.'

'How the other half live.' He paused. 'And what's she like?' he asked again.

'Attractive, you know, reddish hair, green eyes. Funny. Nice. She's not snobby at all.'

I towelled his feet dry and rubbed in some eucalyptus cream. I sat on a leather bench and rested his left foot in my lap. I began by massaging the instep, applying pressure as I worked around to the sole, then back again. I used my thumbs to press out the stress from the heel, turning in close circles with medium pressure before repeating the motion on the ball of the foot.

'Do you drink plenty of water, Pete? You should this weather.'

'All the time, mate. Eight glasses a day.'

'I just gave Carly her massage. She came with a bottle of fizzy drink. She says water leaves a bad taste in her mouth.'

'That's why she's putting on weight.'

'That's what I thought. All these rich ladies I met are just skin and bone.'

'You know what they say, you can't be too rich or too thin.'

The sole of his foot was coarse with hard skin packed around the heel. I rubbed in some more cream and pressed my thumbs into the arch. He groaned.

'Bad case of Postman's Foot, that's what you've got,' I said, and he groaned again.

When people say their feet are aching, the discomfort begins in the bundles of nerve endings clustered in the arch of the foot. I closed my hand in a fist and rolled it back and forth to knead the skin.

'I did another one yesterday,' I told him. 'Vivienne Raynott. She's the one we read about in Wikipedia.'

'You can't believe everything you read on the internet,' he said. 'It's all spin and lies.'

'Now take a deep breath and relax. Your feet are getting all tense.'

'Yeah, past tense,' he said.

'She's actually really nice,' I continued. 'Really generous.'

'When people are generous, they usually want something.'

'My Gran was generous.'

'I don't mean people like your Gran, Ben.'

I shut up and carried on with the massage. Using my thumbs, I pushed up and down in what's called cross-fibre friction around Pete's heel. With both hands, I then moved in a circular motion around his ankle bone. I moved on to the toes, extending each one with a gentle tug. I rubbed the base of each toe with my index finger, then slid my finger between the toes, stretching them out and giving each toe back its individuality. Finally, before treating the other foot, I inserted my fingers between the toes and massaged them all at the same time.

I had started learning about reflexology, an ancient form of Chinese massage designed to relax the whole body, even treat internal disorders, just by massaging the feet. With a quarter of the body's bones in our feet, misalignment can lead to aches in the hips, knees and lower-back, causing neck and shoulder pain, even headaches. There are reflex points, mainly in the feet, but also the hands and ears. By applying appropriate pressure to these points, a good reflexologist can heal the pains and improve a patient's general health.

'How's that?'

'I feel like a million dollars.'

'Shame it's only a feeling.'

'I don't know, never been rich. Don't want to be.'

'If you were rich you could give it all away.'

'Yeah, but that's not what they do is it? They hide it abroad and don't pay their taxes.'

Pete dipped his feet back in the bowl of water, dried off and slipped on some shoes. We crossed the road to look at my new car.

He got in, turned on the ignition, released the bonnet and listened to the motor running.

'Purrs like a baby,' he said, and looked back at me. 'How are your kids doing?'

'Good. Everyone's great. Little Claire says no, no matter what you say to her.'

'That doesn't sound a bad thing. How's Kelly?'

'She's good.'

'You look after that girl, be hard to find another one like her.'

He stretched his shoulders, then shoved his hands in his pockets.

'Thanks for the rub. I'm going to have a snooze before everyone gets home. You look after yourself.'

As I watched him cross the road, I felt as if there was something left unsaid, that I had deceived him in some way. Members of my own family had called me a class traitor when I used the inheritance from Gran to do a massage course instead of blowing it on a holiday in Las Vegas, as my cousin did. Most working people want to get on, they want their children to do well. I knew how proud Pete and Carol were that Lynne was at university. But it seemed sometimes as if every time you tried to pull yourself up, someone wanted to drag you back down again.

9
YOU CAN NEVER SAY NO

With the VW's air conditioning and a CD player, I was a new man in old trainers; I didn't want to damage the new ones. I picked up Kelly from her afternoon shift at the laundry and left early for work so I could go easy on the new motor. The sun beat down from above and reflected up from the black tar on the road to Egham, packed and polluted; I always wondered how many millions of man hours were wasted in jams and how insane we were destroying the planet for our children.

Icy air swirled up from the footwell, the four speakers were balanced, smooth as chocolate, and a mellow voice was reading Napoleon Hill's self-help book *Think and Grow Rich*, a title that implies that the guide is only about making money. It's not. It is more about personal development, on training the mind to think and be positive.

I had been given the CD by Rudy Johnson, whom I'd met when I was giving free massages at the gym. He was a business associate of Rufus, his opposite in every way. Rudy was short, mixed race with a shaved head, incredibly white teeth in a broad smile and he was the only man at the gym who insisted on paying for his massage.

Rudy sold mortgages. In two years, he had gone from being a complete beginner to the number one salesman in London with commissions that had allowed him to buy a flat in Chelsea and a house in the country. He told me he had played *Think and Grow Rich* every day for two years driving to work and driving home. It was like a meditation, a massage for the mind. You had to be absolutely clear about what it was you wanted to acquire or achieve, then channel positive energy into your daily life until the goal was reached. Rudy believed there was no such thing as lucky or unlucky people, only positive and negative people. Positive people were observant and saw opportunities when they appeared.

It had all sounded convincing to me, but after playing the CD once, I had never got round to playing it again. There was never any time at home, not with the kids, and the van didn't have a CD player. With a new car and new prospects, I resolved to listen to Napoleon Hill on my daily drive to The Lodge and see if I could emulate Rudy. The voice on the disc was confident, convincing, optimistic, the words like mantras that I tried to memorise:

Don't wait. The time will never be just right.

Whatever the mind of man can conceive and believe, it can achieve.

Every adversity, every failure, every heartache, carries with it the seed of an equivalent or greater benefit.

We had faced plenty of failure and adversity, a lot of heartache. We were always broke. I was ready to grab any opportunity that came my way. I sympathised with Pete Taylor, but I had three kids to bring up and it seemed to me that if you wanted the best for them, you had to do whatever you had to do to earn the money to pay for it.

The road was busy coming up to six when people were making their way home. I indicated, slowed through the gears and negotiated the potholes outside The Lodge. Vinnie Castro watched me drive in, ten minutes early, which always put him in a good mood. He trotted down the steps scratching the bristles on his cheek.

'You robbing cars now?'

I changed the subject.

'Do you know what *cazzo* means?' I asked him.

'*Cazzo?*'

'Yeah, *cazzo*, what's it mean?'

'Everything and nothing. Prick, cock, fuck, stupid. *Che cazzo vuoi?* You got an Italian girlfriend?'

'Absolutely.'

Marley emerged between the double doors. He looked grey and tired.

'Hey, look,' Vinnie said. 'This *cazzo's* got a new motor.'

'My favourite colour,' Marley said.

'It's on lease,' I explained. 'The van died on me. How are the boys?'

'They hot,' he replied. 'And when they hot ...'

'They're not pissing on Billy again?'

'Not yet.'

We high fived and he wandered out the gate to catch the bus home.

The lights flashed and a double beep pulsed as I locked the car in the shade under the tall sycamores. I followed Vinnie up the steps to start another twelve-hour double shift feeling oddly content to be back in my own world.

Andel Svoboda was playing Monopoly with Chris and his mates.

'How's it going, Chris?' I called.

'Mayfair,' he shouted and punched the air.

Del and Jordan did the same. Red hotels had been erected on Mayfair and Park Lane. Chris had piles of money laid out in military formation and I knew because it always happened when people were speculating on property there would be tears before tea time.

The usual suspects clutched the iron bars as they gazed from the window, dust strewn from the dry heat. The two lads weren't like lions in a cage dreaming of freedom. They were looking out because they didn't want anyone to look at them. Troy was rocking on his blue chair. I watched Alex switch channels on the TV and caught a glimpse of the man in the white suit who had said in the Great Hall that day that it was nice to hear the sound of women's laughter; the man who had made the bet with Maggs about whether or not I would be sleeping under her roof by the weekend

'Go back, Alex, go back. There's something I want to see.'

He paused, thought about that for several moments, stared back as if wondering who I was, then clicked back four channels to the BBC News.

I recognised him now. The man in the white suit was James Chipping, a Minister under Tony Blair. He had a concerned expression on his angular face and gave the impression of being wise as he peered over his half-moon glasses. He was supporting a group of investors who wanted to revive an old race course on land that, according to the spokesman for the Wildlife Trust, was home to numerous endangered species. As they debated the subject, it seemed to be one of those insoluble problems: save the wildlife, create the jobs the Minister predicted, or find a compromise that would benefit no one.

The news rolled on. The ping pong ball smashed across the table. Alex changed channels, confirming his authority over the remote control. Then, unexpectedly, it was always unexpected, all hell broke loose. The table where the Monopoly game was in progress skated across the day room, shedding counters and cards along the way, and Alex turned up the volume on the TV to a deafening pitch.

Chris yelled 'Fuuuuuck,' in one long scream, then stamped out and ran along the corridor with a fistful of play money in his hand.

Like a forest fire, the chaos spread. A table tennis bat whizzed by my ear and hit the wall. Tyson, one of the few black lads, pulled all the books from the shelf. Troy rocked faster on his chair and Vinnie came rushing in as Andel chased Chris upstairs.

'Now what?' Vinnie yelled.

'Monday madness,' I replied.

I spoke to Del and Jordan. They were more cooperative when Chris wasn't there.

'Put the table back, lads, and pick up all those cards.'

They nodded in unison and did so while I crossed the room to the TV.

'Alex, turn down the volume,' I told him and waited while he let that sink it. 'Thank you,' I added when it was done.

I picked up the table tennis bat.

'Who threw this?'

There was no way of knowing because every boy in the day room lowered his head.

'Don't do it again.' I flapped my ears back and forth. 'I've only got two ears and I want to hang on to them.'

There were a couple of smiles. Vinnie let out a sigh. The commotion had run its course.

'Nice one, Ben,' he said and left me to it.

We managed to get through the evening meal without any fuss. Andel dished out the drugs and the lads climbed the stairs to the bathroom, cleaned their teeth and filed into the dorms.

I was having a cup of tea, feet up with the *Mirror*, when my mobile rang with a number I didn't recognise.

'Hello, is that Ben?'

'Yes…'

'It's Angela. I'd like you to come tomorrow at six. I'll text the address.'

She hadn't given me time to speak and I wasn't sure who it was.

'Angela?' I said.

'Angela Hartley. We met on Friday. Have you forgotten already?'

Now I remembered. She was the woman who had been sitting on the antique chair, the politician with the strident voice.

'No, no. Not at all. The thing is, I'll be at work tomorrow…'

'Work,' she repeated. 'I can't imagine it's more important.'

'It's my job. I'd be letting people down…'

'And you would rather to let me down?'

'I don't want to let anyone down.'

'Then you have a choice,' she said. 'You must decide on your priorities or you'll find you won't be receiving any calls at all.'

The line went dead. Someone screamed out in their sleep, then it was quiet again.

I walked up and down the corridor.

You must decide on your priorities.

What were my priorities? My family, my future, their future. I remembered one of the things Napoleon Hill had said: *Don't wait. The time will never be just right,* and I thought: the time is right. This is my chance.

When I called Angela back, there was no answer. She was there. She was making sure I knew my place. I left a message and looked out through the barred windows at the sky. It was clear, full of stars, and reminded me of nights at sea when life had seemed so simple.

My phone buzzed with a text that contained an address and a single instruction: Don't Be Late.

Vinnie was in his office writing reports. I told him something important had come up and I needed to take the two weeks holiday I was owed starting the following day.

'You have to book, mate, you can't just announce it out of the blue.'

'Sorry, Vinnie, it's one of those things.'

'You're letting me down, you know that?'

'It can't be helped. There's something I have to do and I'll never forgive myself if I don't do it.'

'*Che cazzo.* Must be that bloody Italian girlfriend.'

My last night at The Lodge was unusually quiet and I drove home at six with the sun rising and a feeling that everything was going to be all right.

10
ANGELA

When I found an empty parking meter opposite the Imperial War Museum, I was a good half mile from Angela's flat and arrived out of breath a few minutes before six. The entry-phone was on a polished fascia with two rows of brass buttons. I pressed her number and the door opened before I finished saying my name.

'Sixth floor,' she said. 'You'd better hurry.'

Even the lift was under pressure and rose in one quick gasp. The door to the flat was open.

'Come,' she called.

I manoeuvred my massage table along the passage and found her staring out the window. She snapped her fingers.

'Here,' she said.

I leaned the table against the wall, closed the door and stood at her side peering over the grey slate rooftops sloping down to the Thames. The sky was criss-crossed with the arms of cranes and the skeletons of new buildings. She tapped the window and pointed into the distance.

'What's that?' she asked.

'The Houses of Parliament.'

'Ten out of ten. And what's next to it?'

'Big Ben,' I said, and she laughed.

'Your reputation precedes you.' She glanced at her watch. 'Be quiet now,' she added.

A moment later, I heard the faint sound of ringing bells.

'When you hear the six o'clock chimes you know all is well in the world.'

We lived in different worlds, not that Angela would have appreciated my saying as much. She turned and gave me a long, penetrating look as if she might find something shocking hidden behind my eyes.

'This is my little hideaway. It's our secret. Are you good at keeping secrets?'

'I don't really have any to be honest.'

Her expression softened. 'Then let's keep it that way.' Her hair was blunt cut around her cheeks with a long fringe that she swept from her eyes. 'Now, what's all this about the Oriental twist, is that what it's called?'

'I think it's a misunderstanding. My Swedish massage is a full-body treatment, but I like to think of it as more of a meditation. It's a system of healing that comes from India and China.'

'Nothing good has every come from India or China. How long does it take?'

'Forty-five minutes.'

'That's much too long. What else can you do?'

'I can do an abbreviated version ...'

'Good, you get ready.'

'Would you like some music, some candles.'

'I want it all,' she replied, and hurried briskly into the hall.

I secured the table and glanced around the room. It was sparsely furnished with files on every surface and a box of empty wine bottles in the corner. The flat was in a modern building, more modest than I had expected, and coldly impersonal without pictures or photographs. I lit a teakwood aromatherapy candle, scrolled down my iPad and chose Musicazen, a mixture of wind chimes and flutes.

'What's that noise?' Angela said as she marched in wrapped in a towel.

'It's supposed to be soothing.'

'Whatever gave you that idea?'

I turned it off. She gave me a steady, defiant look as she removed the towel. She was naked, small, five feet without heels, her hard body bursting with energy. Even her thatch of pubic hair looked furious.

'Do your worst,' she said.

'I can only do my best.'

'You don't have a sense of humour, do you?'

'I do, but I take my work seriously.'

'Your work at The Lodge?' she asked, and it threw me for a second.

'Well, yes, that too,' I replied.

Angela looked me up and down, as if she might be having second thoughts about me, about the massage. She wasn't vulnerable or self-conscious. She was totally in control. I wondered how she knew I worked at The Lodge and must have read my mind.

'You don't think I invited you here without knowing who you are, Ben,' she said.

'No, I suppose not.'

'You do know who I am?'

'Yes…'

'Good. Now, let's get on with it.'

There wasn't a spare moment to wash my hands. I held her arm as she levered herself up onto the table and wedged her head in the opening. I ran some oil into my palms and added a few drops to Angela's back.

'Take slow breaths, then hold a long deep breath for the count of ten.'

She didn't like being told what to do. Her shoulders tensed, but she followed the instruction.

'Do you have any pains anywhere?'

'If you don't have pains at fifty you haven't lived.'

'Nothing specific?'

'Tony Blair,' she said, and I smiled in spite of myself.

This was what she was famous for, the one-liner, the instant put down. Angela Hartley was always on television, never stopped talking and was renowned for the outrageous things that came out of her mouth.

I applied light friction, or effleurage, sliding my palms in long strokes to spread the warmed oil over her back and up towards her heart, the direction in which the blood flows. I brought my hands back down, maintaining contact without applying pressure. I would have continued the motion for ten minutes, but sensed Angela's impatience and moved on to her shoulders. I switched to circular, petrissage strokes with more compression than effleurage.

'That feels good. What about my neck?'

'That's next. Just relax. It's best not to speak.'

'Is that a fact?'

Angela always had the last word. I had watched her talking over newscasters and rival politicians. But on the massage table, the masseur takes the lead. You are partners in a duet. You can't describe it. You have to be a part of it. I thought briefly of Vivienne in her white room and pushed the image out of my mind. With massage, you must be in the moment. You dance with the one you are with.

The pressure I applied through my hands rose from my waist, my core, which allowed me to work steadily without tiring. This creates an energy exchange that releases a shot of oxytocin, the 'love hormone' that makes massage intimate and helps people bond. Not that there was much chance of my bonding with Angela. In the way that people imagine they know celebrities, I felt as if I knew Angela Hartley. That made it all the more implausible, more weird, that she was stretched out naked on my massage table.

The flat must have been closed up all through the July heat wave. The room was stuffy and the scent from the candle made my head spin. My hands were on auto-pilot as I gathered my fingertips in a cone and applied percussive strokes, called tapotement, swift, repetitive drumbeats in the stress triangles at the top of her back. Angela sighed and wriggled. She clearly liked this and I continued down over her saggy bottom and thighs.

From the head of the table, I placed my hands just below her neck, and used a fanning motion, running my thumbs down towards her lower back. I alternated the pressure from one thumb to the other, moving from the top of her back all the way down to her hips. I massaged the muscles on either side of her spine – you never work directly on the spine, which can be uncomfortable, even unsafe. Moving to her side, I added a drop of oil to my palms and gave Angela's hips a series of 'twists,' a fluid motion pulling one hand towards me, while pushing the other away.

'Yes, that will do,' she said. 'I'm cooked.'

Angela was coated in sweat. She slipped down from the table and hauled me by my shirt across the passage to the bedroom. The blinds were half-closed and the way the lines of shadow crossed the sunlight from outside made the room shimmer in a heat haze. She pulled off my clothes and we fell across the bed. She straddled me and pushed my cock up between her legs. She rode me hard like it was a steeple chase. She was panting, drawing long breaths through her open mouth.

She rolled over, cried out: 'Yes. Yes. Yes,' and dragged her fingernails across my back as she climaxed.

She screamed and I screamed, for different reasons.

'Jesus! What are you doing?'

She leaned over and bit my neck in the vampire spot.

'You are such a baby,' she said, and began running the loose skin up and down my cock. 'Big Ben. That's so clever.'

I went to speak and she put her finger to my lips, which I didn't like.

'Red or white?' she asked.

'What?'

'White.'

She left the room and returned after a few minutes with two glasses of white wine that she set down on the bedside cabinet. She left again and came back with a small bottle of cream.

'Turn over,' she said. 'And don't move.'

As she applied the salve to the scratches on my back, I bit my lips. Tears welled into my eyes. The cure was worse the pain.

'Does it hurt?'

'You're telling me.'

'Witch hazel. The scratches will be gone by tomorrow.'

'Why did you do that?' I demanded and she shrugged.

'I couldn't help myself.'

She waggled my cock back and forth then stopped and reached for the two glasses of wine.

'Cheers,' she said.

'What am I going to tell my wife when she sees those scratches?' I asked, and she thought for a moment.

'Does a carpenter ever hit his thumb with a hammer?'

'What?'

'You think about it,' she replied, and touched the rim of her glass to mine.

The wine slipped down. The way the light crossed the ceiling made it feel as if the room was moving. Sex with Maggs had been surprising, pornographic. Sex with Vivienne was dreamlike, a fantasy. Sex with Angela was brisk, clinical, an exercise to release her pent up energy and anger. The scratches on my back, stinging still, were an industrial accident and in this, my new job, it occurred to me that I would face the same dangers I'd faced at The Lodge, clients with a psychopathic lack of logic followed by sudden violence and a complete absence of respect for anyone else's feelings or well-being.

When we emptied our glasses, Angela went to get the bottle and refilled them. I felt dazed more than drunk. It was the oddest thing in the world to be sitting in bed at seven on a sunny evening with Angela Hartley.

The Angela Hartley.

I remembered something she had said about unemployment on some discussion programme, *Question Time*, most probably, with David Dimbleby.

'Did you mean that about giving everyone who's unemployed a free bike?'

She remained tight-lipped and glared back at me.

'What?'

'Sorry, I thought …'

'People pay taxes for other people who don't want to work. It's ridiculous. Give them a bicycle instead of benefits and they'll get fit while they go out and look for a job.'

'But there aren't enough jobs …'

'Rubbish. If a man wants to work, he'll find work. Haven't you?'

'Yes …'

'Who pays for their big televisions? Why are they all so fat?' She leaned closer. Her eyes were intense, glassy with passion. She lowered her voice. 'I have seen the files. I have studied the files.' The wine trembled in her glass. 'People are not sick. It's all psychosomatic. We don't need a public health service.'

'What about people with cancer?'

She shook her head. 'People with cancer should have paid for their own health insurance,' she replied. 'And let me tell you something else: when people pay for their health care, they are more careful. They don't get sick. They don't get cancer.'

There was no arguing with her. It was like talking to a machine. Angela Hartley embodied the opposite of everything I was brought up to believe, what Gran called fairness and common human decency. Gran would pose the question: What happens if someone is born blind? Do you send them out into the street to beg? Or do we pay our taxes in order to provide schools with teachers paid a fair salary? For my grandmother, that was the measure of how society should be. Angela Hartley would have closed all the schools and pushed the blind down the road on a bicycle.

There was so much I wanted to say, but I couldn't find the words to express myself and Angela wouldn't have listened anyway. She had never struggled, never gone without. She had no idea what it was like to live day after day with the dull pain of poverty. Was I a class traitor? I certainly felt like one. But while I carried that feeling in the back of my mind, I also felt lucky to be earning fifty quid for an hour's work and having this insight into the politics of Angela Hartley.

'You're Annabel Lee Hartley's mother?' I said and she looked offended.

'What has that got to do with you?'

'Nothing. It's just that Rufus said ...'

'Rufus says too much and Annabel's wasting her time.' She paused and her tone changed. 'You have a chance to make something of yourself. Be aware of that at all times.'

Her words struck a chord in me, but I didn't have a moment to think about what she had said. She put her glass down and started to play with my cock, rubbing it slowly up and down.

'Big Ben,' she said and smiled up at me. 'Did you know that's what Maggs calls you?'

I shook my head. 'What's the Committee?' I asked her.

I knew she didn't like being asked questions but couldn't resist answering them.

'Why do you want to know?'

'I asked Maggs. She said it meant nothing.'

'That's a first for Maggs. She was being modest. We are a group of friends who like to ride and quietly rule the world. Does that answer your question?'

She went back to what she'd been doing. She massaged my balls and sucked my cock until it was hard again. She looked up.

'They call it a trip around the word,' she said. 'It's seems to make men feel dominant.'

I had no idea what she was talking about and watched as she dipped into the bedside cabinet and withdrew a tube of KY Jelly and a condom. She used her teeth to open the foil and ran the rubber down the shaft of my cock. She squeezed some lube on to her index finger and swirled her finger around the opening of her anus. She then rolled over, went up on all fours and stared back over her shoulder with her teeth clenched.

'Now fuck me,' she snarled.

I pushed in through the back door, another first for me, and we went at it doggy fashion for what seemed like forever before she screamed, her body quaked and we both gasped to a climax. Our limbs gave way and we collapsed in a jumble of sweating flesh.

'You're something else,' I said, and she laughed.

'I'll take that as a compliment.' She slid straight from the bed and gave me two tissues from a box of Kleenex. 'There's a bin there,' she added, pointing. 'I'm going to take a shower.'

I removed the condom. I would have liked to have taken a shower myself, but it wasn't on offer. I dressed, folded the massage table and packed my bag. Angela appeared at the living room door combing her hair. She was wrapped in a towel patterned with Union Jacks.

'Have you given up that job at The Lodge?' she asked.

'No…'

'Then do so. Vivienne has plans for you and what Vivienne wants Vivienne gets,' she said and I sensed the resentment in her tone. 'And another thing, Kate will probably call you…'

'Kate?'

'Lady Catherine. Be a nice boy when you are with her. Be kind…'

'I'm always kind,' I said, interrupting for once.

'Then let me put it another way, be the perfect gentleman. Can you do that?'

'I can try.'

'Come. Come.'

I followed her back to the bedroom. She dressed in ivory-coloured underwear, black stockings and shoes with four inch heels. I ran the zip up the back of a fitted, wine red dress with a square neckline. She turned and it was the formidable Angela Hartley from the television talk shows staring back at me.

'How do I look?'

'Elegant, really…'

'You're supposed to say beautiful.'

'I was about to.'

'I love it when men lie. They're so bad at it.'

Her eyes glowed. She smiled and seemed natural, almost friendly. She took her notebook from a black leather handbag, tore out a page and gave it to me. On it, was the name, Raul, and an address in Jermyn Street.

'Be there at ten tomorrow. Ask for Raul.'

'What do I have to do?'

'It's a tailors. You just have to wear clean underwear and be on time.'

There was a lot I might have said and bit my tongue instead. I followed her into the bathroom and watched while she applied make-up. She rubbed cream around the corners of her eyes, applied a shade of lipstick that matched the dress and brushed her hair in place. She was quick, efficient, not a wasted movement or moment's hesitation.

'Beautiful,' I said.

'Liar,' she answered.

She handed me a gold cross on a chain, bent forward and held her hair out of the way. As I hooked the necklace in place, the buzzer in the hall sounded. She went to answer.

'Just wait. I'll be two minutes.'

I collected my table and bag.

'You haven't paid me,' I said.

'What?'

'It's fifty pounds for the massage.'

'Oh, is it now. I don't have any change,' she said. 'And, another thing, it's vulgar to concern yourself with petty sums of money.'

'Not if I'm going to give up working at The Lodge. I have to earn my living.'

'Ben, are you a patient man?'

'No, not really.'

'It is a virtue. Trust me. Everything comes to he who waits.'

She pressed her finger against my lips as I was about to speak. She grabbed her handbag, locked the flat and we travelled down in the lift to the ground floor. A black Jaguar, engine running, stood outside the building. A driver wearing a peaked cap opened the passenger door and she stepped in without a backward glance. I watched the car disappear and thought Kelly was dead right: I should always ask for my fee in advance.

I felt disorientated and couldn't remember where I had parked the car. I could smell sweat on my clothes. At least the heat had gone out of the sun and there was a breath of cool air.

Men say things like 'I know what she needs,' and 'I'd like to give her one.' I am sure there were men all over the country who would have given a week's pay to have given it to Angela Hartley doggy fashion as retribution for being who she was. I had lived their fantasy. But I couldn't help thinking the roles had been reversed. She was the stalker. I was the fox. Metaphorically, I had done the bending. Even while I was giving her the massage, I had felt her aura dominating the room.

A young couple passed. They were attractive, casually dressed, the new breed of Londoners with open faces and nice accents. I asked for directions to the Imperial War Museum. The moment the man pointed at the corner where I had to turn, it came back to me and I headed for Lambeth Road where the car was parked. The meter only operated until six thirty. I locked the table in the boot and looked about me as a man from another planet might have done after stepping from his spacecraft.

I wasn't used to drinking. I wasn't used to having sex with famous politicians for that matter. I needed to clear my head before driving home. I bought a bottle of water and drank it as I looked up at the museum's façade. Standing in front of the entrance were two huge guns with long grey barrels that reminded me of one of the photographs on the wall in Vivienne's apartment.

The church on the corner reminded me of St Margaret's, where Kelly and I were married. The young wives club met every Thursday and there was a bring and buy sale the following Saturday. New tower blocks were going up, dwarfing the terraces of Victorian houses. Lights were coming on in kitchens and living rooms, windows into unknown worlds away from the frenetic life of the city. During my days laying paving stones, I had enjoyed working in different parts of London. I could see how each area had been a village, but it was beginning to blend now into one giant metropolis where it was going to get harder for the little people to survive.

If I stayed working at The Lodge, I would always be one of the little people. I would always be working double shifts for the minimum wage and living in fear of the hot water boiler breaking down. Kelly would never escape from the laundry. I had spent a long time refining my skills giving free massages. It was outrageous that Angela hadn't paid me and, yet, I couldn't help having a grudging respect for her. She was a woman who knew what she wanted – she certainly knew what she wanted from me – and knew how to go about getting it.

Worrying about what 'people are going to say' and 'what the neighbours might think' was always in the minds of working people. They aren't afraid of failure. They are afraid of success and how they would have to make excuses to their friends if it ever came their way. This attitude ground people down. It made them dull, anxious, afraid. I was like that myself. Angela Hartley radiated energy like a lit fuse about to explode a bomb and didn't give a damn what anyone else thought about her.

She had said. 'You have a chance to make something of yourself. Be aware of that at all times.' I wasn't sure if this was encouragement or a warning, but it had stayed in my mind. My family came first. Their well-being was all that mattered – bikes for Ollie and George, dancing lessons for Claire when she was old enough. A holiday. Tiny things. Simple things that make a family a family. I had a new car, a few quid in the bank and a bizarre choice: to remain trapped on a treadmill of relentless poverty or choose a new life providing rich women unemotional sex. I could have kidded myself that this was just an extension of my massage practise, but it wasn't true. In four days I had slept with three women. I wasn't just a masseur. I was a gigolo.

At the Elephant & Castle, I found an ATM machine. I checked the balance. With my last wage transfer, I had more than £500, not enough to make you rich, but enough to make you feel rich. I withdrew £50 to give to Kelly, another departure from the truth to add to the list when I arrived home.

There was dinner waiting for me in the oven, shepherd's pie with vegetables. I found stains on the back of my shirt when I took a bath, and thought that's typical: Tory MP Angela Hartley had drawn blood, screwed me out of fifty quid and forced me to throw out a good shirt with the rubbish so Kelly didn't see it.

11
SHOPPING

My Gran worked in a warehouse packing yogurt pots and puddings into boxes that were trucked to the supermarkets. She did four hour shifts on her feet and loved the gossip shouted up and down the production line, that sense that the workers were 'all in it together.' When one of the girls got married, she'd put two £20 notes in an envelope as a wedding present. There were times after she had seen on the news hungry children displaced by famines and floods when she gave her entire wage packet to the appeal.

I was with her once in Twickenham High Street when it started to snow and we saw a man standing on the corner shivering. He was a resident of a local nursing home where the men were given cereal for breakfast and a couple of pounds every day to buy fish and chips for lunch. They were expected to stay out until nightfall, when they returned for a meagre supper. It was called care in the community which meant no care at all.

Gran asked the man why he didn't have a coat. When he said he didn't have any money, she marched him straight into the nearest charity shop and we watched while he tried on numerous overcoats. When he found one he liked, he buttoned it up and his eyes filled with tears when Gran took the money from her purse to pay for it.

There was nothing unusual in this. Gran was kind to everyone. She crocheted woollen squares to make blankets for the church fair and her three-layer coffee and walnut cakes raised a fortune in the raffle. She had standing orders for Oxfam and Save the Children, just £5 each, but it was every month for as long as I could recall.

Everyone in the family thought I had moved to London when Grandad died to look after Gran. The truth is, I'd left Lowestoft because there wasn't any work and she was looking after me. Gran had an edge. An attitude. People listened when she talked. She was stubborn, independent and was still going out with friends to play bingo twice a week a month before she died suddenly of a massive stroke. I missed her without being sad. She had died as she lived: on her own terms. She would have hated being in a wheelchair or having carers coming in every day.

Gran never lost her marbles, as she liked to say, pausing from her crochet and tapping two fingers against the side of her head. She wasn't particularly vain, but coloured her hair that she wore in a bouffant and at seventy was proud that she could still touch her toes, which she demonstrated in case anyone had any doubt. She had a sharp tongue and strong opinions. She couldn't stand the Queen but admired Lady Diana for her work trying to ban the use of land mines. She liked Mario Lanza, Frank Sinatra and the Rolling Stones because one of the women she worked with was related to Keith Richards.

When Gran made cakes and pies, she never used a recipe or measured the ingredients. It was all done on memory and instinct. She rolled the dough with a milk bottle and left floury prints on the radio when she turned up the volume to sing along with a song she liked. Her roast beef and Yorkshire pudding could have won prizes, and she couldn't stand what she called 'foreign muck' – curry, sushi, spaghetti bolognaise. 'If you can't spell it, don't it eat,' she said, quoting someone on the telly. She made one exception. She liked Chinese food and had it delivered every Saturday when she watched *Blind Date* with Cilla Black.

Gran's legacy had set me up as a masseur and I couldn't help wondering what she would have said had she known I had massaged Angela Hartley, not to mention the rest. Like Pete Taylor, Gran believed there were Them and Us and Angela Hartley was definitely one of Them.

I missed her. I missed her stories, her humour, the way she stabbed the *Daily Mirror* with her finger when she read something that made her angry. Gran had been evacuated to Torquay during the last war with her younger brother, Jack. At the funeral, he talked about their childhood and there was a catch in his throat when he ended by saying: 'I'm going to miss you, old girl. I suppose if I don't see you in heaven, I'll see you in Devon.'

It always made me smile when I remembered that.

The back door was open. A wedge of sunlight crossed the kitchen and the pair of blackbirds that had adopted us perched on the fence watching Ollie and George kick a ball around the garden. Claire was giving me a rare treat sitting on my knee as she ate pieces of orange from a bowl. I was a lucky man. I could have been down the coal mines getting black lung. I could have been on the trawlers with the constant risk of getting washed away in a storm. I had made a break from the past. There wasn't a working class movement as there had been in Gran's day. You have to live in your own times. Morals and codes had changed. It was hard just to survive, and it seemed to me that sunny morning in 2006 that surviving was more important than how you did so.

Kelly had finished folding clean clothes ready for the kids to dirty again. She stood beside the table with her hands on her hips.

'What are grinning about?' she said.

'I didn't tell you. I gave Angela Hartley a massage.'

'Who?' she asked and I laughed.

'That Tory MP always running off at the mouth.'

She shrugged. Kelly didn't follow the news, she was too busy, and seemed to be getting used to the fact that my clients were all rich women. Who else could afford to pay for a massage? I never kept secrets from Kelly. Now my whole life was a secret I couldn't share with anyone.

'Me. Me,' Claire said as she struggled to get down.

It was coming up to nine. I was dressed in clean jeans, new trainers and a short-sleeved white shirt from Gap. I slipped on a pair of imitation Ray Bans as I glanced in the hall mirror.

'Is that cool or is that cool?' I said.

'You need a haircut,' Kelly replied.

'You think so?'

'You don't want to look scruffy for all those rich ladies.'

We kissed cheeks. Claire was watching.

'Me, Me,' she said, and I suddenly realised who she took after: my Gran.

I bent down. 'When are you going to learn some new words?'

'Me. Me,' she said again, and I gave her a kiss.

The tap of my fingers on the roof of the Golf reassured me that the car wasn't a mirage. This wasn't a dream. This was my life. The indicators bleeped twice when I pressed the key fob. I even liked the vinyl-smell of the interior when I slipped into the driver's seat. The van had the sound of an old man coughing when I turned the ignition. The Golf purred like a kitten when you stroke its belly. I snapped into the seat belt and pressed the play switch on the CD for another session with Napoleon Hill.

Most people were at work by nine and it was a good time to drive into London. I parked in the National Car Park in Brewer Street and wandered through Soho. The clubs appeared rundown and seedy below the morning sky with its wisps of white cloud burning off in the sunshine. I watched a girl in a short skirt and

big heels polishing a display case showing shots of the pole dancers punters would find inside the club when it opened. I had
never been to a strip joint and didn't imagine I ever would.

Dustmen emptied overflowing bins and a street cleaning machine rumbled by sucking up fag packets behind a pair
of swirling brushes. There weren't many people about, just the
drunks and runaways leaving empty doorways where they had
spent the night. At least it wasn't cold.

Tourists were taking photographs in Piccadilly Circus.
Decades of grime and graffiti had been cleaned from the buildings. Cranes stretched into the sky, the same as in Lambeth
and Westminster. London was booming. Not for everyone, the
rich were getting richer. The poor were falling behind. But you
could taste the optimism in the air. It was like a drug. Young
blokes in black jackets stood on street corners speaking into
their new generation mobiles. Girls armed with backpacks
marched by with intense expressions. There was a pulse, a
tempo. It made you feel that you had to meet the same beat or
get left behind.

Jermyn Street was lined with tailors, shirt-makers, a theatre.
Someone had placed a multi-coloured hat on the bronze statue of
Beau Brummell, 'The arbiter of men's fashion,' I read.

I glanced into Rowley's, a restaurant that could have been
frozen in a different age as an example of how people used to live.
A woman sat at a table set with shiny silverware. She was alone
except for the company of her multiple reflections in the long
gilt mirrors. I shielded my eyes to take a second look and felt
like a Peeping Tom catching Vivienne Raynott in an unguarded
moment. She was in profile, legs crossed, her gaze fixed as if she
were studying the arrangement of pink roses in an oversized
white vase. In her hand she held a closed book, her finger marking the page. I wasn't sure what to do, whether I would be intrud-
ing if I joined her – stupidly, whether it was my place to do so.

I was still undecided when she turned. Our eyes met and she tapped her chest as if her heart were beating faster.

She placed the book on the table as she stood and opened her mouth to huff warm air on the window. She drew a smiley face that faded as I entered the cool of the restaurant and we touched cheeks in a way that was more intimate than if we had kissed on the lips. She was wearing white, I had only ever seen her in white. Now with a short skirt, cropped top, trainers with thick soles. Her pale blonde hair swayed about her shoulders and her blue eyes grew brighter as I stared into them. It was an odd sensation. Looking into her eyes was like looking into my own.

'This feels like an assignation. Would you like some tea?'

We sat. I tucked my sunglasses in my pocket. She waved her hand and a waiter, an older man in an old-fashioned costume, hurried towards us.

'More tea, please.' She fluttered her fingers over the pot on the table. 'You can take this away.'

The gloom that had marked her features when I first saw her had gone taking ten years from her age. She seemed thrilled to see me. It wasn't an act or a pose. She behaved as if we were lovers meeting in secret. Not that it was like that at all. Angela had made the appointment, but Vivienne had been waiting for me in Jermyn Street. According to Angela, Maggs had christened my penis Big Ben, while it was Vivienne who had shaved my pubic hair, a memory that still sent a shudder down my spine. They were like parts of the same person, although the part sitting across the table from me was the one I liked being with most.

The tea arrived and she poured two cups.

'Milk?'

'Please.'

'Sugar?'

'No thank you.'

'The moment I pour a cup of tea, I see a picture of mummy serving the vicar. Always the same picture. It's funny those things.' She leaned across the table as if to share a confidence. 'Can you swim?' she asked and looked relieved when I answered.

'Yes, I can.'

'I'm hopeless. I bet you're a good swimmer.'

'I wouldn't say that, but not bad for a fisherman.'

She gasped. 'A fisherman!'

'I was once, when I was young.'

'And you're so old now, a hundred at least.' She paused. 'Have you read *The Old Man and the Sea?*'

'No.'

'Hemingway. It's about a fisherman, a very old man, like you, struggling to land a giant fish.'

'I've done that a few times,' I said, and she smiled.

'You really were a fisherman?'

'On a trawler, herring, cod...'

'That's so romantic.'

She looked thoughtful as if she were filing this a way. I glanced at the book on the table. It was *The Piano Teacher* by Elfriede Jelinek.

'It's about a piano teacher who likes sex and has a rather odd relationship with her mother.' She sat back and laughed, a wild, hysterical laugh that made her blush. She became serious again. 'Women who read are suspect. Women who write are dangerous. Do you know who upset the applecart?'

'No.'

'Eve, of course. She was the one who bit into the forbidden fruit and tempted Adam.'

'I imagine he was waiting to be tempted.'

She brought her hands together. 'That is *so* revealing,' she said and sat back in her chair. 'What were you saying?'

'I imagine Adam was waiting to be tempted.'

'Undoubtedly. But it took Eve to get the ball rolling. Did you know, every time you have an orgasm, an angel comes to life?'

'That I didn't know.'

'It's true, cross my heart and hope to die.'

Vivienne was candid, clever, confident, silly, defenceless. I wanted to sit her on my knee and hold her tightly. I stared into her eyes, blue pools deep as the ocean, and thought about the scars on her back. She sipped her tea. Her long white arms were awkward and angular. Her skin was shiny, unblemished, except for the parts you couldn't see. She placed her cup back in the saucer.

'Isn't this civilised,' she said. 'How's our dear friend Angela?'

'Not so civilised,' I replied and again she laughed.

'She's adorable. I love her.'

I couldn't conceive of anyone loving Angela Hartley, but then, I had never met anyone like Vivienne Raynott. She tucked her book into a black leather bag and waved her hand, scribbling in the air. The waiter came with a bill for £16, which I paid, leaving the change from a twenty as a tip. It was vulgar to worry about small sums of money.

Vivienne's sleeveless top revealed a band of bare flesh that appeared in glimpses as she took long strides in her white trainers. Her yellow Ferrari was parked across the street where a warden was writing a ticket.

'Oh, please don't. Do be a sweetie,' she called and he shrugged hopelessly.

He showed us his machine. 'I've already done it. You can't take it out.'

'Oh, well, never mind. You have a lovely day.' She leaned closer. 'And don't work too hard in this weather.'

'I'm sorry,' he said, and we left him sliding the ticket into a plastic sleeve and sticking it on the windscreen.

She grabbed my arm. 'Karma,' she whispered. 'We went to Nigeria and stole all the land, now the Nigerians are getting their own back. I think they're all from the same tribe.'

The car was practically outside our destination, a double-fronted shop with big windows showing square-jawed dummies in hunting clothes on one side, shorts and polo shirts on the other. It had just gone ten. Raul was waiting for us. He was a short, broad man with swept back silver hair and an immaculate silver-grey suit I'm sure Beau Brummell would have approved of. He nursed his hands and bowed low as if to monarchy.

'How nice to see you again, My Lady,' he said with a strong accent, Spanish or Italian, I wasn't sure.

'You look very well, Raul. Have you been away?

'Just in the garden on Sunday.'

'How nice. This is Ben,' she said, introducing me. 'We're going to start downstairs,' she made a climbing motion with her fingers, 'and work our way up.'

He laughed as if she had made a brilliant joke and I wondered if Vivienne knew the effect she had on people. Even the parking warden with his scarred cheeks and a coat that was obviously too heavy for the weather had seemed drawn to her and would have torn up the parking ticket if he could.

Vivienne moved around the basement picking out sports shirts and holding them against my chest. She settled on a Hugo Boss polo with four buttons. The changing room was about the size of the box room at home. There was a green leather chair, mirrors in gold frames, a print of hunters chasing dogs across open fields, a brass rail for hangers. Everything smelled of quality and polish.

'Come and show me. I want to see everything.'

I stepped out like a runway model.

'That's perfect, perfect. Now trousers.'

I tried on jogging pants, chinos, cotton sweaters – 'Summer never lasts forever,' she said.

'Nothing lasts forever,' I replied and a cloud crossed her eyes.

'Stop being so profound or you'll get a smack.' She drew breath. 'It's short and brutal and pointless. It was God's sense of humour to give us a brain.'

She went to the table where she had amassed various items. She went through them, selecting and discarding in a way that reminded me of watching women at jumble sales in the church hall seeking bargains among the clothes their neighbours had thrown out. She picked up the polo shirt, white jogging pants, a pair of trousers and reeled off numbers: ten of these, six of these, plain white trainers, four pairs of Sebago deck shoes in different colours. Raul was nodding, writing a mental list.

'Have you got that?' she asked.

'I think so, My Lady,' he answered, and her hands went to her chest.

'Oh my God, I almost forgot. Bathing trunks.'

She rushed over to the Ralph Lauren collection and we added four pairs, red and white striped, dark blue, pale green and pink – a colour I would never have chosen in a hundred years.

'Put one of the pairs in a bag for me, Raul. That would be so kind,' she said.

While Raul was wrapping the blue shorts in layers of tissue paper, we climbed the stairs. I used this moment to tell Vivienne that I did not have the money to pay for the new clothes.

'Oh, don't worry about that,' she said.

'I don't want you to pay for them, Vivienne, you've done so much.'

She stepped closer. 'I haven't done anything. Really, you don't have to worry. They all go on an account.'

'You mean like a tax adjustment?' I said and she smiled.

'You're catching on. Now enjoy it. We're just getting to the good part.'

I was having a makeover. It was *My Fair Lady* in reverse. Vivienne was my Professor Higgins.

I tried on suits – linen, pure wool, a cashmere blazer with plain brass buttons; 'you should never have designs or engravings unless you were in the military.' I tried on shoes – loafers, Chelsea boots, brogues, cap toes, wingtips; shirts with pointed collars and straight collars, button downs, plain and striped. Only long sleeves. Except for sports shirts, short sleeves are a no no. When it's hot you roll them up to just below the elbow, never above. You leave two buttons unbuttoned, never three. It was implicit, rather than regimented. There were codes, formulae, things you do and things you must never do. Things that are said and things that are left unsaid. Everything told a story. Those in the know could read between the lines.

Vivienne was eccentric, Maggs and Angela were eccentric for that matter. But their eccentricities fitted within conventions that were recognised and understood. When two Frenchmen speak, they know that the other is French and has not learned the language. It was like that with Vivienne and her friends. You could dress the same, speak the same, attend the same parties and regattas. But you remained always an outsider clinging to the fringes and cut loose if you ceased to amuse. It was an exclusive club and associate members consisted of beautiful young women because they were beautiful young women, the famous because they were famous and the new rich because they were very rich.

Raul watched with Vivienne as I paraded in shirts and suits, chinos and jackets, brown shoes and black. They stroked their chins and scratched their cheeks. They glanced at each other with quick, decisive nods when something was suitable, a frown and a shake of the head if it wasn't. Vivienne preferred plain shirts, plain suits without a pattern in the weave, everything simple, understated. Raul wore a striped shirt and there was a herring bone pattern in his silver suit, but praised Vivienne's choices as if they were holy edicts. We added a dozen pairs of Calvin Klein boxers, socks and silk ties. Shopping is fun, especially when you don't have to pay the bill.

There were trousers to take up, jackets to take in. Raul took my measurements so they had them on file for when there was more time and I needed new things to fit new occasions. I wasn't sure what had happened to my clothes and was dressed now in an off-white linen suit, the jacket tailored at the waist with narrow lapels, a soft white shirt without labels or logos, two buttons unbuttoned, and dark brown deck shoes without socks. I brushed my hair back with my hands and stood in the reflections of a three way mirror.

'Well?' she said.

'I need a haircut,' I answered and she hissed through her teeth.

'Are you out of your mind? You look beautiful.'

'It's only the clothes.'

'Clothes maketh the man.'

'I thought it was manners?'

'Not in Italy,' she replied and burst out laughing. Then she became serious and ran her fingers through my hair. 'Don't you dare touch it.'

As Raul wrote down my address, Vivienne copied it into her phone. Tailors would work through the night and everything would be delivered the following day. Raul disappeared for a few moments and returned with a plastic bag he held in the tips of his fingers. It contained my shirt with short sleeves, jeans and the Nike trainers I'd just bought.

'What shall I do with these?' he asked and Vivienne fluttered her long fingers.

'Throw them away.'

Fifty quid down the drain, I thought to myself, and my £5 at the market shades gone, too.

Raul handed me the swimwear in a bag with long handles. I was exhausted. We had been in the shop for almost two hours.

There were more people in Jermyn Street and I noticed several heads turn to watch us as we crossed the road to Vivienne's Ferrari Spider, hood down and gleaming like a streak of sunshine on the grey asphalt of the road. She removed the plastic sleeve containing the parking ticket from the windscreen and added it to the pile of identical plastic sleeves in the glove compartment.

'I don't mind the fines, it's just the bother paying them.'

The engine roared like a lion. She eased through the gears and wove through the back doubles to Dean Street where she parked outside a pale grey building with limp flags on flagpoles and no name plate as far as I could see. The doors stood open, letting in the sunshine. A man and a woman, both young and attractive, rose from behind the reception desk with eager expressions.

'Be a sweetie,' Vivienne said to the man. 'If you see a warden trying to fine me again, tell him I'll be two minutes. Can you do that?'

'Be a pleasure. Are you dining?'

'We'll be at the bar. I can pop out. Thank you so much, you are a darling.' She glanced at me. 'This is Ben Foster, my favourite person in the whole world.'

The girl opened the inner door and I followed Vivienne into Groucho's.

12
GROUCHO'S

We sat on high stools at the far end of the bar.

'Are you hungry? I'm starving,' Vivienne said.

'Me, too.'

'I wouldn't care if I never saw the inside of another shop again.'

'I was thinking the same. Great minds…'

'Great bodies,' she said with a little shimmy. She placed her finger on her lips and her expression became thoughtful. 'In our own way, we are all masterpieces. Everyone is unique.'

She kissed her finger and placed it on the tip of my nose. It was strange and thrilling.

If unique means a one off, no one I knew fitted that description better than Vivienne. She looked like an exotic bird perched at the bar, back straight, legs hooked behind the metal ring of the stool. Beautiful women usually give off a vibe that says stay away, don't touch, I'm much too special. Vivienne wasn't like that. She radiated an energy people were drawn to and made everyone feel comfortable. Just being with her made me feel more alive, more able to reach beyond myself.

We were the only two people sitting at the bar. A couple speaking in low angry voices shared a table with unmatching chairs. A man in black, an actor whose name I couldn't recall, was bent over a manuscript like a vulture about to swoop. He kept grunting and taking small swigs from his beer like it was cough syrup. The music drifted in softly from another room and I could just make out the gravelly deep voice of Leonard Cohen.

The barman emerged from attaching a new barrel under the bar. He was short and broad like a boxer with strong features and green eyes, an actor between roles, I imagined. Vivienne ordered two spritzers, 'the way I like them,' she said, and he tapped his temple to show he remembered. He put measures of white wine in two glasses, added slices of lemon, ice cubes and filled them to the brim with soda water. He placed them in front of us with a pair of red and white striped straws.

'Voilà,' he said.

'Vous êtes trop gentil.'

'That's about as far as my French goes,' he admitted.

'Mine too,' she replied, and glanced at me. 'I know what I fancy, a BLT?'

'Sounds good to me.'

I was going to eat it, whatever it was.

The barman strode off with the order and Vivienne said she would be back in two ticks. The actor with the manuscript continued to grunt. The couple hissed at each other like snakes. I studied the stranger reflected back at me from the mirror behind the bar. My thoughts were like a handful of confetti thrown in the air on a windy day. My conversion from care worker to a guest at one of the most exclusive clubs in London had taken less than a week. I was suffering vertigo.

Just as there was more to Vivienne than first meets the eye, I had a feeling that Groucho's was the same. It was an iceberg, more hidden than could be seen floating on the surface. The blue walls were hung with different sized paintings. The wood floor reminded me of a ship deck. Natural light seeped in through frosted windows that allowed no one to look in from outside. It could have been any club in the West End. But it wasn't any club. It was an oasis where actors and actresses, writers and directors, megastars and their lawyers could chat without being bothered by their fans, the public, the great unwashed, as Rufus Bradley had called members of the gym where we'd met, the group to which, in his eyes, I obviously belonged.

I glanced back at my reflection. My hair was tossed about from the open car, but it went with the casual chic of the white shirt and jacket. I looked like someone who would be taken more seriously than the man who had left his house that morning in a Gap shirt and five quid sunglasses. Like the new car, the new clothes gave me a look of composure I didn't really own. The white suit was a disguise, the Emperor's New Clothes. Packaging over content.

Why Vivienne had arranged for me to have a new wardrobe – paid for in some covert way – and why she enjoyed my company, remained a complete mystery. The scars on her back defined her passions, her pleasure in intense, uninhibited sex. But why me? A woman like that can sit at a bar and go home with any man she wants. Apart from massage, I had nothing to offer. Nothing at all. It made it all the more ridiculous that, in some way, paranoia most likely, while I was doing all the taking, I felt as if I were being used.

I kicked these thoughts around my head without reaching any conclusions. In truth, Vivienne had done nothing except make me feel good about myself. The way she looked into my eyes when she was speaking put me at ease and created a mood I only ever felt when I was giving someone a massage. I relaxed. I became serene, assertive, and transferred positive energy to the person I was massaging. I knew I was good at my job. People came away from treatments on an emotional and physical high. The massage table was my home turf. When I closed the table, my confidence drained away. I became me again, the monkey with the wandering mind and low self-esteem.

There is a difference between self-confidence and self-esteem. Self-esteem is how you feel about yourself. Self-confidence is how you project that feeling to others. With self-confidence, you trust in your decisions, believe in your abilities, and learn to accept your limitations. In the yoga books, the first lesson is 'be yourself' or 'be true to yourself.' It is difficult to know what that means exactly, or how to put it into practice.

Was I being myself sitting at the bar in Groucho's? Or was I playing the version of myself I wanted to become?

It was hard to know and the thought fled from my mind the moment Vivienne returned with a new sparkle in her eyes. She climbed up on the stool, crossed her long legs and sipped her spritzer.

'That tastes so good.'

We clinked glasses and sucked at our straws. Then she turned with an intense expression.

'I was reading the other day about an experiment at Cambridge,' she began. She rocked her hands from side to side. 'They put lots of metronomes on a stage and set them in motion at different times. You'll never guess what happened.' She took a breath. 'In no time, they began to beat together. Metronomes are not individuals. They are herd creatures connected to the rhythms and thoughts of those around them. Isn't that amazing?'

I wasn't sure what she was talking about and was saved by the barman. He appeared with two plates containing the BLTs, thick slices of toasted bread filled with bacon, lettuce and tomato, then cut in four. I tried not to eat like a starving man and watched Vivienne pick out the bacon and lettuce from the four quarters of her sandwich.

'We have a dark side,' she continued. 'Mysterious places hidden even from ourselves. Once you discover those places, you stop ticking along with all the other metronomes.'

'And become unique.'

'Exactly. You are so clever.'

'Hardly.'

She slid a piece of bacon between her lips and ran it between her teeth like a circular saw.

'I love bacon. I adore bacon. Don't you love Samuel L. Jackson?'

'He's great.'

'*Pulp Fiction's* my favourite film. *Pulp Fiction* and *Repulsion*. Catherine Deneuve is *amazing*.' That thoughtful look came to her face and she went on. 'It's lost time that matters, the time between time, the moments when you forget time and things just happen.'

'That's how I feel right now,' I said and she shook herself as if with a sudden burst of joy.

She nibbled a piece of lettuce like a rabbit. I eyed the bread she'd discarded. I didn't dare take it from her plate and eat it, yet knew, at the same time, it was the sort of thing she would have found amusing. That was the difference between us. I sat there in my linen suit pretending I belonged. Vivienne did belong. She could be outrageous and everyone would find it charming, eccentric, original. If I behaved badly, I'd be labelled a lout, an upstart. I was constantly aware of myself. I watched myself. Vivienne was herself.

While we were talking, people poked their heads around the door, gazed about the bar, then left again, probably for the dining room. I identified a couple of minor celebrities, a quiz show host with silver hair. Then, I recognised one of the biggest celebrities in the world, not from British television, the entire world. She was global, not merely a star, more like a supernova, a superstar, a household name.

She strode straight up to me with a curious, vaguely accusing expression.

'Do you play the sax?'

I was shaking in my new Sebagos. The BLT felt like lead in my stomach.

'No, I'm sorry.'

She threw out her palms as she turned to Vivienne. 'What are you doing here?'

'I'm leaving tomorrow. I didn't know *you* were here.'

'I'm not *here*. I'm in Paris. If I don't find a sax, I'm gonna kill someone.'

'I wish I could help.'

'Looks like it's you who needs some help, babe.' As she spoke, the star reached for the napkin on the bar and held it to Vivienne's nose. 'Either sniff or blow, one or the other.'

Vivienne took a long hard sniff then pinched her nostrils together. She shook her head, looked at me, looked back at the star, and smiled.

'I wish you were my mother,' she said.

'If I was your mother, I'd give you a spanking,' she replied, and they burst out laughing.

The star looked back at me. She had strong features, wore no makeup and made the air about her throb with her energy.

'Do I know you?'

'This is Ben Foster,' Vivienne said. 'He's a highwire walker.'

The star wasn't listening, which was just as well. She continued to look agitated, as if in some distant strange way I was responsible for her dilemma.

'Sax players! All full of piss and wind, the whole fucking lot of them. How does a guy pull out a day before a gig? Un-fucking-believable. What's the time?'

As I lifted my arm to look at my watch, she grabbed my wrist. 'Coming up to twelve-thirty,' I said.

'Are you staying for a drink?' Vivienne asked, and the star shook her head.

'I got my chess teacher waiting upstairs.' She paused. 'You going to the islands?'

'Aegina.'

'Sounds good. I'll give you a call. Fucking sax players.' She kissed Vivienne on the lips. 'I love you, you know that,' she said.

'You'd better,' Vivienne replied.

The star made a gun from her fingers and pointed at me. 'Don't fall off,' she said, and marched out.

My mouth had gone dry. There was sweat under my arms. It felt as if all the air in my body had been sucked out of me.

'Isn't she darling?' Vivienne remarked and sipped her spritzer.

I was about to ask her why she had said I was a highwire walker. But it didn't matter and the moment passed. I wasn't good at reading between the lines and had a feeling that in Vivienne's world that's where the message was hidden.

'Is she really learning to play chess?'

'Making up for lost time,' Vivienne said and that thoughtful look came to her face again. She brushed at a curl of hair that had fallen over my eye. 'Is there such a thing as lost time? Or is time lost spent doing something else? You only lose time when you're sleeping.'

'Or sitting in a traffic jam.'

'That's the time to listen to Pink Floyd.'

She finished her drink and sucked the juice from the lemon. The hissing couple sat in silence eating sandwiches. The actor scribbled in the manuscript on the table in front of him. Another young couple came in, both dressed in black, the 'in' colour, black clothes, black backpacks, black shades. Even Vivienne, always in white, carried a black handbag on a long strap.

She threw up her arms, stretched them above her head, then called the barman. He looked at her uneaten sandwich.

'Everything okay?'

'You can put it in a doggy bag … No, wait, I don't have a dog.'

He laughed. I laughed. She signed a chit. We had an appointment and she 'hated being late.'

'I won't be a moment,' I said.

I climbed a curving staircase to a wide hall decorated with a vase of pink lilies. The toilet was pink lit with linen hand towels and shiny taps on shiny sinks. The air had the smell of perfume too expensive to bottle. I called Kelly and told her I didn't know what time I would be home. I was going to tell her who I had just met, she was one of Kelly's favourite performers, but decided against it. I still hadn't worked out how I was going to explain away the new clothes for one thing and, for another, I couldn't quite believe I had just met who I had just met, and that person was a friend of Vivienne Raynott.

13
THE GOLDEN RULE

Southley is a sprawling country house outside Bagshot behind high red-brick walls that hide several acres of mature gardens. Golf buggies zip around curving paths to cabins that are rustic on the outside, high-tech luxury once you enter. In addition to the ancient oaks, hawthorns and banks of flowers, there is a grove of banana plants and palm trees in a conservatory where green parrots live the tropical life unaware of the English winter.

A hut built to look like a country cottage stands inside iron gates at the entrance. Guards on shifts watch who comes and goes and monitor tiers of video screens with footage from cameras placed discreetly throughout the grounds. The moment you enter Southley, the air instantly tastes sweeter and the world slows down, becomes serene and elegant.

From Groucho's, it is thirty-two miles on the M4 and M3 to Bagshot, a forty-five minute drive on a clear road, one hour and ten minutes in traffic. With the sun on fire, the hood down, the needle drifting over 100 miles per hour, Vivienne weaved a kamikaze path through the trucks and tankers to reach Southley in thirty minutes. I had kept my eyes closed all the way.

She slowed for the speed bump, waved to the guard and stepped out of the car exhilarated.

'Were you terrified?'

'Absolutely.'

She grinned and opened the boot. My bag with the new swimming shorts was there with another bag. She insisted on carrying them both.

My eyes strayed across the gardens. Not a daisy had dared poke its head above the snooker table green baize of the lawns. Every flower stood to attention. The big-leafed ivy shimmered as if every leaf had been polished by hand and tumbled down the walls of Southley like a green waterfall.

Bethany Bolter was waiting for us in the reception and hurried towards Vivienne as if they were long lost sisters. As she kissed her cheeks, Bethany jiggled her weight from one foot to the other.

'Vivienne, how lovely. How nice to see you. You look wonderful. Wonderful. It's always such a treat …'

'Thank you, that's so kind.'

'Such a treat. How was the journey? Not too busy?'

'Not bad. This is Ben Foster.'

Vivienne took half a step back as I shook Bethany's hand. Her smile dropped and her expression changed. She was in charge of Southley. I was a potential employee.

'A recommendation from Vivienne is a recommendation indeed,' she said.

'Thank you. It's a pleasure to meet you,' I replied.

Her expression changed again as she turned away. Bethany was squeezed into a fitted dress – black again – and wore lofty heels to streamline her legs. She was about forty with dark blonde hair held back from her soft rounded face with a black velvet bow. She wore a heavy gold watch and lots of gold bangles glittered as they swivelled around her wrist. She leaned into Vivienne's space and Vivienne leaned back as if they were dancing a tango.

'How's Lady Margaret? I haven't seen her for ages.'

'She's away, I think.'

'Do give her my regards,' she said and her busy eyes fell on the quilted leather bag hanging from Vivienne's shoulder. She took a deep breath. 'That *is* gorgeous. Is it Lulu Guinness?'

'I don't know.'

The bag was now clutched in Bethany's hands. She studied it like it was a rare find at the *Antiques Roadshow*.

'It is. It's gorgeous. I must get one.'

Bethany grinned and grimaced. Her features were mobile, as if she were seeking the right expression. She wanted Vivienne to feel comfortable and behaved in a way that had the opposite effect. Nothing impressed Vivienne. She liked you or she didn't and seemed to make up her mind instantly one way or the other. She smiled. I knew it was phoney.

'You are always so kind. I'm going to take a swim, if that's all right. Perhaps Ben could join me.'

'Of course, my dear, of course. You know where everything is.'

'Thank you.'

Vivienne took her phone from her bag and we watched her long legs propel her down the corridor to the spa.

The reception area was a new addition, the same as the extension housing the gym, treatment centres and pool. It was cool and airy with diamonds of glass in the leaded windows to follow the style of the main building. The walls were white with panels painted pale green, the same shade as the staff uniforms. A circular Oriental carpet woven through with threads of green and gold had been placed immediately below a chandelier that hung from a rose decorated with lion's heads, a reminder of Southley's former life as the family home of a very rich family.

A couple was checking in. The girl at the counter wore a pale green waistcoat and a white blouse buttoned at the collar. A porter, an older man with a seen-it-all expression stood by with suitcases on a trolley. He caught my eye and gave me a nod as if he had seen beyond my new suit and knew I was not a guest. I followed Bethany into her office. She dropped into a swivel chair behind a desk with eight mobile phones laid out in formation on the glass surface. I sat opposite and peered up at the aerial photograph of Southley on the wall behind her.

'Such a lovely person,' Bethany said. 'Now, how do you know Vivienne?'

'I used to work in a gym and became friends with one of the members. I give him a massage at his house every week. We met there,' I said, probably explaining too much. 'Vivienne's a friend of Lady Catherine, his mother.'

She made a mental note. 'We spoke yesterday. She often calls me. She said your Swedish massage was the best she had ever experienced.'

'That was nice of her.'

She stiffened. 'She happens to be a very nice person.'

We discussed my career. It wasn't overwhelming. I had the Intensive Level 3 Diploma in Body Massage from St Mary's, and had completed introduction courses in reflexology and sports massage. Bethany only employed staff with the Level 4 certificates, but would make an exception and give me a four week trial through August, a busy month when staff were also taking holidays. It would mean that I wouldn't be having a holiday that year, but there was nothing new in that.

Bethany's eyes ran over my shirt and jacket as she told me that her staff were expected to be well-dressed and well-groomed at all times. The image I conveyed, she said, was the image guests took away with them from Southley. There would not always be clients for massage. In my downtime, I would be expected to help out in other areas of the spa. There was always wet towels to pick up from the changing rooms and dry ones to deliver to the pool.

'You're not above that sort of thing?'

'No, of course not.'

She continued in a softer tone. 'Now, I have to ask you this, don't be offended,' she said. 'What is your sexual orientation?'

'I'm married. I have three young children.'

'Ah,' she said with an intake of breath. 'How very lucky.'

I wasn't sure who it was that was lucky, me to have three children, or Bethany who needed a straight guy in the spa. Then it occurred to me that she may have been relieved because she had been unable to work out what my relationship was with Vivienne and didn't want to believe the worst: that we had a relationship. It was that English hang up, a class thing. Bethany felt flattered to have Vivienne's number in her smartphone. She wanted to count her among her friends and would drop Vivienne's name into conversations as a sign of her own status. She pictured Vivienne with lords and ladies at society balls, not on the M3 chauffeuring a masseur to a job interview. She pursed her lips.

'One last thing. Can I see your hands?'

I spread them on the desk and she examined them like they were two slices of liver in the butcher's.

'Thank you, very nice. You have nice fingers, long and slender.' She looked back at me. 'So, four weeks, starting Monday. Then we'll assess the situation. Would that be suitable?'

'That'll be great.'

She suggested a salary almost twice what I had been earning at The Lodge and promised that it would be increased if the trial period worked out, which she was sure it would. She stood, brushed out the creases from her dress and seized one of her army of mobile phones.

'Your accent,' she said. 'It's not London, is it?'

'Lowestoft,' I replied. 'East Anglia.'

'Very interesting,' she added. 'Let's go for the tour, shall we?'

We left the office and made our way through reception and down the corridor to the spa. People with wet hair wandered by in white towelling robes and flip flops that made a slapping sound on the stone floor. We entered the massage centre where a girl in white like a nurse sat at a reception desk. The surface was ringed with price lists and stacks of glossy pamphlets. She stood.

'Tiffany, this is Ben, he'll be joining us next week,' Bethany said.

We shook hands. She was pretty with short dark hair and dark eyes.

'Are any of the treatment rooms empty?'

'There's nobody in number 2 at the moment,' Tiffany said and consulted a list to make sure.

There were three treatment areas accessed through separate doors. Each had their own changing room with a waiting area equipped with a water cooler, coffee machine and magazines fanned out on a wooden table. As we entered the massage room itself, I felt as if I had stepped into a place I had seen before, but only in my dreams. If I had ever had the opportunity to design a massage room, this was how it would have been.

When patients are undressed for massage, they quickly become cold, while the therapist warms up moving around the table. The ideal temperature is 25 degrees centigrade. That was what the air-conditioning was set at. The pale green light that emerged from a recess below the ceiling kept the room in semi-darkness, producing a sense of peace and equanimity. Moving water has a soothing effect, as does sea air, one of the reasons why people go to the seaside. That same sensation had been created with the briny fragrance of aromatherapy candles and the sound of water running continuously over a rock pool where flat stones were kept warm for stone massage. There was a music centre, every oil under the sun and a neat pile of clean towels. The massage table was long and wide with a removable face cradle and an adjustable backrest. From a control panel, you could modify the height and warm the cream-coloured upholstery.

'You like it?'

'It's fantastic,' I said. 'This is the best table I've ever seen. I love this room.'

She closed the door, threw the bolt in place, then unlocked the door again. She did it twice.

'What plays in the massage room stays in the massage room,' she said. 'That's the Golden Rule. You understand what I'm saying?'

'Of course. It's confidential. It's like being a doctor.'

'I hadn't thought of it like that, but, yes, in a way.' She took a step closer. We looked at each other across the table. 'Not all, but a lot of our clients have *very* busy lives. They arrive in need of some TLC. Some Tender Loving Care. We provide the services that allows them to return to their busy lives feeling rejuvenated. You do know kundalini massage, I assume?'

'Very much so. It's the spiritual aspect of massage …'

'I would say the spiritual supported by the physical.'

'Well, yes.'

'Clients may choose to have their chakras realigned, that sort of thing. I'm not the expert. What I do know, and what you must be aware of, is that our clients have certain expectations. Our job at Southley is to meet those expectations. You know what they say, the customer is always right?'

I nodded. 'Yes …'

She made a zipping motion across her lips. 'Just remember the Golden Rule.'

'I will.'

'Do that, Ben, and you will be very happy here.' She paused for a few moments to make sure I had understood exactly what she meant, which I didn't, then opened the door. 'Shall we?'

We continued along the corridor. The sunlight was strong through the windows that faced the gardens on our left. To our right were the various treatment centres. We passed the hairdresser, the nail salon.

'Do have a manicure whenever necessary,' she said.

We reached the pool. Vivienne was in the Jacuzzi. She remained expressionless.

'I'll leave you to it,' Bethany said. 'I'll see you on Monday at ten. We'll go through the paperwork then.'

A plump woman clung on to the rail and kicked her feet on the surface of the water. Other than her, the pool was empty. I approached the Jacuzzi on the far side where Vivienne sat in a froth of bubbles.

'You've been ages,' she said.

'Bethany's very thorough.'

'I bet she is.'

As she stepped out of the bubbles, the water ran off her skin like oil from a shiny surface. She wore a white one piece costume, hair held back with an elastic band. She was slender rather than thin and, as she had said, stronger than she looked. She slipped into a white robe that she tied at her waist. Behind the Jacuzzi, the bag containing my new bathing shorts hung from a white plastic chair. She grabbed it and led me to the men's changing room.

'Back in a tick,' she said.

The changing room was decked out in white tiles, every fourth or fifth one with a pale green flower motif. Below the long mirror, the shelf was stocked with soaps, sprays, body creams, hair gel, combs and brushes still in their packets. You could have robbed the lot but, as a client of Southley, why would you? I hung my clothes in a locker, stepped into the blue shorts and went back to the mirror. I usually wore black Speedo's, small and tight. The Ralph Lauren swimwear was less showy. I stretched my arms into a robe, slipped the locker key in the pocket, and Vivienne sang out as she entered.

'Is there anybody in there?'

'Only me.'

'Is there anyone at home?'

In her hand, she carried a paper package about the size of two postage stamps. She unfolded the package on the flat surface between the sinks. Inside, pressed flat, was some white powder, about the amount you would get from one crushed aspirin. From her pocket, she produced a red and white tube three of four centimetres long cut, I guessed, from a straw from Groucho's. She stirred the powder with the tip of the straw, then separated it into two lines. She leaned over, clamped one nostril shut with her finger and held the straw to the other. She sniffed back the powder in one quick noisy snort, pinched both nostrils together and vigorously shook her head.

Vivienne gave me the straw. I hesitated.

'First time?' she asked, and I nodded my head. 'Lucky you.'

Was this a test?

I wasn't sure, but I had no intention of failing.

I copied Vivienne and snorted back the remaining line of coke. She licked the surface of the paper and rubbed her index finger over her gums. She flushed the paper down the toilet, sucked out the residue from the red and white straw and put it in her pocket. The smile about her lips reminded me of Claire.

If you were supposed to get high from the cocaine, I didn't sense anything except pins and needles in my nose and mouth.

We went back to the pool. We dropped our robes on plastic chairs and Vivienne dived straight in the deep end. She had assured the barman at Groucho's that, like him, her French was non-existent. When it came to swimming, she had told me she was 'hopeless.' I watched as she sliced the water freestyle in steady strokes, did a flip turn and swam back to where I was standing.

'The water's delicious. It feels like silk.'

I dived in. I swam a length underwater. I felt as if I could have held my breath forever and she was dead right, the water was as slippery as massage oil and felt like silk softly stroking my skin. I came up at the shallow end. I took a breath and hugged the bottom of the pool as I swam back to where Vivienne was waiting. The woman was still doing her kicking exercises but I didn't care. I kissed Vivienne on the lips and our bodies glued together like magnets.

We tore ourselves apart and swam another few lengths. Jets of water fired out about a metre below the surface of the pool. By clinging to the rail and holding your feet apart against the side wall, you could direct the jet at your genitals. Vivienne showed me. It was sensual, silly, fun. I laughed. I wasn't trying to be anyone.

We raced to the shallow end and I made sure we arrived at the same moment. We sat opposite each other in the Jacuzzi entangling and disentangling our feet. My mind was spinning and popping like the bubbles in the circular whirlpool. Her eyes were bright in the steamy light. I wanted her. She wanted me. It wasn't love. Love is like being burned in flames then plunged into icy water. Love leaves scars and broken hearts. Your emotions change from one second to the next. It wasn't like that. Our hormones were exploding. Our adrenaline was pumping. It was mating season in a wildlife documentary.

There was another woman in the sauna sweating out toxins. She reminded me of a seal, her big body wrapped in a towel. We stayed for two minutes.

'I love the sauna, it's so boring. It's like being a galley slave.'

I thought of Marley for one second. He said strange things but not like Vivienne.

We collected our robes and went back to the men's changing rooms. We stepped into the shower. We slathered our palms with soap from the pump container and washed the chlorine from each other in long lazy strokes. I adored her skinny body, her pert breasts, the dark mysterious slot dividing the dome of her pubis. She ran the tip of her finger over the scratches on my back.

'Beautiful,' she said. 'Does it hurt?'

'It did. It doesn't now.'

'Did it feel good?'

'Not really.'

She went down on her haunches.

'*Cazzo,*' she said. 'Poor baby.'

As she took me into her mouth, I thought: there is just this moment. This now. Buddhists say live every day as if it may be your last. If this was my last day and we crashed at 100 miles per hour on the M3 going back to London, I would die with a smile on my face. I pictured that smile behind closed eyes and remembered the smiley face Vivienne had drawn on the window at Rowley's back in another lifetime.

The water beat down on my skull. Vivienne ran her tongue over every part of my cock as if it were a memory machine that would hold the shape inside her forever. She moved up and down, finding rhythm. I sensed the quickening beat of my heart and heard the milling of my breath through the sound of the shower.

She stopped before I came, heightening my arousal. We switched positions. I bent her forward. I inserted my tongue in her pussy, her bottom. I licked every fold and curve. I wanted to enter every part of her, her head and her soul. She was Eve. I was Adam. My serpent was a rod of iron. I felt a sense of invincibility, of madness, a desire that was extreme and overpowering. I lifted her into my arms. She clung to my neck and her legs locked behind my back as I pushed up inside her. She was as light as a bird. She rocked up and down, gaining pace in a pulsing rhythmic motion. There is when making love a moment when the body defies gravity. This is the moment to strive for. This was the moment we had reached.

When we came, it was fierce and dramatic like nothing I had experienced before. I didn't have a feeling of loss, a little death. On the contrary, I felt reborn. My mouth tingled. My body tingled. I was still hard and she sucked me beneath the driving rain of the shower until I thought my heart was going to burst. She swallowed the last dregs of my semen. Then we kissed and I wasn't sure if it was my taste or her taste that filled my mouth, and I thought: if sex has a taste, this is the taste.

'Did it feel like silk?'

'You feel like silk.'

'That's the nicest thing anyone has ever said to me.'

It felt as if time was suspended until she turned off the shower and the clock started ticking again. She opened the glass door and vanished like a ghost through the steam-coated mirrors. I dried and dressed. I placed my wet swimwear in the same bag with string handles and sat in one of the plastic chairs watching the woman still kicking the surface of the water. I didn't know where she was going but I reckoned she was going to get there.

There were hairdryers in the changing rooms, but Vivienne's hair was wet still and combed back in a way that emphasised the curve of her cheekbones. Men stole looks at her as they passed on the way to the pool. She didn't seem to notice. As we approached the main reception, her phone buzzed with a text.

'Perfect timing.'

'Your inner metronome,' I said, and she grabbed my arm.

'Were you really a fisherman?'

'Yes, really.'

We reached the café where a man was waiting for us. He stood and kissed Vivienne's cheeks.

'This is Flippo,' she said. 'Flippo, Ben Foster.'

We shook hands.

Flippo was Italian and spoke perfect English with a sunny accent. He wore green shorts, a white shirt (the long sleeves rolled up to just below the elbow). Ray-Bans with mirror lenses held back his black, swept back hair. His face was full of light and energy. I wondered if it was from Flippo that Vivienne had learned the word *cazzo*.

We ordered cups of cappuccino and carrot cake. I watched Vivienne gobble hers down as fast as she had snorted back the coke.

'Wow, you going for a world record?' asked Flippo.

'Sometimes, I don't eat for a couple of days, then everything tastes so good.'

'You're a crazy girl.'

'Thank you.'

She had a foam moustache on her top lip as she drank the cappuccino.

Flippo had a case at his feet that he opened on the table and removed about twenty watches wrapped in cloth bags.

'When we choose something, it is a process of elimination. I love this coffee.' Vivienne took another sip from her cup and wiped away her moustache. 'We don't choose with our eyes, we choose with our psyche.'

'Wow, deep,' the Italian said.

She looked at me. 'Eliminate those you don't like and see what's left?'

'Me?' I said.

'Do it for fun.'

I gazed down at the watches. They weren't new, they were classics, antiques, collectables, each unique in its own way. I instantly discarded three that were monstrously large and two more with gaudy gold straps. I liked the Rolex, but it was heavy. The De Grisogono was too fussy, and I wasn't sure I liked the square face of the Cartier. The Longines Heritage 'looks right whatever the occasion' and 'John Travolta wears a Breitling Navitimer every time he flies.'

During the process, I rejected the watches with metal bands and was left with three with leather straps.

'This is like the Miss World contest,' Vivienne said. 'I know exactly which one you're going to pick.'

I looked down again and indicated one of the three watches.

Vivienne gasped, and I shook my head.

Flippo put the Longines back in its bag.

Two remained. I studied the Tiffany Chronograph for a long time. The dial was blue, the chrome colour of Vivienne's eyes, with silver numerals and a blue alligator strap.

'Self-winding, water resistant,' Flippo said.

I shook my head and he slid it back into the bag.

The watch that remained was the most simple, a wafer thin gold-faced Omega De Ville on a brown leather strap. Vivienne threw up both arms and shook them like a football fan who has just watched her team score a goal.

'I knew it,' she said. 'I knew it. It's so you. Try it. Try it. You must try it on.'

I removed my plastic Casio to do so. Flippo placed the remaining watches back in the case and snapped the locks shut.

'Hang on,' I said, and Vivienne placed her hands over my wrist to prevent me unbuckling the Omega.

'It's for you.'

'No, no, no. I can't.'

'Why not?

'It's ... I don't know.'

'It's only a watch.'

I held up the Casio. 'But I already have a watch.'

'Now you have two.'

'Wow, you English. So good at *matematica*.'

Vivienne finished her cappuccino and placed her cup decisively in the saucer. I wouldn't have felt so awkward allowing her to buy me a watch if Flippo hadn't been sitting there, but if you accept the gift you have to put up with the discomfort. A car, clothes, a gold Omega. Where was it going to end?

'Vivienne, thank you,' I said, and she turned to Flippo as if she hadn't heard.

'Do you have something for me?'

'Always,' he replied.

He reached into his top pocket and removed something small enough to keep hidden beneath his fingers as he slid it across the table. Vivienne covered the unseen object with her mobile phone.

'I want more cake,' she said, and waved her hand to the waitress.

As the girl went off with the order, Bethany Bolter arrived smiling her smile. Flippo immediately stood. I copied him. I was learning.

'Bethany, I had a gorgeous swim, thank you,' Vivienne said. 'Can I introduce you to Filippo Borghese? Bethany Bolter.'

He bowed and kissed her hand. She jiggled from foot to foot.

'What a pleasure...'

'The pleasure is all mine,' he said.

'Filippo's my dealer... watch dealer,' Vivienne added, and Bethany wasn't sure what to say.

'That's marvellous. How marvellous.'

Bethany had an inbuilt radar that allowed her to pinpoint a person's place on the social map the moment they met. Even with an accent, the usual giveaway, Flippo – Filippo – with his bright eyes and good manners was clearly what Bethany would have called 'people like us.' I would come to learn that she was right on target: Filippo Borghese Pecci was from an aristocratic family with princes and Popes on the family tree. He sold coke and watches because lots of those old families had lost their money without losing the desire for all the things it buys.

The waitress returned with a slice of cake for Vivienne and three more cappuccinos.

'Put it all on the complimentary list,' Bethany said grandly.

Vivienne's head dropped to one side. 'Thank you,' she said in a tiny voice.

That was something else I would come to learn. Vivienne did not pay to use the spa at Southley. Bethany had given her a pass in order to buy her friendship and with the prospect that Vivienne would bring her friends. When people are titled or in the public eye, other people, normal people, get a kick out of doing things for them. Their generosity is not flouted or taken for granted. They become fringe members of the court and are repaid by occasional invitations to, say, a large cocktail party – what Vivienne called a 'rat fuck' – where a celebrity would be present. It gave those people a name to drop in the eternal game of who's who, who knows whom, who do you know and how do you know them.

Vivienne ate some of the cream from the carrot cake and left the rest. Likewise the coffee. She stood, gathered up her phone and the little package hidden beneath. She placed them in her Lulu Guinness bag and slung the bag slantwise across her chest.

'You are driving back to town, Flippo?' she said.

'Sure I am.'

'Can you take Ben? I've got so much to do. I'll be in touch.'

She kissed his cheeks. She kissed my cheeks. I watched her pace from the café and heard the Ferrari roar as she accelerated back to the gate. I didn't see her again for a month.

14
POSITIVE THINKING

In my dream I was swimming underwater. When I looked up, I couldn't see the light and realised I had gone down too far to swim back to the surface.

I woke coughing and covered in sweat.

Dance music blasted from the radio in the kitchen. Kelly was clattering around making breakfast. Claire was having a screaming fit. I sneezed. I had a sore throat. My eyes hurt. I couldn't understand why. The previous day at Southley I had felt like a super hero.

I pulled the pillow over my head. I was trying to doze off again when my mobile buzzed angrily. The name 'Angela' appeared on the screen.

'You haven't replied to my email,' she snapped.

'I'm sorry…'

'Are you too busy?'

'No, I…'

'If you're not busy, why don't you answer your emails?'

'I don't have a computer.'

'That's the worst excuse I've ever heard in my life. You're not messing me about, are you, Ben?'

'No, I'm not. I'll go to the library and my check my mail.'

The tone hummed in my ear as the line went dead. My linen suit was hanging on the side of the wardrobe. It didn't look like me at all. I pulled on an old shirt and shorts and went downstairs.

'You look like something the cat's dragged in,' Kelly said.

That made Ollie laugh. Claire was still screaming and bit me when I tried to pick her up.

'What's wrong, baby?'

'Me, me, me, me, me,' she cried.

'She wants George's police car,' Kelly said, 'and he doesn't want to give it to her.'

George was on all fours making the siren wail as he pushed the car between the table legs. The noise put my teeth on edge and I resorted to bribery, the only thing that worked.

'George, Georgie. If you let Claire play with your car, I'll take you to the park for pizza.'

Ollie paused from eating his cereal and punched the air. 'Yeah, pizza.'

George took after me. He was always agreeable. He immediately gave his sister the toy and Claire did exactly what he had been doing. She made the siren wail as she pushed the car across the floor. When Claire wanted something, she used charm and rage, smiles or tears, whatever it took until she got it. I couldn't help admiring her for that.

'Georgie,' I said. 'You've won the prize. Double cheese.'

Kelly shook her head. 'Pizza in the park again. Can we afford it?'

'Yep, no problem. I've got my regular tomorrow.'

She poured me a cup of tea from the big brown pot that used to belong to Gran. We had kept her mugs and a set of six plates, the first with a whole apple, the second with an apple with a bite taken from it and so on until the last one showed just three apple pips.

'There's food to buy, we're out of everything,' Kelly continued. 'Bills to pay…'

'Look, don't go on. Everything's under control.'

She took a long noisy breath. 'What do you want for breakfast?'

'Nothing, darling, I'm all right. I've got to pop out and check my emails.' I burned my tongue drinking the tea. 'Remember, I've got some parcels coming later. I'm not sure what time.'

'I'll be here till I start work, same as always.'

'Soon as we're on our feet, you're going to give up that job.'

'Let's see how it goes, shall we? You've only got a trial, don't forget.' She came to the door and gave me a kiss. 'You look after yourself.'

Kelly had seen how working double shifts at The Lodge had taken its toll. She was pleased I had found a new job with more money. Finally, I would be doing something I was trained for and wanted to do. I had told Kelly I had been obliged to buy suitable clothes to conform to the spa's dress code and would be paying for them out of my wages. Another lie. I was getting good at it, or used to it, anyway.

As for my extra-curricular activities, they had been rationalised, justified, tucked away in a box in the back of my mind. I was paid for sex. It sounded like a bad joke. I had to pinch myself to make sure I wasn't still in a dream forty fathoms down in deep water. I was going to have to split myself between two very different roles, the good husband and loving father at home, Casanova for ladies with special needs when I went to work.

What plays in the massage room stays in the massage room.

It had taken me a while to work out what Bethany meant exactly by the Golden Rule, but I'd got there in the end.

People confuse kundalini massage with tantra. Massage is sexy. When you are rubbing your oiled hands over a naked body, how could it not be? But massage is not sex, even if that's what results.

Tantra is sex. It is a love-making technique originated by Hindu masters in India 5,000 years ago. It is designed to create a mind body connection that can result in powerful climaxes, although that's not the central point. Tantric sex is slow moving. Couples can remain joined for many hours, the purpose being to empty the mind and take a step on the road to nirvana, enlightenment, ultimate bliss. The original meaning has fallen by the wayside and what remains is no longer a spiritual pursuit, but a quest for bigger and better orgasms.

I drove to the library trying to focus on Napoleon Hill and thinking instead about Vivienne. She could be moody if she didn't get her own way, and didn't care about anything except her own passing whims and pleasures. That's what made her such fun to be with. She was like a spoiled girl you wanted to punish so you could lick away her tears. Vivienne was trouble. I knew that. But once you get up on the highwire it's not easy to get off.

Flippo had driven me back to Soho. I had tried to pump him on his relationship with Vivienne but, like her, he was discreet and gave nothing away except that he had met her in Tuscany where her family owned a villa. Gossip is a form of currency and I didn't have anything to exchange. Flippo did talk about his family's princes and Popes, but kept coming back to the one subject dear to his heart: cocaine. The industry was on the 'verge of collapse' because dealers were 'bashing' it so hard that users were snorting poison.

'Coke's everywhere except where it should be, in cocaine!'

He shrugged passionately as he made his points and the car jerked across the lanes.

'People think they've died and gone to heaven paying £40 a gram. What's the big deal if it's only two per cent pure?' He was outraged. 'My white lady comes straight from Peru. None of that Colombian shit. She's from the source, the same coke the Incas have been using for thousands of years. Say what you like, at £100, that's a bargain.'

'You're right,' I said.

'You need anything, you know where to find me.'

Flippo didn't drive as fast as Vivienne, but we were back in London in under an hour. He was seeing customers in Groucho's and drove me straight to my VW in the Brewer Street car park.

Angela's email had given me instructions to pick up Kate – Lady Catherine – from her home on Saturday at eight-thirty. I had a dinner reservation for nine in the name of 'Alan Ingram' at the *Cock and Bull*, a pub about eight miles from Kempton. I was to dress well, pay the bill and 'be the perfect gentleman.' She also told me to send her my bank details.

I apologised for not answering earlier and promised to follow the instructions 'to the letter.' I slowly copied the sort code and account number from my debit card. My fingers that stroked out stress clusters were all thumbs on the keyboard and I read through what I had typed twice before pressing 'send.'

While I waited to see if Angela responded, I Googled 'cocaine side effects.'

I was relieved to discover that, without actually having flu, the symptoms were the same: a sore throat, runny nose and aching limbs. Coke increases your blood flow, heart rate and brain activity. You feel more alert, confident, intoxicated with energy. It didn't say sex on cocaine is astonishing, but I already knew that. The cure is to eat well and, predictably, drink plenty of water. The worst thing you can do is take another hit. That's the cocaine merry-go-round. Once you are on it, it's hard to get off.

Was Vivienne an addict? It was hard to say. It was another area in which I was totally inexperienced. But I did recall that in Groucho's, when she left for 'two ticks,' she had returned with her blue eyes glittering and twice as big. She'd talked rapidly about time and metronomes, then drove like a getaway driver to Southley. She had grown bored waiting in the Jacuzzi and we

snorted the last of her supply before we swam, before our performance in the shower, before coffee and carrot cake. She had been
witty, charming and had left the café with another package from
Flippo in her bag. Vivienne thrived on speed, action, constant
change. She was as demanding as she was generous.

I glanced at the gold watch on my wrist. It was a statement. I
wasn't entirely sure what it meant, but those in Vivienne's circle
knew the secret codes. I hadn't seen her pay for the watch, or
the coke, for that matter. But her relationship with money wasn't
the same as mine. Parking fines double if you don't pay them
straight away. Vivienne didn't concern herself with the cost, only
the inconvenience. Bills and debts were handled, dealt with, put
off for some other time. Talking about money, except in abstract
terms, in millions and billions, was vulgar. Nothing should be
allowed to cast a cloud over life's main purpose, to be amusing
and to be amused.

For me, for the poor, for most of us, money is the one thing
you never have enough of. Money is something you try and save,
you borrow from parents, lend to mates and are anxious about all
of the time. With remarkable modesty, or a lack of imagination,
what most working men dream of – aside from winning the lottery and sleeping with beautiful women – is having an extra £40
a week in their wage packet. For Vivienne, for the rich, money is
the means by which one doesn't have to worry about money.

There is a myth I grew up with and heard so many times that
I had believed it. They say money doesn't buy you happiness. This
is a delusion the poor cling to and the rich find comical. Money
does buy happiness. Money equals freedom, the highest form of
happiness. Money equals pleasure. The more you have the more
pleasurable life is. People with money can never know what it is
like to be without money. And something I would learn in the
next two years: money is a magnet, it doesn't trickle down, it is
sucked up.

Where did Flippo fit in the great scheme of things? He came from what they call a 'good family' and had an essential skill: supplying Inca coke. Where did I fit? It's not easy to see yourself as you really are but, if I am honest, it was the apparatus Maggs had named Big Ben.

The computer pinged. It was Angela with three words. Don't Be Late.

I pinged back: I won't be.

That felt good. I had not forgotten that Angela still owed me fifty quid.

From the library, I wandered down King Street to Starbucks. My flu symptoms were fading and had just about gone by the time I'd finished my cappuccino and almond croissant. I went to Curry's and bought a Toshiba laptop. It was time Ollie had a computer at home. He knew the alphabet and was just about starting to read. Ollie was good with his hands and I was sure, once he got his little fingers on the keyboard, it wouldn't be long before he was teaching me how to build a website.

The Asian lad put my card through the machine and the box in a bag. He wrote his name, Mo, and a phone number on a sheet of paper, then slid it across the counter in the same way that Flippo had passed his product to Vivienne.

He spoke in a whisper. 'If you have any trouble getting on line, give me a call.'

I was running through our nest egg and decided to emulate Vivienne and not think about it. Through repetition and conviction, I was making myself believe that when you stop fretting over money, it slips like a breath of fresh air under the door. On my way back to the car, I passed a shop with the windows plastered in signs: Summer Madness, 20% off. My bleary eyes were drawn to the display of sunglasses. Ray-Ban Wayfarers. The real deal. £69.99. It would have been a mistake not to get them.

Was I aware that I was spending all the spare money on myself, not my family? Of course I was. But I didn't feel guilty about it. They say you have to speculate to accumulate. I was putting the tools in place in order to build a better life for them. I slipped on the shades as I left the store and already the world looked a little better.

Think and Grow Rich filled my ears driving home. You have the power to achieve what you want to achieve. It is all in your own mind. Tell the universe what it is you are seeking. Say it out loud. Repeat it again and again. Write it down. Be clear and precise. The only thing between you and your goal is your own self-doubt.

The depression and aching bones I'd woken with that morning had gone. I knew what I had to do: work hard, harder than I had ever worked before, *and never take cocaine again.* Drugs and alcohol didn't suit me. They never had.

There had been too many mornings when I had set off on the trawler from Lowestoft harbour with a hangover. I remembered the lows after the highs, the empty feeling and paranoia from smoking dope. Drink and drugs turn you into a different person, a projection on a screen that looks like you without being who you really are. After the momentary high, your confidence dips and you want to dig a hole to climb into.

That feeling of low self-esteem was something I had suffered all through my childhood. When I was eight, my father was dragged overboard by the nets and drowned before the rest of the crew could pull him back on board the boat. When I returned to school in September, I found it hard to concentrate and was diagnosed with Attention Deficit Hyperactivity Disorder. It was fashionable to label kids with ADHD at the time. It marked me like a tattoo in school and still, at the age of thirty, one particular incident continued to come back into my mind.

Miss Pelham was our class mistress, as well as our arts and crafts teacher. She was a middle-aged lady with small bright eyes behind rimless glasses. She wore a cameo brooch to fasten her high-necked blouses and her hair was always tied back with a tartan ribbon that matched her tartan skirt. She liked girls because they were neat and polite. She didn't like little boys because we were noisy and clumsy with scabby knees and shirts hanging out of our trousers. I was the biggest boy in the class, gangly and awkward. I had started to stammer and Miss Pelham seemed to delight in asking me confusing questions so that she could then lean forward with her two hands cupping her ears as if in an attempt to gather in the words spluttering from my mouth.

At the end of the year, we were introduced to sculpting clay and made ceramic figures for Christmas presents. Most of the children made angels, shepherds, the Virgin Mary or Father Christmas. I decided to make a fisherman for my mum. I'm not sure what went wrong. My hulking creation was grand and ambitious, the largest by far. I was the last to finish and the clay figure was still moist when it went into the kiln. When our precious objects came back shiny with glaze, my fisherman was hunched forward with long arms and a small head. Miss Pelham took it from the tray and balanced it in her palms for everyone to see.

'What's this?' she asked.

'It's a, it's a fish, fish, fish, fisherman,' I stuttered.

'I thought it was a monkey,' she said.

All the children in the class laughed.

'You'd better not take it home, Ben, it will frighten the life out of your poor mother.'

She opened her palms and let my figurine fall to the floor where it broke into countless pieces.

I had told mum I was making her a fisherman in the arts and craft class, but I never told her what had happened to it. It was too ashamed. The experience was humiliating and long lasting. It killed what little confidence I had and shaped my understanding of how the world works.

It was years later when I started my first massage course that I discovered that I had never had ADHD. Like many children of eight, I only concentrated when I had a teacher who made the subject interesting and inspired the class. Many people ask themselves when they look back why they didn't work harder at school, why they didn't do the homework and pass the exams. They blame themselves, when it is not their fault. You don't make these life-changing decisions when you are eight.

Children are wet clay and it is up to teachers and parents to show them what they can make of themselves. In underfunded and failing schools with underpaid, overburdened teachers, opportunity is in short supply. No one was going to inspire my children except Kelly and me. Whatever potential Ollie, George and Claire had, I intended to do everything I could to encourage them to reach that potential.

Patience, persistence and perspiration make an unbeatable combination for success.

As I arrived home, a blue Mercedes van pulled away from outside the house and I slipped straight into the vacant spot. That's what positive thinking does for you. I let myself in and found Kelly and the kids standing in the living room gazing at the piles of boxes filling every space. The children were teary-eyed and it broke my heart to see their sad little faces. It was like Christmas except every present in the room was for me.

'You're not serious, are you?' Kelly said.

'What?'

'Hugo Boss. Tom Ford. Giorgio Armani. Only the best for Ben?'

'That's just the labels. They're all fakes.'

'I didn't know fakes came in boxes and suit bags.' She shook her head. 'Why did you get so much?'

'I don't know.'

'You don't know?'

'The image I convey is the image customers take away from Southley.' It was something Bethany had said. 'I have to look the biz.'

'Why all the suits?' She counted. 'Men buy one suit. There are six here. Look at these shirts. I've never seen anything like it. And the ties.'

'I'm going to have to go to receptions, that sort of thing. All the people are rich. They expect it.'

'Yeah, but you're not rich. Bloody hell, Ben, what's wrong with you?'

'Nothing's wrong with me …'

Her eyes swooped down on the Curry's bag I was carrying. 'What's that?'

'A laptop.'

'Is that for your image as well?'

'As a matter of fact, it's not for me. I only check emails. It's for everyone. It's so Ollie can learn …'

'Is it for me, dad?'

'It's for everyone,' I told him.

'You're getting in over your neck,' Kelly said. She had her hands on her hips. Her eyes narrowed. 'We don't want to lose the house, Ben. We've got three kids, for Christ sake.'

'We're not going to lose the house. I've got a new job, more money. Everything's going great. Don't ruin it.'

I must have raised my voice. Claire started crying. 'No, no, no,' she sobbed, and Kelly picked her up.

'Pizza, dad,' George reminded me, and I didn't know whether to laugh or cry.

I followed Kelly to the kitchen.

'Don't ruin it, Kells. Be positive. Everything's all right. Everything. Just give me a chance.'

'Don't forget who you are, Ben.'

'It's not for me, it's for us.'

Ollie and George were peeking around the door. We didn't argue often but it upset them when we did.

'I want the children to have a decent start. I want them to have all the things we didn't have ...'

'That's why you need six suits, is it?'

'Forget the damn suits. They're just suits.' I took a deep breath. 'Look, I'm not going to argue. I'm going out for a run. Then we're all going out for pizza.'

I winked at my boys and they punched the air.

15

WHAT CLOTHES SAY

There was a shift in Rufus's attitude when I gave him his weekly massage on Friday. Was it my new clothes? Was I more confident? It was difficult to put my finger on it exactly, but something had changed, and for the better.

It was change, too, that was needed in Rufus's treatment. I had meant to tell him for a long time that his back pain was caused in part by bad posture. But Rufus always kept a distance between us and I had never found a way to bridge the gap. He was sitting hunched over on the side of the massage table in his boxers.

'Rufus, are you aware that you slouch?'

'What?'

'I saw you riding last week. You were leaning awkwardly to one side. You looked as if you were trying to keep balance.'

'You don't ride, so how would you know?'

'That's the whole point of massage, it's to keep your body in balance. Your shoulders are hunched up even now.'

'That's just the way I'm sitting.'

'It's not the way you're sitting. It's your posture.' I remembered something I had read. 'Imagine there's a piece of string hooked to the top of your skull being pulled up into the universe. It would hold you erect. That's how you should be at all times.'

'So what you're saying is I need surgery to have a hook implant?'

'No, you need a different treatment. I'm going to try Rolfing…'

'What?'

'It's a deep massage. Every time we have a session, I'll work on a different set of muscle groups.'

'You're the so-called expert.'

'One more thing, no oil,' I explained. 'With oil it's harder to penetrate beyond the surface. Today we're going deeper.'

He gave me a long hard look. 'It's taken you long enough,' he said, then rolled over.

'Hold your breath for a count of ten.'

I flexed my fingers and began on Rufus's lower back.

Rolfing literally takes the therapist under the skin of the patient by working the soft tissue that holds the muscles in place. The process was developed in the 1950s by Ida Rolf, who treated musicians and athletes suffering RSI, repetitive strain injury. Rufus did have back pain, but self-inflicted by a combination of bad posture and the RSI of lying about doing nothing. A course of Rolfing sessions would realign his muscles. Once his posture improved, the back pain would ease.

Another benefit of Rolfing, as with all massage, is once the body is in balance, you are less likely to become tight or tense from minor pressures, or injured through everyday activities like bending or turning from the front seat of a car to reach into the back, a major cause of neck and shoulder strains.

Rufus groaned in pain a few times during the session, but left the table without complaint and stepped straight into the shower when I had finished. I folded my kit and stared out at the grounds. I could see the horses in the field off to the left. A red BMW was parked behind my car on the drive, the gravel shiny as a streak of white paint across the green landscape. The Met Office had said it had been the hottest July on record and it didn't look as if the heat wave was ever going to end.

Rufus returned, brushing his hair with his hands. He was casual in shorts, a shirt with bold blue stripes and old loafers with the backs pushed down.

I told him I was starting work at Southley. Naturally, he knew the spa and didn't appear to mind that I would have to fit our sessions into my new schedule. Rufus had always behaved as if he was doing me a favour booking a massage. That day, for the first time, he said he really felt a difference from the treatment and placed the fee in my hand, not on the table.

'Still £25?' he said.

'It's going to have to go up soon,' I replied with a surge of courage.

'I'll tell you what, Ben, next time we'll make it £50. Is that all right?'

'It's a deal,' I said, and he returned a rare smile.

All those months when I had spent two hours in the car and an hour bending over the massage table for £25, he probably couldn't believe I had never asked for an increase. I had always felt victimized by Rufus. But it was my own deficiencies that had made me afraid to put up my prices. That and the fact that £25 had made a big difference to our weekly budget. It was my own fault.

Until you have formed the habit of looking for the good instead of the bad in others, you will be neither successful nor happy.

I followed Rufus downstairs, and was shocked to find Rudy Johnson waiting in the Great Hall. Not only that he was there, but the coincidence that I had just been thinking about Napoleon Hill.

Rudy was studying a red-coated general in a gold frame on the wall. He turned with a beaming smile and we shook hands.

'Looking good, man,' he said.

'You're looking even better,' I replied, and we laughed.

Rudy looked you straight in the eye and you thought: I want to be friends with this man. He was dressed in a white shirt, blue chinos and slip-ons with buckles. I was six inches taller than Rudy, but the way he stood, shoulders back with his feet apart, I felt as if I was looking up at him. Something Rudy had said once had stuck in my mind: there is no such thing as lucky and unlucky people, only positive and negative people. It was Rudy who had given me the audio book I played every day in the car.

'By the way, you remember that CD you gave me ...'

'Napoleon Hill.'

'I was thinking about something he said a moment ago. Then I walk in and here you are.'

'Synchronicity? Serendipity? Collective consciousness?' He tapped the side of his head. 'There's not more going on in here than we imagine. There's more going on than we *can* imagine.'

'Sometimes less than we imagine?' Rufus said in his deep voice, and we laughed.

I usually watched myself and checked myself to make sure I didn't do or say anything out of place. It makes you stilted, unnatural, a bore. It was either Rufus's changed attitude towards me, or the epic energy created by Rudy, but for once I felt at ease in my own skin. After the hand shaking, it was clear that Rudy was there to talk business.

'Good to see you again,' I said. 'I'll leave you to it.'

'Are you in a rush?' he asked and I shrugged.

'No, but you guys want to talk.'

Rudy shot Rufus one of his powerful stares. 'Do you mind if Ben sits in on this? It might be useful.'

Rufus tensed up. Having money is one thing. Talking about it made him nervous. He twitched and ran his hand through his fine hair.

'No, I suppose not.'

Rudy dropped down on the grey sofa facing the walk-in fireplace and we sat either side of him on wine red armchairs. The girl in pink gingham materialized with a pot of mint tea and a plate of ginger snaps. I had not seen Rufus ask for anything, but had a feeling that servants in great houses are all mind readers.

I poured the tea.

As a mortgage broker, Rudy acted as a middleman between the person needing credit and the bank or mortgage lender. He assembled the borrower's financial and personal details and charged a fee for organizing the loan.

As they talked, a question welled up inside me and I couldn't stop myself asking.

'It's obviously none of my business, Rufus,' I said. 'But why do you need to get a loan?'

The cup he was holding froze before it reached his lips. Rudy answered for him.

'It's what rich people do,' he explained. 'If you've got capital, you make it work for you. Capital's hard to get. And harder to keep. Once you've got it, you don't use it unless some amazing opportunity appears.'

'Oh, really. Like what?' Rufus asked him.

He sat back and crossed his legs. He was perfectly relaxed, totally undaunted by the generals with their swords surrounding us on the walls. Rudy didn't have Rufus's reluctance to talk about money, quite the contrary.

'My first house in the country belonged to an Italian diplomat,' Rudy answered. 'There was some scandal or other. He was transferred and had to sell up and get out quick. He wanted seven-fifty. I'd built up some savings. I went to the bank for a bridging loan and offered the guy five hundred thousand. He took the cash. I flipped the property for seven hundred in two months and bought the place I've got now.'

Two hundred thousand pounds profit in two months. I swallowed hard as I thought about it. Rudy was smart. Now, I was determined to get smarter.

'Opportunities are out there.' He grabbed at the air. 'You have to recognise chances when they appear.'

'I've been waiting all my life and they still haven't appeared,' Rufus grumbled.

'Ah, but you weren't born with the advantage of my disadvantages.'

'What?'

'My black daddy left when I was three and went back to Jamaica. Mammy was an alcoholic. So was her new companion. Billy. He was a dustman, a really big guy with big hands. Every weekend, they'd drink away his wages. When they'd spent it all, every penny, he got mad because there was no more money for drink. Nothing for the bills. Nothing to buy food. We moved every three or four months because they never paid the rent. Those things made Billy angry, and when Billy got angry he swung his fists at anything that moved.'

'He hit you?'

Rudy leaned forward. 'Me. Mammy. The wall. If you got in the way when Billy was drunk, you got a hiding. I had to learn how to duck and dive. How to look after myself. Every adversity, every failure, and every heartache, carries with it the seed of an equivalent or greater benefit,' he said, and looked at me.

'Napoleon Hill?'

'He's the man.' He grinned. 'You have to learn how to turn life's disadvantages into advantages. Once I realised no one was going to help me, it was liberating. The only path open to me was to help myself.'

'Well, you're doing bloody well at it,' Rufus said.

We drank our tea and ate the ginger snaps.

'Money's flexible.' Rudy demonstrated with his hands, moulding the air. 'It's like the tide. It comes and goes. It grows and shrinks. You think Harvey Weinstein uses his own money when he makes a film? He doesn't. He uses the investors' money. Rufus is buying another buy-to-let flat, the seventh isn't it?'

'Eighth,' Rufus corrected.

'The renters will pay off the loan and Rufus still has his capital for when the big chance comes along.' He shot Rufus a beaming smile. 'Keep your eyes wide, it's out there.'

'As long as you don't grab it first.'

Rudy laughed. 'I will if you let me,' he said, and glanced back at me. 'What's needed is a long-term strategy and the ability to make decisions quickly. The poor are always spending their money enjoying themselves because they never know when they're going to have full pockets again. What we have to do is learn to think like the rich. There's a housing shortage. Prices are going up and they are going to keep on going up. If you don't get on the ladder, you'll be left hanging.'

Rudy Johnson gave me a look like a laser beam and then smiled. It was a great smile. He knew that and used it to make others feel good. His smile made you smile and all's well with the world when everyone's smiling.

'I'd better leave you to it,' I said, and stood.

Rudy jumped to his feet and gave me his business card.

'You need anything, just give me a call.'

I left them to complete their business and drove back to Twickenham thinking about everything Rudy had said. I wondered if it had all just been a pitch to make sure I went to him if I ever needed a mortgage. Not that I imagined I ever would. But that was negative thinking – negative on both counts. You have to look for the best in people and you have to believe that, one day, you're going to buy your own home. Rudy was giving me a life lesson because he knew I needed it. As to why Rufus required a mortgage to buy property, his money was probably locked away in an offshore trust.

The atmosphere at home was still tense. It was beyond Kelly's comprehension that I had bought six suits at once, and I had been unable to invent an excuse that would explain that I didn't pay for them at all. After giving Carly her massage that morning, Kelly had watched as I emptied the wardrobe and drawers of everything I owned. I filled six bin bags with my worn out clothes and took everything to the Oxfam shop. I only had new things now, new clothes, new car, new watch, new shades. I was going to have to grow into my new image.

Clothes are a flag, an emblem, a walking notice board. It doesn't matter if your shirt is stained or frayed, as long as it was custom made to begin with. Shoes are a personal signature. You can wear torn jeans and your shoes may be worn out or pushed down at the back, but the jeans are Levi's and the footwear is hand-stitched by Crockett & Jones Hallam, Church, Barker Alderney.

What you wear has its own glossary, gauche, gaudy, loud, kitsch, overbearing, frumpy, dowdy, subtle, unassuming, flattering, tasteful, discreet. It is easy to get things wrong but sometimes, as Vivienne would say, 'when it's wrong, it's right.' Clothes don't maketh the man. They do say who he is, or who he is trying to be.

Clothes, your accent and your choice of words are class indicators. For the PLU folks (people like us) flashy displays of wealth are signs of new money, *nouveau-riche,* social-climbers. The old rich never say 'pardon.' They say what or sorry. It is never the toilet. It's the loo or lavatory. The word serviette makes high class ladies wince as if they have just bitten into a lemon. The word is napkin. The rich eat dinner. The poor have their tea. That place for resting your backside is called a sofa. Never a couch or settee.

You don't invite guests into the lounge or living room. It is the sitting room or drawing room. Sometimes the parlour. The rich stay thin by eating pud or pudding. The poor get fat filling up on sweets and dessert. Just a word can make all the difference.

The poor use the word posh to describe people and items beyond their reach. The PLUs use posh for irony, as in: Are you going to the Russian Debutante Ball? No, it's much too posh for me. The poor describe the rich as snobs. The rich describe the poor as oiks, clods, louts, those people and the great unwashed.

I wasn't sure that I wanted to know these things, but once you know them they can't be unlearned. Class indicators are the way by which everyone in that world knows who's who and who matters, while everyone else is placed outside that particular box. They see society as a top down structure. A pyramid. Those born at the top – the Queen, the upper classes – are there because that is the natural order. It is the way it is meant to be. It. They believe social harmony is preserved by knowing and keeping your place. They do not believe in fairness, equality or equitable distribution. They view the notion as ridiculous or, worse, socialist. People have duties and responsibilities. The workers are responsible for working hard without complaining or forming unions. The duty of the rich is to keep the pyramid exactly the way it is. The old rich believe in something called *noblesse oblige*, which inspires spates of generosity like attending charity balls. The new rich don't bother with that sort of thing.

Remarkable people, the super rich, working class stars, sportsmen and very beautiful women are raised up the pyramid because they are remarkable. Rudy Johnson belonged in the group of remarkables. He was the exception that proves the rule. He was himself and that is a category on its own.

I was reluctant to put Rudy's crisp white card with raised black lettering in my wallet. It was dirty, stained and worn out. Another expense. But you mustn't think about that sort of thing.

I now had two invaluable contacts. Rudy Johnson when I needed a mortgage. Filippo Borghese Pecci when I needed Inca quality cocaine.

When I drove Kelly to her afternoon shift at the laundry, she wore trainers, old jeans and a charity shop blouse with a stain I think was already there when she bought it. I dropped her off and went straight to Topshop. I bought a cornflower blue dress with a strappy top and flowers decorating the skirt. Summer sandals were in the sale and I found the perfect pair of mules with a navy blue material top, thick soles and a four-inch wedge heel.

She took the dress out of the bag as we were driving home.

'Only one?' she said, and I had to smile.

'Look, I got the suits in a special deal. Their last year's fashion. It was a clearance sale.'

She opened the box containing the sandals.

'These are lovely,' she said. 'Can you remember when I last had a new pair of shoes?

'No.'

'Nor can I.'

'That's going to change, Kelly. Trust me.'

'I do trust you, Ben, you know that. But people bite off more than they can chew. They get carried away. Don't let that happen.'

'I'm not going to. This job is going to change my life, our life. It's what I've been waiting for. I'm totally positive.'

My hair had fallen forward and she leaned over to push it back in place. 'I thought you were going to get your haircut?'

'I can't afford it,' I replied and finally she laughed.

As soon as we got in, she rushed up to the bathroom to take a shower. She put on eye makeup and lipstick. She lifted her freshly-washed hair so I could attach the cross on a fine gold chain she always wore when we went out. It was part of the modest collection of jewellery that had belonged to her mother, her wedding band, thin as a wafer, two pairs of clip-on earrings and a cameo brooch like the one Miss Pelham always wore. She kept the pieces in a box made of seashells, the hinge loose, the shells chipped, but none the less precious.

I zipped the back of the new dress. The blue matched her eyes. She stepped into the sandals and did a twirl. The strained look about her lips from the constant worry about money and the kids had gone for a moment. Kelly was pretty, slender, feminine. She was just as beautiful as the beautiful women I had met at the Great Hall that day a lifetime ago, with one big difference. She didn't know it.

Carly came over with Lily, her little girl, to babysit and we drove into town to see *Pirates of the Caribbean: Dead Man's Chest*, the big summer movie. The film is like a cartoon. You have to suspend reality for two hours. But Kelly – and every woman in the audience – swooned watching Johnny Depp swashbuckling across the screen, and Keira Knightly was no strain on the eyes.

We walked back to the car, my arm like a wing around her shoulders. We looked like a happening couple, me in my white linen suit and white shirt, Kelly in the blue dress. She was happy and we made love that night, the first time for ages.

16
DEFYING GRAVITY

Saturday afternoon, I loaded the car with my table and a suit bag containing a navy blue suit, a pale blue shirt, and a Ferragamo tie, dark blue with a pattern of rajahs riding elephants decorated in gold and red. The tie was 'playful,' Vivienne had said. I completed the outfit with dark blue knee-high socks – ankle socks are a no-no, and brown Alden tassel loafers.

I felt as if I was journeying back through time when I entered the tunnel of trees and parked in the York stone courtyard at Frowley Manor. The last week of my life had been an intensive social and psychological course in the ways of the world. I knew so little and realised the more you know the more you know you don't know.

Douglas opened the door and I had a flicker of déjà vu as I followed him past the suit of armour in the hall and manoeuvred the table along the corridor with its paintings of stormy seas. Maggs was waiting in the familiar wood-panelled room.

'I'll be away for the rest of the day, Lady Margaret,' Douglas said. 'Is there anything you need?'

'No, we'll be just fine, won't we, Ben?'

'We will,' I replied.

He about turned. Maggs stood back to look at me in my new Hugo Boss shirt, lightweight jogging pants and white trainers without flashes or ornamentation.

'You clean up very well, I must say. I'm glad I was the first.'

'And the best,' I said.

'Oh. So you're learning to be charming now.'

'I mean it.'

'I'll pretend that you do.'

I erected the table. Maggs dropped her gown.

'You like being naked,' I said.

'I once ran starkers through the street of Paris. It was a dare.'

'Did you get arrested?'

'In Paris?'

'I've never been.'

'That's so cute. We shall have to fix that, won't we?' She paused. A puzzled look crossed her features. 'You're seeing Kate, later, aren't you?'

'I am.'

'You're not going out dressed like that?'

I smiled. 'No, I have a suit in the car.'

'Oh, goody. I shall help you dress.'

She stretched out on the table, I coated my hands in oil. She wriggled and squirmed as I ran my stretched fingers down her back.

'Mmm, I like it.'

'You're supposed to keep still.'

'I can't. I love being touched.'

'I'm going to do something different today.'

'Do whatever you want.'

'We're going to try kundalini massage.'

'Isn't that the sexy one?'

'I'll let you decide.'

After my discussion with Bethany Bolter, I had a feeling kundalini massage was going to be popular at Southley. I had never actually given anyone this particular treatment, and could think of no more suitable subject for the trial run than Lady Margaret.

Ancient Indian mystics defined kundalini as the well of potential that exists and remains inactive in every person. It is a metaphysical concept given form in massage workbooks as a sleeping serpent coiled in the base of the spine, usually illustrated by a woman with full rounded breasts, a narrow waist and generous hips, for which Lady Margaret was the perfect model.

The spine has seven chakras, or energy centres. Kundalini massage is designed to awaken the sleeping serpent so that the dormant energy comes to life and flows up the spine. The exercise realigns the chakras and brings about a higher state of consciousness and well-being. There is a side effect. The awakening of kundalini stirs the repressed libido, resulting in heightened sexual desire. The ancient sages had set out to find a route to greater spiritual growth and discovered the untapped potential in the core of the senses. We are often starved of human touch. Massage loosens inhibitions and feeds a hunger which the Ladies of the Committee appreciated and had the wherewithal to feed.

Using plenty of oil, I massaged Maggs's lower back until her breath slowed and became even. I then glided my open palms up the sides of her spine to her neck, around the shoulders and back down. I slid my hands across the mounds of her bottom, lightly running my fingertips over her rosebud, the spiral of puckered skin at the entrance to the anus. I repeated the motion ten times before rubbing my hands up her back and down her arms to her fingertips.

I continued the exercise along the sides of her body, one side then the other. As I worked on her hips, I pushed the flesh up and held it for a moment. From her hips, I moved to her waist, easing the skin continually upwards. I carried out the same movements on each side of her chest before placing my hands under her armpits. I pulled up and stretched out her whole body. Manipulating the outer, nonvascular epidermis in a rising motion is designed to defy the will of gravity and keep the body youthful, unwrinkled and fresh. The Sanskrit word *tan*, the root of tantra, means to stretch, expand, to smooth out.

Maggs rolled her shoulders as I pulled from beneath her armpits, the muscles relaxing as they eased back into their cushions of protective tissue. I returned to her back. I squeezed the flesh either side of her spine with my thumbs and fingers in the same way that you knead dough. I continued nipping and pinching the fleshy areas of her buttocks with more pressure. I moved down over her thighs, first making long, fluid strokes, then with my fingertips in a circular motion, going randomly from one area to another in a way that Maggs could not anticipate where each new set of strokes was going to occur. Her breath raced. She liked that. I then turned her over on to her back and our eyes met.

'Close your eyes. Don't think of anything,' I said.

'You've got to be joking,' she replied.

Through the next part of the massage, I focused on her stomach and chest. I dribbled some oil into her bellybutton and ran my palms in a circular motion over her stomach, up to her breasts, around her nipples and down again to the whirlpool of flesh marking her navel. I repeated the movement ten times before running my hands with spread fingers down the tops of her legs and up between her thighs. I repeated this ten times. Each time, I allowed my fingers to move closer to her sex without actually touching the lips of her vagina.

Maggs was gripping the sides of the table and breathing faster. The exercise was healing, sensual, invigorating – the goal of kundalini massage. When the serpent rises, it races along the spine, illuminates the chakras and fills the mind with light. The feeling triggers a sense of restoration and can activate the slumbering parts of the mind, fears as well as desires, that may have been blocked for years.

I massaged Maggs's shins and calf muscles, her feet and toes, which tickled and she wriggled like a wet fish on the massage table.

'Enough, enough. You're killing me.'

She swung her legs from the table, took my hand and we hurried up the narrow staircase to the room with the big four-poster bed where I had slept before. The late afternoon sun filtered through trees and painted the walls in pastel shades. I tore off my clothes and we tumbled into the white sheets like two people who have crossed the desert and arrived finally at a watering hole.

Sex for Maggs was like walking, swimming, breathing. It was an act that came naturally, that you did because it was human, instinctive, limbs entwined, skin pressed to skin. She wanted to possess and be possessed. I could smell the briny pheromone scent of her arousal. Maggs was a woman who enjoyed the abundance of everything, food, riding, laughter, sex. She was eternally in heat, her body lush, ripe, wet, the quintessential female form sketched in yoga books and carved on temple walls. She was designed to give and receive pleasure in every way and in every position. She was as supple as soft melting wax and opened her body to be filled to the full in every opening.

Maggs had not needed kundalini massage to spark her desire. What it did do was awaken in her an impulse to draw out each second, to slow down, to transform the act of love from an endeavour to a meditation. We tumbled like acrobats. Like pieces of a Chinese puzzle. I felt as I drilled into her that I was mining a deeper, more dangerous seam within myself. We stained the bed with our sweat, with the liquids I released from her and the liquids she released from me. When I was soft, she sucked me until I was hard again. And when we were done, we rolled in a ball, the puzzle complete.

I lay back, panting for breath, the dying sunlight pressed against my eyelids. She slid from my embrace and took my flaccid cock back into her mouth. She massaged the tender flesh.

'Beautiful,' she whispered. She looked up at me and smiled. Her eyes were bright as stars. I started to harden again. 'Big Ben has grown even bigger.'

She swallowed me down to the root of my penis. She massaged and sucked my balls. We made love again, slowly, gently, like a soft wind through trees. She bit her lips and climaxed in an easy, rolling motion like the tide receding.

'Ah, yes. That was lovely,' she said breathlessly. She smiled mischievously. 'I'd better not wear you out.'

She crawled back into my arms. We closed our eyes for a few minutes. Then it was time to go.

We showered. I collected my suit bag from the car and she sat on the long pink sofa below the window in her gown as she watched me dress. She redid my tie knot to make it smaller. She brushed her hand across my hair.

'Does it need cutting?' I asked her.

'Yes,' she replied. 'But not now. In about two weeks. This is the perfect length. You should have it cut often so it always looks the same.'

'That'll cost a fortune.'

'I wouldn't know.'

'Of course you wouldn't.'

She laughed.

'Good for you.'

What I liked about Maggs was that there was no pretence. She wasn't interested in my life. She didn't want to know how the 'other half' lives. She was immersed in her own passions and pleasures. It was just sex. I stood back and looked at myself in the mirror. She watched me in the reflection.

'Well?' she said.

'It doesn't look like me.'

'Oh, but it does.'

We had arranged the massage for five. When the clock chimed it was hard to believe it was already eight. I noticed as I glanced at the clock that on the dresser, in a glass dish, was a folded white packet identical to that which Vivienne had produced at Southley.

'Do you need anything?' Maggs asked.

'No, no. I really ought to go.'

She kissed my cheeks and brushed down my lapels. 'Ben, that was smashing. Thank you. I'm away for a while. I text you when I'm back.'

I drove slowly, the radio silent, and listened to the sound of the air gushing past the car. I had forgotten to ask for my fee and realised, finally, why Angela Hartley had warned me not fret over petty sums of money – not that fifty quid was petty by any stretch of the imagination. What Angela had meant was that there was a bigger picture and I should only focus on that.

My throat felt constricted by the tie. I remembered Vivienne saying a little pain can lead to a lot of pleasure. There was certainly some truth in that. I wondered if a little pleasure could lead to a lot of pain.

The road was busy, cars weaving in and out of every space like needles stitching cloth. One day, I thought, London would seize up in total gridlock and it would take months to uncoil the snakes of jammed metal. Darkness fell slowly like a dimmer switch being turned down. I curved through the gates. The house at night was lit up with lights marking the drive and beamed on to the stone façade. I brushed my hair back and straightened my tie.

A servant I had not seen before opened the enormous door and led me through to the Great Hall. Lady Catherine was waiting. She wore a fitted white dress with long sleeves and a square neck trimmed in green, emeralds in a string at her throat and glittering from her ears. Her pale blonde hair curved about her cheeks and her legs were slender and shapely in white heels. It was not the way a woman – not the women I knew – would normally dress to go to a pub. But Lady Catherine wasn't like any woman I knew and the *Cock and Bull* was not the sort of pub where I had ever been before.

She stood and dropped the magazine she had been reading on the coffee table. She touched her hand to the stones at her throat.

'You're here. How lovely. Do you need anything?'

I wasn't exactly sure what she meant, but it sounded so formal I gave a little bow.

'No, we can go. We have a reservation.'

'How wonderful. You're so very kind.'

She slipped a dark green jacket over her shoulders and the same servant led us back to the entrance. His face never cracked and gave nothing away. I opened the car door. Lady Catherine was unable to attach the seat belt and I did it for her.

'Thank you, I'm so useless at that sort of thing.'

She seemed to have shrunk into the seat, her knees and ankles rigidly together. She was five feet six in high heels. Sitting she was small, delicate, like a very old child. Our eyes met. I wasn't sure what was expected of me, but I plunged ahead and kissed her cheek. She moved back with a faint smile as if she had never been kissed before.

'Shall we?' I said, and started the engine.

Like teens on a date, Lady Catherine acted as if she wasn't sure how she should behave when, really, it was me who should have felt uncomfortable. There are no guides on how to be a gigolo. It was the first time I had escorted an older woman to dinner and had to make it up as I went along. My heart drummed. I slipped through the gears and accelerated up the drive.

I had left Frowley Manor feeling as if I had been turned inside out and put back together with wings that held me suspended just above the ground. Maggs was right. People take sex far too seriously. Sex is the greatest of gifts. The pleasure of all pleasures.

Only at the point of orgasm do you feel your soul shaking off its chains and becoming one with the universe. That's why the Indian mystics had formalised the quest through yoga and meditation. If every woman was as free and open as Maggs, I am sure the world would be a better place. Sex with Vivienne was like a violent dance, like performance art. It left scars and illusions. Sex with Maggs was visceral, animal, sheer undiluted lust. I felt a soft tugging between my legs just thinking about her.

The night was warm still and close. Clouds billowed across the darkening sky and I remembered old fishermen on nights such as these looking up and warning that a storm was on the way.

'The weather's going to change,' I said for something to say.

'We do need some rain.'

'You're telling me,' I replied, and realised immediately it was the wrong thing to say. What do you say when there's nothing to say?

We drove through the country lanes until the headlights picked out the sign for the *Cock and Bull*. I parked. I released Lady Catherine from the seat belt and hurried around the car to open her door.

The pub was an ancient coach inn, hundreds of years old, perfectly conserved, stone shiny with age, wood waxy with polish. I had watched new buildings going up all over London. The haunts of the rich were dutifully maintained. At the same time, the council estates were getting rundown, the roads were broken, sports halls and youth clubs were closing.

I gave my name, my false name, Alan Ingram. I had no idea why the subterfuge was necessary and didn't ask. I had a feeling that this was all a game, that I was an extra in a film screening in Lady Catherine's imagination. The Maître d' led us to a table in an alcove and handed me a wine list encased in an oxblood leather folder. He clearly knew Lady Catherine, but acted out the charade that he didn't. I assumed this was a regular occurrence, the titled lady, her young lover, an assignation while Lord Bradley was running the country or seeing his mistress. That is if his name was Lord Bradley. Lords often have a different surname when they are elevated to the peerage and women with that special quality impossible to put into words marry many times. It was all new to me and I had to pick up these society intricacies as I went along.

There must have been a thousand different wines on the list ranging from £20 to £2,000 a bottle. We ordered champagne. The waiter poured two glasses. We clinked rims and finally Lady Catherine relaxed.

I am sure that if Rudy Johnson had been sitting there at the *Cock and Bull* that night, he would have found any number of things to talk about. He would have been witty and charming. I racked my brain. The weather. *Pirates of the Caribbean*. England getting knocked out the World Cup?

'I tried a new massage on Rufus. He seemed quite pleased.'

'There's nothing wrong with Rufus's back. There's something wrong with Rufus.'

'I didn't realise ...'

'He imagines he's going to be happy with Annabel. But I don't see it.' She took another sip of champagne and looked back into my eyes. 'Let's not talk about Rufus. Tell me about you.'

'There's nothing much to tell, really.'

'Everyone has a story, even if it's cock and bull,' she said, breaking the ice, and we laughed.

I told her about my career as a fisherman. People were always interested in that. We were on common ground when I said EU quotas had killed the fishing industry. I avoided mentioning Kelly and the kids. This was a date, after all. What I did do after we had ordered the first course was ask Lady Catherine – Kate, she insisted – where she had originally come from. The upper classes don't like direct questions. But I had refilled her glass, her pale cheeks had a flush of colour and she let her story unfold like a romance novel as she picked at her green salad.

Kate Lingren had run away at nineteen from the stony Swedish community in Minnesota where she had grown up to marry a handsome golf instructor. She had known the moment he slipped the ring on her finger that she had made a mistake and rectified the error when she met one of his clients, her second husband, a steel tycoon, Rufus's father. Al Bradley was a 'sweet guy' thirty years older than her who died suddenly of a heart attack on the golf links at Archerfield in Scotland, leaving her with a young son to care for and a billion dollars with which to do so.

Kate was forty, refined and familiar with all that England had to offer a single woman with a very large sum of money. She moved to London, bought a house in Knightsbridge and married Lord Aberstone. He was from a distinguished family of whiskered ancestors (scowling from portraits in the Great Hall), a First World War spy and an adventurer who discovered a Mayan burial site in the Yucatán. With so many ancestors carving out the Empire and exploring the world, the present Lord Aberstone had inherited nothing but debts, a title, the estate with the grand house Kate called 'the castle,' and which she had restored to its former splendour. She had sent Rufus to Harrow and turned him into the textbook English snob.

Lady Aberstone, Catherine, Kate, had the softest, palest skin I had ever seen, blue-green eyes and small, dainty features. She appeared vulnerable but had an iron will that acknowledged no bars or barriers. The aristocracy is not a club you can join. You are born into it or you are beautiful with a billion dollars.

The Maître d' suggested a red wine with an unpronounceable French name to go with the roast lamb and mint sauce. I was starving. I ate everything on my plate and watched Kate eat a couple of peas and half a potato. I took two sips of wine and understood for the first time what all the fuss was about, what a 'fine wine' actually meant. It took all my will-power not to drink more. The last thing I needed was to lose my licence.

I stuffed down baked apple with cream for dessert, or pudding, should I say. Kate snapped a few dry biscuits and slipped a piece of Cheddar between her lips. The bill with fifteen percent added on for service came to almost £180 and I paid with my debit card, as I had been instructed by Angela Hartley.

We drove back the way we had come, through the tall gates and up the drive. The same expressionless servant opened the door and I felt his eyes on my back as I followed Kate up the sweeping staircase to her bedroom at the back of the house. It was not actually a room, but a network of rooms in pale green, full of flowers in tall vases, sofas and tasselled armchairs, table lamps with flower-patterned shades, a black piano, the top crowded with framed photographs of Lady Catherine with various people I recognised including one with Margaret Thatcher, and another with the Queen and the Duke of Edinburgh.

We kissed. It wasn't a tongue and teeth passionate kiss, it was a cold Swedish kiss like we were two birds pecking at a bowl of water. She loosened my belt, ran the zip down my fly and slipped down to her knees to take me into her mouth. She was slow, methodical, well-practised, I thought. I gripped the side of her head, and she eased my hands away. As I was about to ejaculate, she took my cock into her hand and sprayed her face. I looked down and watched in the mellow light of the table lamp as she spread my semen with her fingertips over her cheeks, around her eyes, over her brow and neck.

She came to her feet, kissed me lightly on the cheek and left the main room, closing the door behind her.

After that first night, I visited Lady Catherine once a month, occasionally twice. On occasions we went out to dinner, mostly we stayed in her rooms. Sometimes she played the piano, not particularly well, I thought. Our meetings always ended the same way, with oral sex and a semen face mask.

A few days after our dinner at the *Cock and Bull*, a deposit of £500 from Coutts Bank appeared in my account. That same sum was added by direct debit every month for the next two years.

17
EXTRAS

The rich are always busy. In the early months of summer they attend Ladies Day at Ascot, the Henley Regatta, opera at Glyndebourne. There are parties and barbecues. They throw up the portcullis at their historic houses on Heritage open days when the hoi polloi get the chance to run their grubby fingers over the family heirlooms. The debutante balls may have lost their significance, but not their importance. Privileged young girls at eighteen are not looking for husbands, but an internship at *Vogue,* a place at Oxford, a literary or theatrical agent.

All this pleasure is exhausting and in August, when the rich need to recuperate, they decamp to the Mediterranean – their villa in Tuscany, the chateau in Provence, the converted monastery on the hills above a Spanish village, the yacht cruising the calm seas around the Greek islands.

While the Ladies of the Committee were away sailing and sunning, husbands in tow, I was able to concentrate on my trial period at Southley. Vivienne and Maggs, even Angela and Kate, had each in their own way boosted my confidence. I had the skills. Now I had the opportunity to prove myself.

I joined a team of three therapists. Denny Doyle was Irish, a gym fanatic rippling with muscles, curly red hair, a lyrical voice and the gift of the gab. Anastasia was his polar opposite. She was tall, thin, cold, a Russian brunette with unsettling dark eyes and an abrupt way of speaking that didn't seem to bother her clients, quite possibly the reverse. Rachel, the third member of the team, was on holiday in Ibiza.

We worked eight hour days – which often extended to ten – on a five day rota that gave me one weekend off in three. Massages were set at forty-five minutes, providing a fifteen minute break between sessions, with an hour for lunch. When clients booked a double session, ninety minutes, it usually inferred that massage wasn't the only thing on their mind.

Unless they indicated a preference, male or female, new clients were assigned to whoever was available. Regulars tended to return to the same therapist. Once they had overcome the discomfort of being naked, they felt more at ease in the intimacy of the massage room.

Clients had to fill in a form detailing past illnesses and injuries. We then had to ask them what they wanted to achieve from the treatment, which was never easy for people to define except to say they wanted to feel great. It was serious, formal. More than mere therapists, we were expected to behave like doctors, consultants, psychologists. We were healers taking broken souls and making them stronger as, with our bare hands, we put people back together again – a snip at £120 a session.

After taking off their clothes, clients wrapped themselves in a towel and stepped into the green flip flops provided. They kept themselves warm in a towelling robe with the spa insignia on the top pocket, a mature tree in a loop of green letters spelling the word Southley. Some kept their underwear on. Most didn't.

Once the client entered the massage room, I slid the bolt into place and lowered the table from the control panel. They stretched out on their stomach, face resting in the aperture, eyes closed. It's odd, but now they were unable to see me, they forgot their embarrassment at being naked. They lifted themselves up so I could remove the towel, which I folded in half length-ways and laid over their bottom to contrive a degree of modesty. I finally raised the table to the appropriate level for my height.

The massage rooms were the area of the spa that had impressed me most that day when Bethany took me on the tour. They were warm with pale green light and hazy with wafts of steam rising from the heated water churning in the rock pool. The flickering light and heady fragrance of the aromatherapy candles was mesmerising. The music was ethereal, haunting rhythms that lulled the senses. Everything was calculated to be serene and sumptuous.

When Denny first showed me how to work the console on the massage table, he told me not to go over time, or there would be a backlog of 'impatient patients.'

'They're all richer than God. They don't like waiting at all,' he warned.

He had helped me register my first client and I entered the calm of massage room 3 with an elderly French woman with a replacement hip and stooped back. She moaned softly all the time I was rubbing her muscles and took £20 from the pocket of her robe when I had finished.

'You are here tomorrow?' she asked, and pressed the money into my hand.

'I am.'

'Then I shall see you again.'

I went back into the room to turn off the music and punched the air when no one was looking. I had started. I was a professional masseur. I would have liked to have had a few minutes to reflect on my début massage, but another client was already waiting in the reception area, one long smooth leg rocking restlessly over the other. She had signed without filling in the admission form.

'Would you like some water?'

'No, not now.'

I filled a cup for myself, sat, reached for a pen and asked her name.

'Caroline,' she said.

'Have you had any illnesses in the last five years?'

She look a long breath through her nose and pointed at the signature at the end of the form.

'Write whatever you want,' she said. 'It's legal twaddle to say the spa takes no responsibility – for anything.'

'It's just the procedure,' I explained.

As she re-crossed her legs, her robe opened. She had not wrapped a towel around herself and was naked beneath.

'You're new, aren't you, Ben?'

'First day.'

'Then I'm going to let you into the worst kept secret at Southley: the procedure is a smokescreen. Now, shall we …?'

She stood and led the way into the massage room. She dropped the robe and turned hands outstretched to face me. Her eyes were twinkling in the spectral light and she wore an expression that said: come on, are you a man or a mouse? Look at me if you dare.

It was new to me, but I was coming to understand that some women – Maggs was one – like being naked. They want to be seen naked, and used nudity as a form of empowerment. Women strip to highlight causes: human rights, women's rights, anti-war, anti-fur and innumerable injustices often inflicted on them by men. Most famously, Lady Godiva rode naked through the streets of Coventry a thousand years ago to protest a tax increase imposed, ironically, by her own husband. Men are less at ease being naked, but are more likely to be Peeping Toms, watchers rather than doers. Southley was my university. Caroline my first teacher.

I looked into her eyes and must have sounded like an automaton as I continued to follow the spa's process. This was, as I had said, my first day, and it occurred to me that Caroline could have been a plant, there to test my professionalism.

'What do you want to achieve from the therapy today?' I asked, and she sighed.

'Just work your magic.'

'Did you have something in mind? Did you read the list?'

She glanced at the rock pool. 'Hot stones. My back's killing me from tennis.'

'So you do have an injury?'

'Now you have something to write on your form.'

She wore dangly earring that she removed and placed on the shelf. As she turned, her deep tan was emphasised by the whiteness of her bottom.

'You've spent a lot of time in the sun. You have to rehydrate the skin and use plenty of screen.'

'Thank you, doctor.' She paused. 'It's been so hot this year. We have a place in St Tropez, a bar. We're selling up. My husband's with the lawyers today.'

'And you're here.'

'I am, indeed.'

Finally, she smiled. Caroline was tall and slender with a wide face, dark hair, green eyes and that special kind of poise that belongs to beautiful women used to getting their own way. She sat on the side of the table and raised her knees before rolling over.

I glanced through the music library.

'Norah Jones?'

'If that's what does it for you.'

The music was soothing and seemed to appear from beneath the water in the pool, adding a new layer of sensuality. It was midday but felt like midnight in a night club. When I had worked in the gym where I first met Rufus, the massage room was sporty with wood floors and steel lockers. The spa was more like a temple where the body was the object of worship and everything was designed to arouse and pamper the senses.

I had learned how to give hot stone massage, but this was the first opportunity I'd had to put theory into practise. I told Caroline to hold her breath to a count of ten and empty her mind of everything except the warmth seeping into her skin. The stones in the pool were of various sizes, flat, smooth and heated to a temperature where you could barely touch them. I laid a towel on her back, dried the first stone and placed it on her lumber region.

'Breathe slowly and deeply. Hold an image of the sun in your mind. Imagine its healing rays spreading over your back.'

Most massages originated in the East, India and China. Stone massage comes from native American Indians, who warmed stones in the fire before placing them on and around injuries.

Once I was sure she could stand the heat, I removed the towel. I positioned stones in a T-shape on her shoulders and along her spine. Her skin was creamy and flawless. In the pale light, in the steamy air, her white bottom rose from the small of her back and I had an urge to give it a good hard slap. It was a reaction that would never before have crossed my mind, but that afternoon with Vivienne Raynott had opened doors inside me that may have been better left closed.

As the stones cooled, I scolded my fingers replacing them with hot stones. I did this several times. When the heat had penetrated the first layer of skin on her neck, shoulders and back, I returned the stones to the pool and warmed patchouli oil in my palms. I began by massaging her spinal muscles, an area prone to strains with the jolting movements of tennis. I continued the therapy by adding three stones to each of her legs, one in the middle of each thigh, one in the middle of her calf and one behind the kneecap. When the heat had radiated down her legs, I used a stone as a massage tool, rubbing it over the length of warmed skin, one leg after the other. I repeated the action ten times.

Norah Jones was singing *I'll Be Your Baby Tonight*. I spoke softly in Caroline's ear.

'Keep your eyes closed. Turn over slowly.'

I held her shoulders as she did so and placed the towel in a strip across the area of her hips and trimmed pubis. I positioned hot stones on her bellybutton, heart and sternum, the long necktie-shaped bone that runs down the centre of the chest and connects to the ribs to form the ribcage.

When her skin was pink with heat, I removed the stones and added more oil to my palms. In a circular motion, I massaged her abdomen and chest. As my hands passed over her ribs, her breasts became firm and her nipples hardened from the rush of blood. I massaged her neck, her face and worked my fingertips over the top of her skull with its hidden information on personality, character and health.

I moved to the opposite end of the table. Caroline's feet were long and slender with perfectly buffed toenails painted in translucent polish. She tensed, then relaxed as I dug my thumbs into the acupressure points.

'Mmm, so good,' she murmured.

I rolled the towel up to uncover the full length of her legs. I used long sweeping strokes with firm pressure to stimulate the calf muscles, over and around the knees, hamstrings and hips. As I repeated the movement, Caroline opened her legs so that I could reach the tops of her thighs. Her hips swayed, just slightly, but in a way that my fingertips couldn't help but slip over the lips of her sex. My back was wet. I had an erection. I wasn't sure if she was tormenting me or I was tormenting her.

'Ben, you're giving me goose bumps.'

'Me, too,' I replied.

'Then you'd better fuck me.'

I suppose I was expecting this to happen. There wouldn't have been locks on the door, or a Golden Rule, if there were no rules to break or secrets to conceal. I lowered the table as far as it would go. I slipped from my clothes and slipped without foreplay into Caroline.

'Come inside me,' she whispered.

It was quick, easy, natural, two human animals doing what they were designed to do. I felt no guilt. No remorse. No shame. Too much had happened for me to look back and think about who I used to be. This was my job. If prostitution is the oldest profession, 'rubbing,' as Hypocrites put it, was the second oldest, and the two have always been inextricably entwined.

She was all smiles as we dressed.

'I want more. You're a great fuck,' she said. 'Do you give private massage?'

'I do.'

'Give me your number.'

She went to take a shower and returned with her hair wrapped in a towel. She gave me £30.

'That's all I have on me.'

'I don't expect anything.'

'If you don't expect anything, you'll never get anything. Remember that.'

I wrote down my mobile number and she placed the slip of paper in the robe. She turned to go, then turned back again.

'I almost forgot. Vivienne sends her love,' she said, and made her way down the corridor, flip flops drumming as she went.

Two seconds later, Denny poked his head into the reception area. He wore an enormous grin.

'How did it go? All tickety-boo?' he asked.

'It was fine.'

'She's quite a woman, that one. Very full of herself. She likes to get her own way, I can tell.' He paused. 'Then, don't we all.'

'She had a tennis injury. I used the hot stones.'

'Did you, now. I'm glad to hear it. It's a fine thing when you have a customer leave with a big Cheshire cat grin on her face.'

I did two more massages that morning and took a twenty-minute swim before lunch. I had a piece of quiche with salad, a banana and Greek yoghurt. People don't realise, but massage is strenuous and demanding. When you tease out the tightness balled up inside your clients, some of the tension enters the masseur. You have to be strong and pace yourself.

Over the coming weeks, I swam almost every day. I used the running, rowing and cross-country machines in the gym. I did the occasional skill swap with Vladimir, the tennis pro, thirty minutes on the courts for thirty minutes on the massage table. Jacqui, the hairdresser, trimmed my hair so it was always the same length. Dawn gave me the occasional manicure.

For a masseur, your hands are your livelihood. After several hours a day rubbing and firming fatigued muscles, my palms burned with pressure sores. Before I went to bed, I moisturised with QV Intensive Ointment and gave my hands a reflexology treatment. First, you relax your hands by shaking them and wriggling your fingers. You loosen your wrist the same way, then pinch the fingers and thumbs of each hand with enough force to be firm, not painful. Finally, with the thumb of one hand, you knead the palm and the undersides of your fingers.

Kelly made fun of this nightly ritual. She thought I was 'mollycoddling' myself because I worked at a 'fancy' spa, but the treatment was necessary now that I was giving as many as ten massages a day. Semi-clad bodies passed through the room like it was a conveyor belt. I saw so many beautiful women naked I stopped seeing them at all. My schedule was always full. Repeat bookings became the norm, which pleased Bethany Bolter and irritated Denny Doyle. For the moment, I was the blue-eyed boy, the flavour of the month.

What I soon learned was that some clients were only interested in what they called 'extras.' With those ladies, I put less effort into the massage, saving myself for the rigours of oral sex and intercourse. When men turned over on the table with an erection and the expectation that I would do something to relieve this condition, I left the room for a few minutes. I returned with two cups of water and spoke in my best Broad Norfolk, the language of the fishermen.

'You all right there, mate?'

They immediately got the message and I continued as if nothing had happened. I was more than happy to massage men. It offered a different challenge. Men have harder muscles and often suffer sports injuries that require serious therapy. 'Extras' were not, and never would be, on the itinerary.

That afternoon, on the first day, I did four more massages and had sex once more, with a middle-aged French woman who whispered *oo la la* in my ear. It was the first time she'd had sex in three years, she told me. She gave me £50, bringing the total that day to more than £200 in tips. It was, in fact, a modest day. The money grew over the weeks and months. I had so much cash, screwed up notes and folded in envelopes, every time I was in Twickenham, I deposited the money in our joint account at Nationwide.

Instead of emptying my pockets of small change for Kelly to feed the family, she now marched into the bank and drew out whatever she needed. We had lived from hand to mouth, mending, making do, going without. There had been days when Kelly and I went hungry so there was always food for the kids. Poverty grinds you down. It rips out your self-confidence. It turns you into a different person. I reminded myself of that every time I heard the word 'extras.'

As I drove home from the spa, Napoleon Hill's words on a loop, I would catch a glimpse of my eyes in the rear-view mirror and talk to myself: Ben Foster, you fuck women for money. What do you think about that? You're a sex worker. A prostitute. Are you proud of yourself? Ashamed of yourself?

Why are you doing this?

I am doing this because it is a means to an end. We lived in poverty. Now we don't. I was going nowhere. Now I'm going somewhere.

Every adversity, every failure, every heartache carries with it the seed of an equal or greater benefit.

I was on a merry-go-round. Every day, the money rolled in. Normally, when you look at your bank statement, there is always less than you thought. For Kelly, it was the reverse. Every week when she went to the bank, there was at least £1,000 more in the account than there had been the week before. She bought new clothes for herself and the children. We started to replace the worn out old furniture that had belonged to Gran and Kelly's parents, often the cause of quarrels.

Kelly liked frilly, fancy things. My tastes had become more Zen, stark, simple, minimalist. We weren't growing apart. But I was viewing the world from a different angle. I had moved on and Kelly made me realise that if you wanted to make the most of yourself, moving on is fundamental. It was stereotypically English to accept that we are born with a fixed 'station' in life. It's what keeps the poor downtrodden. If Rudy Johnson could break the cycle, so could I. So could anyone.

Money had always been a problem. We'd never had enough. Now, Kelly thought we had too much. She was convinced I was doing something dishonest, that I was a drug dealer, or I passed secret information to terrorists. I told her a million times that the money came solely from tips for giving great massages. It was normal for rich people. They like service, I told her, and pay extra to make sure they get it. I don't know that she was ever fully persuaded that the generosity was inspired by massage alone, but

I kept to my line. She never saw my shaved genitals and she never knew that there were many occasions when it wasn't only my hands that were damaged with pressure sores.

I had sex every day, twice a day, three times a day. Once, five times in one day. I remember that particular day because I made a remarkable discovery. I went for a swim when my shift was over. After my shower, I sat in the changing room eating a banana and Greek yogurt. Bananas give you a quick sugar boost. The yogurt was creamy, soothing. The changing room was empty. I stepped back into the shower, dipped into the tub and smoothed yogurt over the sides and around the inflamed tip of my penis. Yogurt calms thrush, or yeast, infections, in the vagina. For cock pains, Greek yogurt is the panacea.

Was I ever unable to perform? Sometimes I had to close my eyes and imagine Vivienne naked in her sculpture gallery. But, as a rule, Big Ben never let me down. Sex is addictive. The more you have, the more you want, the more you can. The penis is like a muscle. It grows stronger from use. More important, I learned how to control the environment. The massage room was my temple. I was the alchemist I had always wanted to be.

When women asked for 'extras,' it was obvious what they 'wanted to achieve' from the treatment. Some women showed through their body language that they had come for a massage. Nothing more. Between these two points, women who booked a session with open minds, almost without exception, succumbed to their subconscious fantasies and let themselves go with desires so wanton it surprised them that they could be so wild and uninhibited.

Why did so many women feel the desire to have sex with a stranger? I didn't kid myself that I was special. It was a combination of the seductive aura of the massage room, the touch of caring hands sliding over their naked body. But there were other factors. A lot of women were married to powerful alpha males.

Betraying them was a form of revenge. For others, it was payback because they knew their husband was having an affair. Some women lived with men who were abusive and controlling. In my temple, their wishes were my command. Some were in marriages that had grown stale. Others lived with men who treated them as virgins when they wanted to explore the whore who lived inside them. Older women felt flattered.

Women want to feel desired. They relish foreplay and after-play. For many men, sex is like exercise, something to get over and done with. A lot of the women who came to Southley had partners who had gone to top public schools and a lot of those men seemed more comfortable with their chums than with women. They weren't necessarily gay, but often came from households where their mother was distant, their sisters spoiled, the maids servile, and they had never learned how to treat women.

It is said that every woman is a potential prostitute. I stood the maxim on its head. Those women I turned on, often against their will, were the most thankful and gave the largest tips.

At the end of the month, a little over £5,000 had accumulated in the Nationwide account. I had a plan.

18
SPOILED CHILDREN

received a call from a man with a chopped, military accent.

'Ben Foster?'

'That's me.'

'You know Zara Swift?'

'We've met, yes.'

'She wants to see you.'

'For a massage?'

There was a pause on the line. 'Yes,' he finally said. 'A massage.'

We arranged a time and met the following day at the Knightsbridge entrance to the Lanesborough Hotel at Hyde Park Corner.

When I told Kelly I was going to massage *the* Zara Swift, she wasn't impressed.

'Just make sure she pays.'

I gave her a hug. In the shifting sands of my life, Kelly at least was a fixed point; an oasis.

Zara Swift was one of the women I had met in the Great Hall at Lady Catherine's house that day when I was 'interviewed' by the Committee. She was an actress more famous for being famous than for her roles. She had full lips, a husky voice and a shapely figure continually on the verge of falling out of the dresses she wore at parties and premieres photographed by the tabloid press.

Her fixer was just what I had expected, but six inches taller with shoulders so wide I imagined he had to move sideways like a crab when he entered a door. He was waiting, spine straight, hands behind his back as I climbed the hotel steps with my massage table and bag of oils.

'Ben Foster?'

I nodded and followed him to a waiting car, a black Range Rover, obviously. He turned into Knightsbridge. In ten minutes, we arrived at an apartment building with two uniformed porters and chandeliers in the polished hall. No one spoke. We rode up in the lift to the second floor and he led me along the corridor with its wine red carpet and paintings on the walls. He knocked three times, then unlocked the door for me.

Before I entered, he showed me his mobile phone.

'I won't be far away,' he said. 'And one more thing, her name's Gemma. Call her by her proper name.'

She was waiting in the drawing room smoking a cigarette which she stamped out when I entered.

'Filthy habit,' she said. 'I hope Arnie didn't bully you.'

'No, not at all.'

'So, where do you want me?'

I glanced around the room. It was crowded with furniture, paintings, famous people boxed up in silver frames, chinaware and ornaments judiciously placed and shiny with the hand of a cleaner.

'I'll have to be able to get around the table,' I explained.

She stood and retied the black silk dressing gown she was wearing. She looked at me, as if she wasn't quite sure why I was there, and looked about the room as if it was unfamiliar to her.

'In here,' she said.

She led the way into a bedroom with an expanse of pink carpet between the bed and an alcove with latticed windows. She watched as I lowered the blinds. I erected the table, lit candles and she was amenable to the wind chime music I chose. She wanted the Swedish massage she had 'heard so much about.'

'That takes about forty minutes. I charge £50. Is that okay?'

'Yes, terrific.'

She gave a little shrug as she removed her gown and spread out face down on the table. Zara Swift naked. It was unbelievable. Everything about her was erotic, her body, her voice, her carved hipbones and collarbones. I warmed some jojoba oil in my palms, began with skimming, effleurage strokes and avoided the provocative moves I practised at the spa. Zara had given no hint that she wanted anything more than a massage and there was a gorilla outside with a mobile phone.

Denny Doyle called clients 'fresh meat' and the massage table the 'butcher's block.' I made myself think of Zara Swift in that way, just a body that would age and decay and turn to dust. Like us all. She was relaxed to begin with. She purred when I unravelled the knots in her shoulders. But as the session progressed, I could feel tension rising into my hands.

'Is everything okay?'

'Why shouldn't it be?' she replied.

She turned over. Her breasts were firm with rosy nipples. Her pubes were a tidy dark triangle. I massaged her abdomen. I closed my eyes and skirted the side of her bust. I worked on her hips and legs. Feet in reflexology represent the whole body. In someone as sensual as Zara Swift, it didn't come as a complete surprise that her feet were an erogenous zone where all her passion and sexuality was concentrated.

I massaged her right foot, pressing my balled fist over the arch where tension gathers in the feet of women who always wear heels. When I switched to her left foot, her breath began to race. I dug my thumb into the sole, in the acupressure point symbolising the heart, and she slid forward. She spread her legs, wedged her feet against the end of the table and lifted herself towards me, bowing her back. I lowered my head between her thighs and she rolled in a rowing motion as the tip of my tongue caressed her clitoris. She shuddered, rocking the table, and heaved to a screaming climax that echoed around the walls. It was like a mini-earthquake and I continued massaging the channel of her vagina as the after-shocks receded.

She dropped back on the table, quivering and breathless. Her face was tranquil, passive. Then her expression changed and I watched in amazement as her features morphed to absolute rage. She swung her legs from the table, stretched into her gown and stormed out of the room.

She returned with £50 that she threw down on the massage table.

'Now get out. I'm not a mark,' she said, and disappeared again.

I put the money away and packed up my things. When I left the flat, Arnie was waiting at the end of the hall. His shadow climbed over the walls as he approached. It was like a scene from a horror movie. He reached for my table.

'I'll take that,' he said.

'Thanks, mate.'

The silent porters watched as we passed through the hall and stepped into the black Range Rover. I gave directions to my car. As he eased into the traffic, the automatic locks snapped into place and I took a long breath through my teeth. The drive took ten minutes, just long enough for me to conjure up a vision of Arnie racing out of London to some secret base to pull out my fingernails.

'How'd it go?' he finally asked. I let out the breath I was holding.

'Not bad. She does have a lot of tension.'

'Not surprising, is it, things she has to put up with. That git of a boyfriend. What do you expect?'

'That's true.'

As I transferred my table to the back of the Golf, I felt as if I had survived a war zone. I started the engine and turned it off again when my phone buzzed. It was a text from Vivienne. She wanted to know if I was close by and asked me to drop in 'if I could spare a few minutes.'

My underarms were wet. I was still coming down from the rush of paranoia after the journey with Arnie and felt as if I was being watched, monitored, checked up on. Perhaps the car was bugged? That's one of the problems serving the rich and powerful. You are always off balance.

My gold Omega read five to five. I had wanted to get home and put the children to bed for a change. But I had a feeling that Vivienne was the axis around which the entire circus spun and I did not want to let her down. I tapped out: *Be there in ten*, and hit send.

When Vivienne opened the door, my heart skipped a beat. My knees almost gave way. She was wearing an exact copy of the dress Zara Swift had made famous. Her silvery blonde hair was covered by a dark wig like Zara's hair. She had done her makeup the same. She had the same slightly disdainful look about her features and the identical deep sexy voice.

'I'm not wearing any knickers,' she said, and it made me smile.

'Is that so?'

She nodded in an exaggerated way. 'What happens to naughty girls who forget to put their knickers on?'

I don't know how I knew the script, but I did.

'They have to be spanked,' I replied.

She eased up the tight skirt of her dress, bent over the Henry Moore sculpture and I spanked her white bottom until it was pink. I still had the taste of Zara Swift in my mouth and stirred it in a cocktail as I brought Vivienne to orgasm with my tongue.

Vivienne was like therapy. I had felt as if I needed a massage I'd been so tense when I arrived. Now I was floating. She sucked down my load and kissed me, letting my semen drain back into my mouth.

'I believe in sharing.'

'Really?'

'I'm a Bolshevik at heart.' She paused. 'How's Gemma? I haven't seen her for ages.'

'She's quite … demanding,' I said, and she laughed.

'I adore her. She's wonderful. She's one of my favourite people in the whole world.'

She pulled down her skirt and left the room. I loved watching her. We all have boundless, infinite, myriad potentials. Vivienne brought out the decadence in me. She returned with a little mound of cocaine on a mirror with a straw.

'I won't,' I said.

'That's sad.'

'I get high just being with you.'

'Don't say that unless you mean it.'

'I wouldn't say it if I didn't.'

She smiled. She seemed girlish, happy, a bit lost. I watched as she diced the coke, separated it into two lines and snorted one of them. She held her nose and shook her head. Her eyes went out of focus and came slowly back in again.

'I'm going to stop. Will you help me?'

'Course I will.'

'I'm glad I found you Ben Foster.'

She snuggled up like a child in my arms. My bookings at Southley were full every day. The money kept rolling in. My goal was clear. My world was in balance, except for the feeling of Vivienne breath fluttering like a butterfly against my chest.

The children were asleep by the time I got home. We had moved Claire into the box room. We had bought a small pine bed and a matching chest of drawers on which stood a doll's house with lights that ran on a battery. It gave the room a warm glow, a feeling that there was a joyful life behind the miniature doors and windows.

We had exchanged the frayed carpets in the sitting room for oak floorboards. A decorator who lived on the estate had stripped off the flowery wallpaper, plastered the walls and sprayed them white. Kelly and I exchanged a few heated words, but I had got my own way when we chose the new three-piece suite. It was dark green leather – no fabrics, nothing fancy, nothing to gather dust.

Kelly had taken up cooking and was working her way through the latest Jamie Oliver recipe book. That night, she made sweet potato, chickpea and spinach curry with rice. Fresh pineapple for dessert. When we were digging down the back of the sofa looking for every penny, I bought the kids Crunchies and Milky Ways to soften my shame for being poor. Now that I could afford those treats, we didn't buy them. Ice cream and pizza had been replaced with fruit and carrot sticks.

We used to have a mishmash of old plates, white with blue rings and fine cracks filled with ancient germs. I'd boxed up the lot for the Oxfam shop and bought a set of plain white crockery from Habitat. New cutlery, too. We sat at the table to have dinner, following the rules set for the children. No eating on our laps in front of the telly and no telly at tea time.

Or dinner time, I should say.

Every word you say puts you in a box. I didn't want to be in a box anymore. You don't become confident and positive overnight. You start by acting confident and behaving in a positive way. Slowly, the act becomes reality. You are what you do. If you change what you do, you change who you are. I had been a care worker. Now, I was a well-paid masseur. The educated articulate every word. Working people in Norfolk drop their 'y's and aitches. They say 'bootiful,' 'ouse and 'ammer. I wasn't in Norfolk. I was in London, and made an effort to say beautiful, house and hammer.

Kelly made fun of me and said I was trying to be something I wasn't. I tried to explain that anyone could be whatever they wanted to be. The only limitations are those we set ourselves. I intended to make the most of myself so that it would rub off on our children.

When we were in Habitat, we also bought wine glasses, and with wine glasses you do need the occasional bottle of wine. One glass of red is supposed to be good for you and that's what we had. Kelly put the curry on the table in a serving dish. I dimmed the lights.

'This is what I call tasty,' I said.

Kelly looked up from her plate. 'How was Zara Swift?'

'Bit of a bitch, to be honest.'

'She always comes across as a bit ditzy, but sweet.'

'Course she does. She's an actress,' I said. 'When you see them on chat shows saying how they didn't think they were good enough to do this, that and the other, they want to come across as genuine, like ordinary people. It's all an act.'

She sipped her wine. 'This is nice.' We clinked glasses. 'Is she as pretty as she looks in real life?'

'Nah, it's all makeup. Zara Swift can't hold a candle to you.'

'Who you kidding?'

'I mean it. She's just an empty shell. They all are. You've got inner beauty.'

She gave me a sceptical look and put the plates in the dishwasher. I made a cup of tea and we watched *Newsnight* on the flat screen television.

Jeremy Paxman was giving a chief constable a hard time over his investigations into child abuse. He promised to hold an inquiry. Paxman shook his head. 'Another enquiry?' he shot back. He looked annoyed and that's how I felt. It was always years before enquiries came up with answers and, then, nothing was ever done. Children continued to be abused. Girls were being groomed by paedophile rings. And senior policemen were spending weekends at Southley with their mistresses.

I had massaged one top cop with shoulders as tense as sheets of iron. When he turned over, he had tears running down his cheeks. He had just lost the promotion he had expected and that meant he would probably never get the knighthood he had worked for 'all my damned life.' He behaved as if I were a counsellor, or a vicar. He told me that for years he had been taking Olanzapine, the same antipsychotic drug the lads were prescribed at The Lodge. He was so emotional, I had to walk him back to his cabin where a woman half his age was waiting.

There were times when my job got on top of me and I felt like quitting. Then I reminded myself that my changed finances had changed the lives of my kids. They were growing up happy, curious, confident. Ollie was a wiz on the computer and had started teaching George. Claire had turned three. She had grown into a talking dictionary and was beginning to use logic as well as tears to get her own way.

What I did for a living didn't matter. I wasn't hurting anyone. I wasn't robbing banks. The bankers were doing that and the rich ones had discovered Southley. The spa had become fashionable. Celebrities and people in the public eye were booked into my rota on a daily basis. I massaged movie stars, soap stars, models, judges, footballers, politicians, corporation bosses, oil barons, police chiefs and bankers.

Often, I'd see well-known faces at the spa and, within a few days, they popped up on television. In front of the cameras, they were confident, witty, charming. On the massage table, they lowered the mask. The dance of the massage is magical. The power of *chi* energy cleansing the chakras releases the body of stress and opens the mind to revelations and confessions. Whether they came for 'extras' or a sympathetic ear, the one thing those illustrious clients had in common was fear.

I had an actress in a soap who sobbed because she thought the writers planned to kill her off. A footballer with a knee injury was afraid he would never be picked for the first team again. A renowned chef admitted that he was an alcoholic. He could no longer hold a spoon without his hand shaking. I heard sex secrets, government secrets, confidences that needed to be shared by people who had no one else to share them with. Public figures and fame junkies live in fear of failure, fear of aging, fear of losing their jobs, and most were taking prescription drugs or cocaine – or both – to overcome their fear.

One of the problems for celebs is that they have so much they don't know what they want. Zara Swift had looks, class, money, fame. She had control over her life, her future. Losing control of her bodily desires, even for a moment, had made her angry with herself. She wanted to believe that I had taken advantage of her. That was not the case. Not that there was ever any point in arguing with celebrities. They are like spoiled children.

If anything, the determination to survive and the fear in the famous that drove it made me feel more contented with my own life. It was also financially rewarding. The more tears that flowed, the more lavish the tips. I worked long hours and, on days off, I continued with my circle of regulars, Vivienne, Maggs, Rufus, Angela and Kate.

Caroline called, as I knew she would. I followed the GPS to a remote farmhouse in the Cotswolds. She was waiting with another woman whose face was hidden by a mask. I only realised it was Vivienne when she spoke. Caroline had money; her husband was selling their bar in St Tropez. But Vivienne was not the sort of person who knew the sort of people who owned bars. They connected on another level.

They were dressed in white bunny costumes that covered their heads and entire bodies. Music played from speakers in every corner. It was Ravel's String Quartet, I later learned. The volume deafening. They ran and hopped and bounced from room to room. I chased them, pulling their ears and smacking their furry backsides. They were covered in sweat when we stripped off. I went to bed with them both, a confusing but not unpleasant experience.

19
SECRETS

I was chatting to Tiffany at the massage centre's main reception one morning when an elderly man in a pin-striped suit came to look at the price list. It was the prices, as well as the spa's veneer of respectability, that kept Southley exclusive. A variety of different massages were offered at £120 for forty-five minutes; anti-ageing facials £120; mud wraps £100. The ultimate indulgence was the Four-Hands Massage at £250, one client with two therapists.

He pointed at the last item on the list and spoke like a Shakespearean actor in a deep plummy voice. 'Is that with a man and a woman?' he asked.

'It is, sir,' said Tiffany.

'Then that should do nicely.'

He booked a time. Denny and Anastasia performed their speciality treatment and, by lunchtime, the whole world knew that the client was a high court judge hearing a case vital to national security. His way of coping with the pressure was giving oral sex to a man while receiving oral sex from a woman.

What plays in the massage room, *doesn't* stay in the massage room. The Golden Rule was like a finger stuck in a dike. Gossip is the human condition. It's like water. It finds its way through every crack and gap. It can't be contained.

Denny loved the sound of his own voice and what he liked talking about most was the louche details of his many conquests: the Italian actress with the 38 d-cups, the new weather girl on Channel 5, the hot male lead causing waves in *Eastenders*. He swung both ways and was the source of an endless stream of chatter that ran along the corridors from the massage rooms to the hairdresser, out the window to the tennis pro and groundsmen, and back through the main doors to warm the ears of the porters, reception team, kitchen staff and house maids, girls mainly from Eastern Europe employed for their outstanding bed-making skills.

Bethany behaved as if she were the mother superior in a convent delivering the damaged and distressed into the healing care of her therapists. But as she marched along in her spiky heels and fitted black dresses, the impression to me was more of a dominatrix at a high class bordello. It is not surprising that sex at Southley was the major attraction. For those who can afford to indulge every passion and whim, what else is there?

The spa was a hothouse of rumour, jealousy and politics. Bethany was pleased that I received good reports and had repeat customers, but remained guarded, even mistrustful of my relationship with Vivienne. She would like to have been more than just a listing on Vivienne's smartphone, but must have been aware on a deeper level that that was never going to happen.

What Bethany didn't know was that Vivienne and her circle spotted what they called 'star fuckers' a mile off. They tolerated the *nouveau riche*, money is an equaliser, but couldn't abide hangers on, sycophants, philistines – a new word to me – and those whom they labelled 'middle-class' with their middle-class ambitions and values. It was one of the biggest con tricks of all time. Old money in pin-striped suits and Barbour coats, with their skinny daughters and shooting weekends, were the icons of

British ethics and morals which they themselves scoffed at and flouted.

Something else that Bethany did not understand. You didn't discover them. They discovered you. They took you up because you were amusing, or had something to offer – drugs, sex, secrets – and I always knew that they dropped you the second you didn't.

Vivienne booked me for a double session at least once a week. She roared into Southley, bouncing over the traffic bumps in her yellow Ferrari, and stepped into the spa looking like one of the lost children from Peter Pan. She rarely wanted a massage. She liked to swim, or have bone-shaking sex below the pressure shower, that she called water-boarding.

When the weather was fine, we played tennis. One occasion, a November day I particularly recall, and still have the scar as a reminder, Vivienne was hyped up, eyes big as snooker balls. She unleashed her ferocious backhand and forehand and I could barely see the ball as it crossed the net at 100 miles an hour. I raced around the court like it was a rifle range and cut my knee so badly falling it needed three stitches from the nurse.

Most women are squeamish about blood. Not Vivienne. It turned her on. I, on the other hand, turned as white as a sheet and had to take the rest of the day off. As she drove back to her apartment, she called Maddy Page, the model, Committee member, arm candy to rock stars and billionaires – perhaps arm candy to her – and, according to Vivienne, an accomplished artist.

She was also the rudest woman I had ever met. Maddy had booked a massage with me a couple of days after my experience with Zara Swift. I suspected that Zara had told her some terrible story, that I'd seduced her or attacked her. Had Maddy Page come to wreak revenge? Was I being paranoid again? I wasn't sure, but the moment I locked the door in the massage room, I had a feeling it was going to end badly.

Maddy was beautiful, of course. She was one of the most beautiful women in the country. But she had a hardness about her, like a shell, a stiff set to her lips and a gaze that could turn you to stone. When she stretched out on the table, I asked her to hold her breath and she replied: 'Shush. Just get on with it.'

It is normal during massage to say comforting words and ask clients if they feel okay. When I spoke to Maddy, she either didn't reply, or said 'Be quiet.' When she turned over – that rare vision, a woman more beautiful than her photograph – she stared into my eyes as if she was trying to read my thoughts. I spent more time massaging her face and head than her torso and legs. I applied soft, circumspect strokes with open palms, and she remained frosty throughout the session. She didn't say thank you and didn't tip.

Was Maddy Page bi-polar?

It's hard to say. Having being so impolite at Southley, she couldn't have been nicer that afternoon with Vivienne. The girls were different in almost every way, yet similar in that they were fantasy women, untouchable, as if they belonged to an alien species, eyes deep but distant like tunnels or black holes. They clearly enjoyed each other's company and made me feel as they moved around me as if I were one of the sculptures in the studio, an object merely of interest for aesthetic reasons.

Vivienne gave Big Ben a shave. I then positioned myself on a plastic sheet on the studio floor, naked, my knee bandaged, as if posing for one of the hard core photographs on the wall. Maddy mixed plaster of Paris with warm water in a bowl and stirred the mixture until it was as thick as cream. She then produced a square of cardboard and cut a hole in the centre. Vivienne sucked my cock until the blood ran hot through the veins and the flesh was hard.

Maddy then did an incredible trick with a condom. She removed it from the foil packet, held the rubber in a ring between her lips and unrolled it down the length of my cock.

'That's amazing, where did you learn that?' Vivienne said.

'Don't ask,' she replied.

Maddy threaded my cock through the hole in the cardboard, then slid the sheet down to the base to form a platform. There is a loose bulb at the top of a condom. Vivienne snipped it off with nail scissors, leaving just the eye in the tip of my penis exposed. She coated the sheath in baby oil before Maddy caked my cock in warm plaster, smoothing the mixture around the column with her fingers. Vivienne squeezed my balls to make sure I didn't become limp. Not that it was necessary. The plaster contracted as it dried.

Now came the hard part. I had to remain motionless and erect for thirty minutes while the plaster set. To achieve this, while I remained propped up on my elbows with the beehive shaped mound of plaster rising like some terrible growth above my groin, Vivienne and Maddy kissed each other in a way that was far more sensual than any kiss you will see between a man and a woman.

It is not easy to keep an erection going for half an hour and I was growing soft when Maddy removed the mould. She eased it slowly up and down until it slid off, the hollow image of my cock captured inside. Vivienne unrolled the condom and used some oil to clean off the flecks of plaster stuck in the narrow seam at the top of my penis.

'Christmas presents,' she said, and the girls burst out in laughter.

In bed, they bathed Big Ben with their little pink tongues and I was home in time to read the children a story at bedtime.

It wasn't easy to concentrate.

A *ménage à trois* with Vivienne Raynott and Maddy Page. It was unbelievable. A fairy tale. Hallucinogenic. It was like I had put a pinprick in space and strange, alien things had come tumbling into my life. Vivienne had said I was a highwire walker and that was so clever, so true. I was moving across the void on an invisible thread.

'Why me?' I kept asking myself.

I had no idea then. And I have no idea now.

There were not enough hours in the day to give all the massages that were required and it annoyed Bethany when clients were turned away. Southley was on the lookout for a third masseur. Men were more popular and, truth be told, being stronger, were better at massage.

Rachel, the second masseuse, never returned from holiday. Apparently, that happened when girls went to Ibiza. Not that I knew this from personal experience. I had never been out of England. Rachel was replaced by Diane Dunham, Dee-Dee, a willowy girl of twenty-three with sharp features, short blonde hair and a taste for dark carmine lipstick. She was from a background not unlike my own.

Just as Denny had showed me the ropes, I did the same for Dee-Dee. On the afternoon of her first day, I found her sobbing in massage room 2. A guy had tried to put his erection in her hand and she had frozen in fear. The session had ended with the guy stalking out and Dee-Dee in tears.

'What if he complains?' she cried.

'What's he going to say? I wanted to sexually harass your masseuse and she wouldn't let me?'

'He might.'

'He won't.'

I told her what I did when those occasions arose. I went out and got two cups of water, then continued breezily as if nothing had happened.

'I suppose it doesn't happen with women clients,' she said

'You'd be surprised.'

'I didn't realise...'

'Grateful people give large tips. In the end, that's what it's all about.'

'Making money?'

'What plays in the massage room stays in the massage room. Not!' She smiled. She was learning. 'We are in the service industry. You give whatever service you feel comfortable with. Just do what feels right.'

'Are you saying, you know, that you do it with the clients?'

'Every day.'

Dee-Dee's dark lips fell open.

'Oh my God!'

That was Monday morning on her first day. On Thursday, she did a line of coke with a soap star. She gave him a blowjob. He gave her £200. On Friday, she saw on her schedule 'a very well-known name,' another member of the cast. I watched as they entered the massage room. He must have said something funny and Dee-Dee was laughing. When they left the room forty-five minutes later, her eyes were glassy and bright. He kissed her cheek before strolling down the corridor in his robe back to his room.

Dee-Dee still looked as if she was on a high when we had a few minutes alone later that day. She blurted out that she had once dreamed of 'copping off' with that particular actor and couldn't believe the dream had become reality.

I remembered when I had first got together with Maggs and Vivienne that I had been dying to tell someone, not to boast, exactly, but to share the sheer incredulity of it. That's how Dee-Dee felt. She had wept the first time a man put his cock in her hand. The uncertainty vanished with the £1,000 she started to put in the bank every week from tips.

Sex is not the obvious and only outcome of massage. Physiotherapists with the NHS provide therapies to reduce blood pressure, muscle pain, tension, insomnia. In cancer patient, massage alleviates nausea, anxiety and depression. Sports massage strengthens muscles to prevent injures, restores mobility to damaged tissue, and quickens the healing of sprains and strains. It was a field that interested me and I planned to go for more training when I had the time.

In the massage rooms, the smell of exotic oils in the half-light and the repetitive sound of running water lent itself to sensuality. The American architect who had designed Southley had created an erotic temple to the senses. The touch of warm hands on bare flesh quickened the libido of the most introverted and repressed. Sex was the very air we breathed. I had never wanted to be a gigolo. Dee-Dee never thought when she was studying massage that she would become a sex worker. You take the money once and it is easier the second time. After the second time you are what you do and there seems to be no way back.

According to Bethany, Mr Vijayakumar was the 'richest man in India.' He was the owner of steel smelting plants all over the world, a man in his mid-sixties, short and muscular with a heavy moustache and thick dark hair.

He had just married Lakshmi, a girl in her twenties, the perfect representation of the Hindu goddess of prosperity, after whom she had been named. She was slender, inscrutable, with a haunted expression and creamy, cappuccino-coloured skin. There was something about her green and gold eyes that made me think of a rare animal being hunted to extinction.

Mr Vijayakumar was like a lot of men who came to Southley. They ruined their health working to get rich and, once they were rich, they married beautiful young women and spent their money trying to get their health back. While he played tennis with Vladimir, he had booked Lakshmi for the Ayurvedic massage, a full-body treatment developed thousands of years ago in India and with which, I assumed, she was familiar.

We went through the booking process and she lowered her eyes as she gave one word answers to my queries. I opened the door to treatment room 3, my favourite refuge, and she watched blankly as I shot the bolt. She removed her robe and gave it to me to hang up. I had learned that wealthy Asian clients came from households with scores of servants and were not expected to do anything for themselves.

Lakshmi kept the towel wrapped about herself as she climbed up on to the table. She hesitated for a beat when I asked her to lift up so I could remove it. I folded the towel and placed it over her lower back and bottom.

'Take deep breaths. Relax. Tell me if you need anything.'

'Thank you,' she replied.

I lit fresh juniper candles, said to promote self-assurance, and chose jasmine oil, reputedly an aphrodisiac. I turned the temperature up a notch and played Tantra Trance with strings, a sitar, drums and distant voices that call to the inner ear.

'Are you ready?'

She nodded and I removed the towel. She grew tense but slowly relaxed. She was aware suddenly of her nakedness, aware that she was alone with an unknown man in a locked room, aware of the music drumming hypnotically inside her skull.

'Empty your mind. Don't think of anything.'

'That is not difficult,' she said.

I warmed the oil in my palms and smoothed it over her back and shoulders. I began with reverse effleurage. I moved my hands down either side of her spine, over her bottom, up the sides of her body, then back to the top. I applied more pressure for the second sweep, my hands planing over her skin like a skater on ice, every motion slow, calming, sensual. Eventually, I allowed my fingertips to glide over her rosebud. She tensed, but instantly relaxed and imperceptibly parted her legs.

As we move across life's sea of experience, we collect barnacles, unwanted memories, unresolved wounds that cling to our subconscious minds. Ayurvedic massage is the antidote. The treatment strengthens the nervous system, nourishes bodily tissues and promotes good health. I assumed Lakshmi already knew that. She was as smooth as a glass of milk without a knot cluster to work out of her muscles.

During massage, electromagnetic energy passes between the therapist and the client. I felt her energy enter my hands and move through my body. I had set out to seduce the girl. Why, exactly, I wasn't sure. Perhaps, to see if I could. Perhaps because Mr Vijayakumar was three times her age and stinking rich. I felt ashamed, but also an overwhelming desire which transferred to Lakshmi. It was a feeling of passion mixed with love; love in the sense that we love those rare beasts on the edge of extinction.

She turned over. I coated my hands in oil and massaged her abdomen. As I slid my palms up her chest, she placed her hands over mine. Not a word was said. She looked into my eyes, tightened her grip on the backs of my hands and rolled my palms in a circular motion over her breasts. Her nipples jutted out, dark red like ripe fruit. I took the flaming teats, one after the other, and bit down gently. She sighed and squirmed. I lowered the table. She lifted her legs in an arch. My tongue tip found her clitoris and she rocked back and forth, her breath beating harder and harder.

I stripped from my clothes. When I entered her, she began to moan, the sound growing until she reached her climax and screamed so loudly I would not have been surprised if someone had broken down the door fearing a murder was taking place. Her orgasm went on and one. It was a tsunami. Her voice echoed around the room until it sounded like a choir of voices. Only slowly did she calm down as her orgasm ebbed and faded.

When we left the massage room, I was stunned to see Mr Vijayakumar sitting in the reception area in his tennis clothes reading *The Economist*. He stood, smiling, and reached for his wife's hand.

'How was it, my darling?' he asked.

'I feel better now.'

He looked back at me. 'She hates flying. It's always upsetting.'

'Then massage is always the answer,' I told him.

Next day, I was surprised to see Mr Vijayakumar's name on my list and thought he was probably going to kill me once we were alone. Then, I had another thought. Perhaps he was gay and was expecting to get the same treatment as his wife. I was wrong on both counts. He told me he didn't like massage. It was too static. He was a man of action, tennis, polo, cricket. But Lakshmi had made the recommendation.

'I have learned two things,' he added. 'The old should learn from the young, and husbands should always take the advice of their wives.'

He wanted a chakra massage, a deep-relaxation therapy to still the mind and access positive feelings. The session went without incident and Lakshmi was waiting for him when it was over. It was the last day of their stay. The very, very rich have very rich lives and never stay anywhere very long.

The following morning, before they left, Mr Vijayakumar came to see me.

'Sir,' he said. 'I wanted to thank you personally and most profoundly.' He paused. 'May I speak openly, man to man?'

'Yes, of course.'

'Last night, I was very relaxed. Very serene.' He smiled and his head jiggled from side to side. 'I finally awakened my wife's kundalini. She had an orgasm. Her first. I am sure it is thanks to your massage.'

He gave me a hotel envelope, thick with its contents, and we shook hands.

When he turned away, I realised it was the first time I had seen him wearing glasses. On each arm of the frames was a silver receiver with a miniature speaker that fitted in the ear. Mr Vijayakumar was deaf.

20
COMEDY OF ERRORS

In my teens, I leapt into things without looking or thinking about the consequences. With a family to support, I had largely got over that, but on occasions slipped back into my bad old ways.

After the hottest summer on record, December felt like cosmic revenge with ice rain and freezing fog. I spoke to my mum in Lowestoft where it was -2° C and felt lucky not to be going out that morning on a fishing boat to trawl the North Sea. It was just above freezing in London. Flu had swept through the laundry. Kelly was filling in on the morning shift and I drove to Nationwide with the kids to deposit some money.

It was the Thursday before Christmas. London Road was a blaze of lights and we hurried along with the wind biting our cheeks. The boys were wrapped up in red woolly hats and Timberland puffa coats. Claire had forgotten her gloves. I gave her mine and she walked along pretending she was a monster with giant hands.

When we passed the travel agent's, I stopped for a moment. Just looking at the posters of sunny beaches pasted on the windows gave me a warm glow. In July, we had complained about the heat. How quickly we forget.

'I'm cold,' Claire said.

'Me, too,' I replied. 'Come on, let's take a look.'

We squirreled in and I glanced through the brochures. Two weeks in the Canary Islands in a four-star hotel with flights included would set me back £1,990. It just so happened that in my pocket I had £2,000 in an envelope that Mr Vijayakumar had given me on his last day at the spa. I had worked a lot of extra days. I was due some holiday time. I took out the envelope and was about to start counting out the money, when a vision of Bethany with gritted teeth and an angry red face rose into my mind.

'Won't be a minute,' I said, and the travel agent tapped my arm as I reached for my phone.

'Just let me say,' he began. 'I'm packing this in next year. Hard to make a go of it, what with the internet. If it's a cash deal, I'll give you ten per cent off.'

He was an older guy with silver streaks in his hair and an anxious look in his eyes. He needed a massage

'Sounds good to me. I just have to make a call first,' I said.

When I told Bethany I wanted to take two weeks off from the 3rd of January, her instinct was to say no, even though January was a quiet month. Just as the rich go to the Mediterranean in August, after Christmas they top up their tans in the Caribbean.

Bethany spoke in her brusque, offended voice. 'You've left it late, Ben, I must say. Anastasia's not back until the sixth.'

'It's only a few days.'

'Can't you change the dates?'

'It's a fixed package.'

'You're putting me in an awkward situation. Very awkward.' She paused. 'You'll have to work over the holidays and do some extra days before you go.'

'I'm glad to do that, as many as you want,' I said. 'I really appreciate it, Beth. We've never been abroad before.'

Her tone changed. 'That's nice. The kids will enjoy that. Where are you going?'

'The Canary Islands.'

'Sounds lovely. Try to get in early tomorrow.'

She clicked off and I looked back at the agent. 'I'll take that ten per cent,' I said.

The boys watched the pile of £50 notes stack up on the desk and did a jig like soccer players when they score a goal. Claire looked confused.

'Where are we going?' she demanded and I picked up her up.

'On holiday,' I replied.

'I don't like holiday!'

'How do you know? You've never been on holiday.'

'Where are my gloves?'

She struggled to get down and we carved our way through the squall to the Post Office to collect the passport applications. When I got home and started filling out the forms, I discovered that it took three weeks to process the papers. I rescued the laptop from the boy's room and went online. You can get a passport the same day by lining up, but the offices were closed over Christmas, and I had just promised Bethany to work through the holidays.

Kelly was still at work. Carly didn't answer her phone. I called Pete, apologised that I hadn't seen him for ages, and left the kids with him. I raced back to the travel agent. He scratched his chin and shook his head. I had not read the small print. The only way I could get my money back was if there was a death in the family and I produced a death certificate.

Back again at Pete's, we checked again online. Pete pointed his stubby finger at the box with bold letters on the passport office website: 'Make sure your passport is valid before you book a holiday.'

He glanced at me and it felt as if a fist had snatched at my insides. With Pete, I always felt like a boy trying to be a man. Spending £2,000 on our first holiday ever was one thing. Losing it through one impulsive moment would be the most stupid thing I had done in my life.

We read on. The one day service required making an appointment, taking the relevant documents to the office and returning four hours later for collection. The service had been suspended due to 'exceptionally high traffic' before the holidays, and would reopen on the 3rd of January – the day we were due to leave.

'Right comedy of errors,' Pete said.

'I've never applied for a passport before.'

'Obviously.' He drummed his fingers on the desktop. 'Unless…'

He hesitated and I clung on to this grain of hope.

'Yes. Unless?'

'Unless you've been rubbing them up the wrong way, maybe one of those rich mates of yours can sort it out.'

'You reckon?'

'Friends of the Queen and all that?'

Thoughts spun through my head.

Maggie would have been perfect. Her husband was in the Lords. But she was away. Lady Catherine resided in what they called an ivory tower, which I assumed meant behind a wall of bullet proof glass. She probably wouldn't have been able to grasp what I was talking about. Angela Hartley could get anything done, but on the five occasions I had given her a massage – and all that went with it – she had not once put her hand in her purse to pay me. Angela wasn't so much hard right, she was what I called hard-righteous, a church goer. She felt chosen. The one thing that put a smile on her angry face was seeing working blokes like me messing up. Rufus wasn't the type to put himself out, and I wasn't sure that he had the contacts for such a mission.

That left Vivienne.

She had come into my mind first. Vivienne wasn't ditzy at all. She was smart, but incapable at dealing with tedious daily concerns like paying parking fines. Something as tiresome as getting a passport was so far from her surreal world of costume and BDSM, I could see myself being dropped like the proverbial hot potato.

'It's what friendship's all about,' Pete said, as if he'd followed my thoughts.

'There is someone I can try.'

'Gird your loins, mate. Either that or lose your money.'

I went into the kitchen and closed the door behind me. Vivienne's phone rang and rang. I was about to give up when she answered.

'Call me back in two minutes,' she whispered. I waited and tried again. 'Guess where I am?' she then asked.

'I dunno. In the bath dressed as a goldfish?'

She laughed. I loved her laugh. 'Close. I'm sitting on the loo in Groucho's. You know something, Ben Foster, you never call me.'

'And now I've called to ask a favour.'

'The plot thickens.'

I took a breath and explained my dilemma. There was a long pause. The phone seemed to be holding its breath.

'Are you still there?' I said.

'I was thinking. Have you got photographs?'

'Not yet.'

'I'll call you back in about ten minutes.'

I took the children home before they destroyed Pete's house and checked over the application forms again. I was surprised that Vivienne had seemed so obliging and could scarcely believe it when she called back as promised a few minutes later.

'Just hold the fort,' she said. 'Text me your address and I'll shoot by at about half past two with a photographer.'

'You mean you can get it sorted?'

'It's not as if we need Parliamentary approval. You're not planning to invade the Middle East, are you?'

I explained the entire 'comedy of errors' to Kelly when she got home and she sat in the kitchen piecing the story together like it was a riddle. We were going on holiday. Then we weren't going on holiday because we didn't have our passports. Now Vivienne and a photographer were on their way.

'She's the one you like,' Kelly remarked.

'Do I?'

'You know you do. You've mentioned her enough times. Isn't she the one who made you get all those new clothes?'

'Yeah, she knew I'd need them. She's not like the rest, just snobs. She likes to give people a helping hand.'

'I'd like to see her hands.'

'What?'

'I bet they're not like these.'

Kelly's hands were red raw. I took them between my palms.

'Put some lotion on them. I'll give them a massage later.'

'That'll make a change.'

It was true. Like the cobbler who makes shoes for others while his own children go barefoot, I rarely gave Kelly a massage.

'Tonight. That's a promise. And another thing. Next year, you're going to give up the laundry. That's my New Year's Resolution.'

'We'll see. Now I'd better get ready for your friend.' She turned in the doorway as she left the kitchen. 'The Canary Islands. That is posh.'

The children were washed and brushed in their best clothes. The kitchen was tidy. Kelly wore a cream blouse, black skirt and a tight grey jacket from Gap. I put on a dark suit and tie. We could have been going to a funeral. Claire was still hooked on her monster act. She had found my gloves and we stood in the living room waiting while she entertained us.

We heard the Ferrari roar as it entered the street. Vivienne double parked and I was surprised to see Flippo armed with a camera following her up the path. Vivienne wore a tweed suit, brogues and a button-down shirt with a yellow tie – to match the Ferrari? I wasn't sure. She probably thought of the outfit as 'dressing down.' But the cut of the suit combined with the cocaine confidence of her eyes projected the same head-turning vision she always did.

Kelly was behind me. As I stood back, I felt the tension in the air as they met – the woman I loved and the woman I loved being with. It was irrational, but I felt a jumble of pleasure and terror bringing the two parts of my life together. In that moment, I was wholly me, the loving provider, the bewitched gigolo. Vivienne's big eyes grew bigger as she smiled.

'Kelly, I'm Vivienne, it's such a pleasure to meet you,' she said.

She took Kelly's two hands and the good will she beamed out was so powerful I was sure Kelly fell instantly under her spell. We went through to the living room. The lights on the Christmas tree blinked on and off. Cards were strung in loops across the mirror, the way Gran always used to do it, and for some reason I thought about the thirty foot tree hung with silver decorations in the Great Hall at Lady Catherine's castle.

I introduced Oliver and George. Vivienne shook their hands formally and went down on her haunches to greet Claire.

'Hello, my name's Vivienne. What's your name?'

'Claire Foster.'

'Are we going to be friends, Claire?'

Claire's nature is to say no when asked a question. She certainly thought about it for a few moments before she replied.

'Yes,' she said.

'Have you asked Santa to bring you something nice for Christmas?'

'I want a pram and a bicycle. And a computer. We're going on holiday.'

'That's so exciting. I wish I could come.' She smiled at the boys. They were standing behind their sister. 'I've got a present for you. It's not a computer, but it's almost as good.'

She dug into her bag and produced three Montblanc pens in black leather cases. When the children opened them, Vivienne must have noticed the disappointment in their faces, but didn't show it.

I introduced Flippo. He asked me to turn off the tree lights and turn on the main lights.

'I didn't know you were a photographer?' I said.

'Io sono un uomo di tutti i mestieri,' he replied, and Vivienne translated.

'He's a Jack of all trades,' she said, and turned to Kelly. 'I love this room. It has a real family feeling.'

'Thank you,' Kelly said

It struck me how similar they were, same height, same colouring, same blue eyes and fair hair. But Vivienne had poise, grace. She held herself as if she were the linchpin around which the world spun. I also sensed Kelly's uncertainty, or insecurity. It's the feeling ordinary people get when they meet the famous and titled, their 'masters' and 'betters.' You imagine they are judging you, when in fact they have no interest in you whatsoever.

There was a silence Kelly filled in the only way she knew how.

'Would you like a cup of tea?' she asked.

'Yes, please, that would be divine,' Vivienne replied.

'Sure,' said Flippo.

'Milk and sugar?'

'Just tea,' said Vivienne.

'Lots of milk, two sugars,' said Flippo.

The children were unusually well behaved. Claire seemed fascinated by Vivienne and followed her every move and gesture. The boys watched Flippo as he erected his tripod. He began with the children and shot us in turn sitting on a chair against the white wall. Kelly admired Flippo's camera, an Olympus. She loved taking photographs and everyone who looked through the albums said she had a good eye.

Vivienne glanced through the application forms. Claire showed her the hideous Father Christmas she had painted at playschool, an orange blob with black eyes and a green gash for a mouth.

'That's so interesting,' she said. 'Did you paint it yourself?'

'Yes.'

'It's luscious. I love it. It's brilliant.'

'It's for you,' Claire told her.

'Then I shall have it framed and cherish it always.'

They drank their tea. We trooped up the path. Claire waved until the Ferrari had disappeared from view and we went back in to change out of our best clothes.

Vivienne and Flippo left just after three on Thursday the 21st of December. Twenty-four hours later, on Friday the 22nd, a motor-cycle messenger arrived at the house with five shiny red passports.

Kelly relayed the news to me by text and I called Vivienne the moment I had a break.

'I can't thank you enough. You saved my life,' I said.

'I'm sure you'll have to do the same for me one day.' She paused. 'I adore your children. And Kelly's really rather special. An attractive woman becomes beautiful when she's happy and in love.'

'Then you must be in love,' I said, and she laughed.

'Then everything is quite perfect.'

Vivienne was off that day to stay with friends who had a house in the Dominican Republic, which I had to Google to find out where that was.

I worked the weekend, even Christmas morning. Before going home, I dropped in at The Lodge. I had bought some new table tennis bats, a net and a box of balls, a Monopoly and various other board games. The home at Christmas received more donations than they could handle, but most things were too young for the boys and were quickly broken.

From the day I started work at Southley, my life had seemed unreal. I often felt as if I were an imposter, an actor playing a role. Driving through Egham and parking at The Lodge was like returning home after a long time away. Chris, the bully, had been moved to a secure unit. Other than that, The Lodge was the same, dreary and grey with the pervasive smell of urine and the spirit of hope totally absent.

They were still understaffed and underfunded. There was no time for individual care, no hope that the boys might improve and develop strategies to cope with their disorders. The day room was strung in home-made paper chains. A forlorn tree stood in the corner. Alex managed the TV remote. Little Billy didn't recognise me. The same two boys stared hopelessly out of the barred window.

Marley was a jovial Santa Claus in a red costume. Vinnie Castro seemed older, unless he was always old and I had never noticed before. They appreciated the new table tennis bats and board games. We slapped backs. I ate a mince pie, took two sips from a can of lager and arrived home to carve the turkey.

A lot of lonely people checked into the spa during Christmas and New Year. They gave themselves massages as presents. With no one to give presents to, they were generous with tips. I worked ten straight days. I changed £1,000 into euros and hid £6,000 in an empty ice cream box in the freezer. It would have been more, but I was spending a fortune on Greek yoghurt.

Ahmed, a mate on the estate who ran a cash-only taxi business, drove us to Gatwick on a frosty road through dense midweek traffic. The airport was heaving. People were already in the holiday spirit. Lines snaked across the concourse from the check-in desks. Trolleys swerved around each other like silver insects with shells of luggage. Claire refused to take her shoes off for security because the floors were dirty and ran through the metal detector before I could stop her. I had always thought flying was glamorous. It wasn't. It was like travelling on the Northern Line at rush hour.

We herded through immigration on Gran Canaria. A bus, packed to the gills, the same colour as the pale blue sky, dropped us at our hotel in Maspalomas. We were sweaty, grubby, exhausted. The children were grumpy. Ollie had left his book on the aeroplane. After checking in behind a party of Germans, we rose four floors in the lift to our family room with four beds and a cot that sent Claire into a rage when she realised that it was for her. Ollie and George had decided to race along the corridor, upsetting the Germans, and Kelly dropped down on the bed as if she had been shot.

The briny tang of the sea seeped through the shutters. It awoke good memories. I had felt in charge of my own destiny standing at the prow of a fishing boat. I felt the same way in our family room with Claire having a tantrum and the television rabbiting on in a foreign language. I stepped onto the balcony and gazed out across miles and miles of sand dunes that stretched to the water's edge and out in both directions as far as I could see. We had left home at six. It was now four in the afternoon. The sea was choppy beneath a turquoise sky. Windsurfers bounced over the waves. I was used to seeing palm trees under glass at Southley. In Maspalomas, they emerged out of the dunes and danced in the breeze.

It wasn't as warm as I had hoped, about 20 degrees every day, but the pool was heated and the sky was always clear. The boys had swimming lessons. At the end of two weeks, George, my tough little four year old, could swim a width under water holding his breath.

Kelly did not have a costume. It was not that she had forgotten to pack one. She had never owned one. In the shop she chose various frilly colourful things. I told her to get the plain one piece black costume.

'I suppose that's what your friend would like.'

'It has nothing to do with that. You are a beautiful woman. You don't need anything fancy. You look best in solid colours.'

We compromised. She bought the black costume and also a red bikini with gold trim.

We had dinner beneath the starlight. Claire decided she did like holidays after all. I swam. I jogged on the machines. I had a massage, no extras, and felt ready for 2007 by the time the plane took us back to Gatwick.

21
BASIC INSTINCT

The new guy had started. Christian was from Oslo, straight out of a Viking movie with golden hair in a ponytail, an easy smile, perfect English and a sing-song voice that sounded as if he was gargling water when he spoke. He was twenty-five with a scar on his carved cheekbones and deep-set eyes as blue as the fjords of Norway. He was a gym buff like Denny. They had become chums. Anastasia, always aloof, seemed unusually comfortable with Christian. Bethany Bolter was like a girl in love.

The parrots in the conservatory sat in pairs ruffling their green feathers and staring out at the alien landscape with black beady eyes. Southley with bare trees and frost on the lawns was still pretty, but forbidding. The celebs with their drug problems and florid need for ego stroking and absolution, filled the schedule at weekends, but the overseas visitors were scarce and there was plenty of free time to catch up on manicures and haircuts.

In her black winter suits with bangles like braid about her wrists, Bethany was like the captain of an ocean liner and made tours around the decks to make sure all was shipshape and Bristol fashion. One morning when Christian and I were in the pool, she asked who was the better swimmer. We were about the same, we thought, and Bethany suggested a race to find out. Anastasia and Tiffany, from massage reception, joined her at the side of the pool. Then two couples in Southley robes wandered over, turning the race into an occasion.

'Five to one on the pony tail,' one of the men shouted to peals of laughter. He was a big guy with great hair, the head of an American fracking company.

Christian had rippling biceps and triceps. I had been swimming every day in Maspalomas. I was older, but taller, more aerodynamic. I would have set the odds at evens. We shook hands. Christian's perpetual smile had gone and I noted a glint of determination in his eyes. It went through my mind that I should let him win. He was new, he was younger. I had nothing to prove.

'On your marks, get set – Go,' Bethany cried.

We dived in and raced two lengths freestyle. Christian turned at the shallow end half a second before me and my competitive spirit kicked in against my will. It's a man thing. You can't hold it down. We were neck and neck midway through the home stretch when I stepped up a gear. I touched the bar at the end of the pool a body length in front of Christian and noticed as I looked up that Bethany's lips were gripped in that tight grimace that comes to people when they are trying not to show disappointment.

'Well done,' she said, and turned away.

Bethany knew I was a fisherman from Lowestoft; a nobody from nowhere. The fact that I was on good terms with Vivienne Raynott, Maddy Page and their friends and fellow Committee members, had always puzzled and vaguely annoyed her. Why it was important to her that Christian won the swimming race I had no idea. But it seemed that in this trivial event a seed had been planted and it would come to bear a bitter fruit.

To rub salt into the wound – fertiliser to that buried seed? – when Annabel Lee Hartley waltzed into the spa later that same day, Bethany's pleasure at being in the presence of a major celebrity, was tempered by irritation when Annabel asked for me personally. She booked a double session.

The staff at Southley were used to seeing soap stars, footballers, politicians. Annabel was several rungs further up the fame ladder. She was cut from the same cloth as Vivienne with fine manners, sparkling eyes, a hit TV series and her face plastered across the media having just signed for a movie set in Paris and starring two of Hollywood's leading male stars performing together for the first time with Annabel the third strand of a love triangle.

Beauty is power. Youth is power. Annabel was blessed with both. She had class, privilege, connections, talent. She was kind, generous, self-effacing with a trace of vulnerability and an aware-ness that life is unfair and random. She knew she was lucky and didn't believe she was 'chosen' or special. It was hard to believe she was Angela Hartley's daughter and engaged to marry Rufus Bradley.

Annabel wanted the Swedish massage with 'the famous' Oriental twist – the Ladies' code for reciprocal oral and vagi-nal sex. Celebrities seek out gurus in India, trainers with magic formulae, chefs with esoteric diets, financial advisers with the keys to Wall Street, Feng shui masters to bring their apartments harmony and chi energy. I was on the list. My 'reputation had preceded me.'

Annabel could have sex with any man in the world. She had driven to Southley to have sex with me. I wasn't fooling myself. I didn't think I was special, a super stud, God's gift. It wasn't like that. Those beautiful upper crust girls like Annabel have prodigious energy, an irrepressible sex drive and a tendency for kink. They like their sex uncomplicated, less an emotional than a bodily function. They have an excess of dopamine, the 'cuddle drug' chemical that brings pleasure and the desire for more plea-sure. They swim, they ride, they dance from dusk till dawn, they don't eat and they like to fuck.

It was the best kept secret in Britain, a truth that would be so shocking to working men and women, they would find it impossible to believe or comprehend: yes, the upper-classes enjoy their power and money, but they are addicted to sex. Sex and more sex. Sex in role play, bondage, masks, sadomasochistic sex, discipline and multiple partners. There were exceptions, of course, but all those well-heeled and titled people I met were hyped up, often bored and flirted with drugs. Sex was a safety valve, an obsession. Like all well-kept secrets, they didn't talk about it. They just got on and did it.

Why was I invited into the secret? I was married with children. I was discreet. I didn't sell stories to the tabloid press. In order not to say the wrong thing and make an idiot of myself, I didn't say very much at all. This had given me a reputation for being the 'silent type.' Women like to chat. I had learned how to listen.

Annabel dropped her robe. Her demeanour was calm. Her muscles were tense. I dug deep and loosened the knots. She shivered and writhed like a butterfly breaking from its cocoon. The sex was healing and vibrant. Our lips met, a seal of approval, a connection. Prostitutes, I'm told, never kiss the clients. It's too personal.

The second half of the session we swam, then sat in the sauna. I massaged her feet. Feet are intimate, perhaps more intimate than a kiss. She had gone in twelve months from playing Shakespeare on stage to seeing her face on magazine covers all over the world. She was reading scripts to play opposite Brad Pitt, Hugh Jackman, Robert Downey Jr, stars so big, the contracts so complex, she sometimes felt like 'walking away from it all.' I wasn't a psychologist, even a confidante. I was just a sounding box.

'What does Rufus think?' I asked, and she laughed.

'Oh, he's the last person I'd talk to.'

She explained that while she was engaged to Rufus, she was protected from the advances of actors, studio heads, 'greedy' lawyers and the 'money.' It put a hole in my theory that these upper-class girls were sex mad. But not entirely. Annabel, Vivienne, Maddy, were not seeking favours or enhancements like poor girls on the casting couch. They took their sex on their own terms. They were the predators.

Annabel thought Rufus was probably more gay than straight, but didn't worry about that sort of thing.

'Gay men make great husbands. They don't interfere with a woman's private life.'

'Don't you want to have children one day?' I asked her, and she nodded.

'That would be nice. One day. You have three, don't you, two boys and a clever little girl.'

'Too clever by half,' I said. 'You know everything about me.'

'Everything.' She sighed as I dug my thumb into her the arch of her left foot. 'Mmm. I love that. I received a super bronze *thingy* as a present. Vivienne always does the cleverest things.'

'I would probably blush if I wasn't so hot,' I said. 'But if Rufus is gay…'

Annabel laughed. 'All the best people are conceived on the wrong side of the bed sheets.'

'It doesn't surprise me.'

'Ben, you're becoming jaded, poor thing.'

After she had changed, Annabel did something other women had done and I didn't really like. She opened her purse, took out all of the cash, dollar bills and £20 notes, and shoved them in my hand. It was patronizing. Not that I complained. My savings were mounting. My plan was on course.

If the Committee Ladies were playing Professor Higgins with the passive little flower girl, or Svengali with Trilby, I could assume now, at the start of 2007, that I was ready to be launched on society. I returned with Vivienne to the store in Jermyn Street. I was fitted out with a dinner suit, winter suits, shoes, a cashmere over-coat, and became what they call a 'walker,' an extra man.

I had got to know the rich naked on the massage table. The rich dressed at dinners, art auctions, book launches and receptions were far more revealing and what they revealed, as they saying goes, is the rich *are* different. Apart from the obvious, that they have more money, and the less obvious, that they are addicted to sex, they have advantages that the rest of us never fully grasp: money creates networks of contacts with others equally privileged. It nurtures self-confidence, a subtle brand of charisma, and a sense of entitlement.

Rich people don't like waiting. When they want something, they want it now. If they want it badly enough, they don't care how much they have to pay for it. Money is for spending, for buying the best, for all those pleasures small and large that the meek and humble who, they say, will inherit the earth, can't even begin to imagine.

The old rich hide their wealth in shell companies set up in tax havens managed by advisers who they went to school with or who someone they know went to school with. Old school ties are pivotal. It is a cloistered world, impenetrable except to the super rich (or *nouveau riche*, as they say disparagingly with a French accent) who emulate old money by sending their children to the same posh schools where the networks are formed.

Kids when I was growing up thought of school as a place to get away from. For the middle-class, school is where you pull yourself up by your bootstraps in order to distance yourself from the deprived and underclass. For aristocrats, school is where you go to make connections. If a young toff wants to work hard and go to Oxford, the hinges are quietly oiled and the doors slide open.

Money, real money, unearned money, money you can't pin a number on, gives people the freedom to take risks and offers a continuous array of opportunities and choice. Life is a long road with lots of junctions and every time you choose to go one way, you may just have easily have gone the other. The wrong choice for the poor can be fatal. For the rich it is a learning experience. Self-assurance makes people more daring, more open to new ideas and, in turn, more fun to be with. That day when Annabel entered Southley, we were strangers. In ninety minutes, we made love, we laughed and, by the time we parted, I knew more about her than Rufus did.

Wealthy people enjoy their yachts and high-performance cars. But they are not attached in a sentimental sense to material things. Property is an asset. Today's new car is second-hand tomorrow. They respect the past, invest for the future, but live in the present.

The rich stay healthier and live on average ten years longer than the poor. Rich men take the adage 'you're as young as the woman you feel' to heart by continually paying off old wives to take on new, fresher young models. Rich ladies love their dogs and horses, often more than their children, a potential asset and a potential disaster, quite aside from the fact that babies can leave unsightly stretch marks. When they find a good nanny, butler, chef, groom, gardener, an ex-special forces sergeant with a gun licence, they pay them well and hang on to them. There are a lot of perks serving the rich, but woe betide anyone who forgets that they are only servants and will always remain so.

The moneyed classes are rarely contented except when they win something or beat someone at something, tennis or golf, the number of shot grouse, a bet or a business deal.

One night at a black tie reception in the Great Hall, Vivienne introduced me to a property developer named Hal Peret. We all shook hands and Vivienne, for my benefit, my education, asked Hal why he kept working when he had 'a charming wife' and was already high on the Forbes rich list.

'It's just a game,' he said. 'I've got, I don't know, $4 billion. If I'm at a party and some jerk's got two, I win.'

We laughed.

Hal Peret was from Arizona, as wide as he was tall – about five foot six inches – with a shiny shaved head and dark glasses. He had just acquired several buildings from a housing trust in Kensington and planned to 'amortise the asset' by moving the residents out in order to convert the blocks to 'luxury apartments.' He was well into his sixties with a wife of about twenty-five, a petite Southern Lady with lots of blonde hair who said out of the blue that she had a terrible pain in her lower back.

'Too much damned tennis, what do you expect?' her husband told her. He held up his untouched glass of Louis Roederer Cristal. 'Why is it these people always serve the same monkey piss?'

Again we laughed. Vivienne lowered her voice. 'I happen to know where there's rather good whisky. I'll have one myself,' she said.

She led him through the throng leaving me alone with Mrs Peret. In her green eyes there was an inquisitive expression.

'Now, tell me,' she said, 'is that right, you are an authority on back pain?'

'It's normally caused by irritated large nerve roots,' I replied. 'Serving at tennis will do that. But you should really speak to a doctor.'

She was wearing a strapless red dress that quivered like fire as she drew closer. 'I have been given to understand you have magic hands.'

I glanced at my palms to avoid gazing down the front of her dress. 'Not really,' I replied. 'People tend to exaggerate.'

'Modesty. I like that in a man.' She paused, nodding her head. 'Vivienne tells me you could put the life back into a stone statue.'

'Now that is an exaggeration.'

Her expression remained thoughtful. 'She has obliged me with your number,' she added. 'May I be so bold as to send you a text?'

'Whenever you want.'

She held out her hand, as if we had made a deal, and gave a little shimmy. 'Missy Peret, from Birmingham ...'

'Birmingham?'

'Alabama,' she announced, and we shook hands.

'Ben Foster.'

'It is an honour to *finally* meet you.' She stared into my eyes. 'Now do tell, Mr Foster, do you enjoy your work?'

I wasn't sure what to say and was saved as Vivienne and Hal Peret approached, whisky and ice rattling in glass tumblers.

'Now look at him, we've got a happy bunny,' Mrs Peret continued and smiled for the first time. 'I will tell you something, Mr Foster, it is my mission to spread a little pleasure wherever I go.'

The way Vivienne held up her glass and raised her eyebrows made it appear as if the two motions were connected.

'Look what we found, an absolutely charming double-malt,' she said.

She tapped the rim of Missy's champagne flute and the women exchanged looks which I understood, although I'm sure Hal Peret didn't.

He glanced at the glass I was holding. 'What's that you're drinking?'

'Just water,' I replied, and he threw up his big shoulders.

'You know what they say about water, the fish piss in it.'

I'd heard it before, but laughed, of course, a courtesy extended to billionaires. It was my job to be good-humoured and obliging. Like those who sourced rare wines, found yacht berths in Montenegro, supplied helicopters or tickets to sold-out shows, like all the dog walkers, personal shoppers, night doctors, caterers, party planners and coke dealers, I was a service provider, a tiny cog in the wheel of wealth, the money circle, the network.

Kate appeared with Lord Aberstone, a twinkly man like Father Time with a silver beard and a cane with a naked figurine handle in shiny silver. I noticed Kate's accent wavered back to her native American talking to the Perets. Hal was happy with his double malt and the arrival of Lady Catherine. Just as footballers like chatting with footballers, billionaires are most comfortable in the company of billionaires.

Vivienne took my arm and we were drawn into the ebb and flow of the crowd. A cocktail party is like the universe, trajectories changing continually, the magnetic pull of stars and money drawing others into their orbit. Rufus and Annabel were amusing J-J, shorter in real life and wearing a brown leather jacket, jeans and a Che Guevara tee-shirt. He was one of the two Hollywood A-listers about to appear with Annabel in her new film.

Maggs looked relaxed between her husband, Jasper, a Tory peer, enemy of the health service and the BBC, and her lover, James Chipping, the Government Minister with a partiality for white suits. That evening, he was dressed in a tartan rather than a black dinner jacket.

'Have we met before?' James Chipping asked me.

'Yes, right here, in this hall,' I replied.

'I never forget a face.'

'What a liar, you are, James,' said Maggs. 'You have the worst memory on the planet.'

'But I will never forget you, my dear.'

Maggs turned to her husband.

'Jasper, Ben Foster, he's our favourite ...'

'Highwire walker,' said Vivienne, and the women laughed as I shook hands with Lord something or other.

I was often bored at those parties, although I could see they were indispensable for internet giants, corporate heads and global power brokers. Meeting socially and looking each other in the eye was a tacit pact to protect their own well-being at the expense of the 99 per cent; the rest of us.

It occurred to me that whoever invented the 24-hour day might have thought again and made it 30 or 36 hours. Up on my high-wire, I juggled time trying to keep the minutes and hours in the air.

After swearing on my own internal Bible never to take coke again, I slipped on occasions. When everyone's hoovering up lines of white powder, it seems eccentric not to join in. Just as I had crept into bed at daybreak after the midnight to six shift at The Lodge, the parties or, more accurately, the after party parties, meant I often arrived home as Kelly was stirring ready for another day.

She did not object to my long hours and late nights. If she suspected that it was more than just massages that I gave my clients, she never said so. I suggested she quit the laundry, but Kelly insisted on keeping it up; she even did extra shifts. She enjoyed working with the girls and wanted to add her contribution to the fighting fund mounting in Nationwide.

Like Gran, like my mother, like most working people, Kelly had grown up believing that we 'are what we are' and trying to improve yourself was somehow phoney, or dishonest. There had been a time when she made fun of me smoothing out my Norfolk accent. Not anymore. During our holiday in Maspalomas, sparkling wine and dinner beneath the stars, her eyes were opened to another way of being and living. A Canary Islands package tour is not the life of the rich. Far from it. But it is a long step from the poverty of empty cupboards and empty bellies.

Kelly enjoyed buying new clothes in regular stores instead of castoffs in charity shops. In your own clothes, you are in your own skin. It's a confidence boost. You become who you are. Our kids were smart and always dressed smartly. You had to wonder if the two things were connected. Ollie was reading by the time he started school and came home with rows of ticks in his exercise books. A year before, we'd had no future. Now, we had one.

My main gift to Kelly at Christmas was a course of driving lessons with the British School of Motoring. I tried to ensure my days off coincided with her agenda and the last minute bookings at the spa. Bethany knew when I changed my rest days it was because I was seeing the VIPs in Vivienne's circle and was sympathetic, or at least obliging, when I had to rearrange my diary. Annabel Lee Hartley and Maddy Page had not visited the spa simply to have a massage. They had come to see me. Both had allowed their photographs to be used in brochures showing they were patrons of Southley. Bethany still had a crush on the Viking Boy. But I was the link to the society set she wanted to belong to.

I worked the Sunday morning after the reception at the Great Hall, but was able to take the afternoon off in order to make a private call at Claridge's, the Mayfair hotel known as the 'Buckingham Palace annexe.' The Perets were staying in the £4,000 a night penthouse. Hal was playing 'big stakes' golf eighty miles away in Sandwich and Missy Peret needed some work on the large nerve roots in her lower back.

Claridge's provided a massage service. The hotel also kept tables for clients who sent out for massage consultants or travelled with their own masseur, not uncommon in the world of the superrich.

One evening as I was about to go home, Bethany came clacking into the massage centre on her heels. Lowering her voice as if to whisper a confidence, she told me that one of the world's 'biggest stars' was flying in on her own helicopter and had asked for me personally.

'It'll be nice to see her again,' I responded. 'We met at Groucho's.'

'Did you now! Well, make sure you're ready.' She clacked out again.

Southley didn't have a helipad. While I took a break and dipped into a tub of Greek yoghurt, Bethany rallied the maintenance staff. In less than an hour they assembled the temporary dance floor used for weddings and receptions on the flat stretch of lawn. The electricians added spotlights along the sides of the platform and the grounds looked like a scene from a Second World War film when spies land behind the lines in the dead of night. Receptionists straightened their ties. Cleaners polished the corridors. Denny should have gone home when Christian arrived, but he wasn't going to miss this.

The flight was due at eight. It arrived exactly on time. It seems like it should be the reverse, but megastars are ruled by the clock and are notoriously punctual. The trees around the lawn rocked as if caught in a hurricane. I had never been close to a helicopter before and, as it landed, it sounded like a train crashing. The side door opened and a short flight of stairs descended automatically. She stepped out while the blades were still spinning and had to yell to be heard.

'You learned to play the sax yet?'

'No, but I'm still blowing my own trumpet.'

'You go for it, buddy. No one else is going to.'

She grabbed my arm as if we were old friends and talked non-stop over the noise, her gaze focused solely on me.

Bethany blocked the way and tried to get out her welcoming speech.

'We are so happy to have you. It's a privilege ...'

'Yeah, yeah, thanks a lot. Listen,' she said. 'I need two big bottles of Evian. Can you handle that?'

'Straight away ...'

'Thanks, honey, you go for it.' She turned back to me. 'You seen Vivienne? I love that chick.'

'Why?' I asked.

She stopped in her tracks. 'That's a good question.' She thought for a moment. 'Why do we feel close with one person and not another?'

'Chemistry?'

'Could be. Then, most people are assholes. What's to like?'

She kept a tight grip on my arm as we entered the building and made our way down the corridor. This was not for protection, I realised, she was afraid of nothing. It was to say that she was occupied with me at that moment. She did not want to be bothered by anyone else.

She changed and we entered massage room 3 with two cups of water I filled from the cooler. I locked the door.

'Am I safe in here?'

'Of course ...'

She held up her palm. Her gaze moved around the walls. 'Not from you. No eyes in the sky? No Cameras?'

'No. No. Nothing like that.' I smiled with relief. 'Now, what about music? I've got some of yours ...'

'You think I'm than vain?'

'Just asking.'

Lines crossed her brow. She was pensive again. 'People try too damn hard to do the right thing. That's why Vivienne special. She doesn't give a shit.' She paused. 'Bach. Can you handle that?'

'Sure can.'

I played the Brandenburg concertos. She took from her robe a familiar white packet with a pinch of coke which we shared. It was one of those times when I needed it. I did the full Swedish massage, working out knot clusters and smoothing weary muscles. She found it hard not to talk. When I oiled and massaged her stomach, she leaned up on her elbows.

'Forget the sax, stick with the sex. Do what you're good at.'

She widened her knees. I dropped my tongue over her clitoris and the most famous of the famous sighed with contentment. She liked it doggy fashion. She sucked my cock like she was trying to swallow me whole. She was naked except for a watch with a big dial. When it hit nine, she swung her legs around and sat on the edge of the table.

'You like your job, eh?'

'I do,' I said.

'How much do you make a year, 100K?'

I shook my head. 'No, not as much as that.'

'I'll tell you what I'll do, Ben, I'll double it. I've got to go back to LA. I've got a big tour coming up, a lot of dates, and a movie. Come along for the ride.'

'That's the best offer I've ever had in my life.'

She smiled. 'It'll be fun.'

'It would. But I can't,' I said. 'I've got children, and a wife. It wouldn't be fair.'

She was silent for several seconds. Big stars, the biggest stars, aren't used to people saying no. She had to rationalise this, take it all in, decide whether to go ape or accept it.

'You're turning me down?' she finally said.

She nodded for several seconds, then grabbed my shoulders. We kissed cheeks and she stretched her arms into the robe.

Bethany stood outside the door holding two bottles of Evian.

'Grab those, Ben, I'm going to take a shower.'

Later, I walked her back to the helicopter. The rotors started to spin.

'Wait,' she shouted. She rooted around in the dark until she found a manila envelope that she gave me. 'I'll catch you next time. You say hi to Vivienne.'

'I'll do that.'

The door closed. The helicopter lifted into the air and vanished quickly back to London. In the envelope was £2,000.

To get back to Missy Peret, there was absolutely nothing wrong with her back. It was sexy and smooth without knots or pain. She was another of those women who liked being naked and being seen naked. She moaned and wriggled on the table for thirty minutes. Then her mobile phone rang and she leapt from the table to answer.

'Hi, honey,' she said. There was a pause before she continued. 'You come right on up. I have been waiting for you.'

Two minutes later, Missy, naked, swung the door open and Vivienne swanned in dressed as a punk in a black wig with fiery red tips across the crown, a short leather jacket covered in silver studs, Doc Martens, ripped black tights with suspenders, no knickers and a short tartan skirt barely concealing a strap-on dildo.

Vivienne was whatever she wanted to be but, more than that, she was whatever you wanted her to be. The air about her hummed. The black makeup around her eyes was badly applied. Her pink lips were daubed in black and crystal tears were painted on her cheeks. She laid back in a pale blue wing chair and breathed heavily as she masturbated the black rubber appendage. The dildo was brutal and absurd, but funny, outrageous. She turned sex into art.

Missy went down on her knees between Vivienne's spread legs. While she sucked the dildo, Vivienne stared into my eyes and did that thing with her tongue, pushing the tip into the side of her cheek, miming fellatio. It was a scene from a Mapplethorpe photograph – explicit, but enigmatic: a naked girl hidden by a bonnet of yellow hair in a sex act with a false cock that could only have been sexually exciting from the point of view of the voyeur, the eye of the camera.

With Vivienne I always had that breathless, high altitude feeling you get from running marathons and swimming under water. I connected with her in a way I had never felt a connection with anyone else. It was as if she knew me, understood me, that she saw something in my core than no one else could see. Even if it was only in my mind, a fiction I wanted to believe, it was still exhilarating.

She wanted a choo-choo train. Missy leaned over the arm of a sofa. Vivienne made her wet with her tongue then pierced her with the dildo. I made Vivienne wet and entered her from behind. It was like dancing. Thighs touching, knees trembling, we chugged along until the girls screamed in orgasm. Then, we went downstairs to the art deco lounge to order afternoon tea served in peppermint striped china with finger sandwiches, warm scones and pastries, a culinary tradition at Claridge's dating back 150 years.

Conversations stilled when we entered. We had not taken showers, on Vivienne's command. Missy Peret had dressed in tight white jogging shorts and a cropped top revealing her flat tummy and playful breasts. I was in Hugo Boss whites. Vivienne, in her short skirt without underwear, the dildo tucked in her Lulu Guinness bag, kept crossing her legs in the way made famous by Sharon Stone in the film *Basic Instinct*. Sex is a drug. We reeked of it. Every eye strayed to our table, the image multiplied endlessly by the bevelled mirrors and lit by the antique chandeliers above our heads. We ate every finger sandwich, scone and pastry and Vivienne ordered more.

22
THINGS CAN ONLY GET BETTER

The 13th of April 2007 happened to fall on a Friday. Unlucky for some. Not for the Proclaimers. *I'm Gonna Be 500 Miles* was No 1 in the charts and I was beginning to get bored hearing it every time I turned on the radio. Jessica Alba was declared 'the sexiest woman in the world,' a fair call, and Kelly had her driving test.

She hadn't eaten for two days. Her stomach was in knots. Even the massage I gave her didn't help. She did three hours of extra lessons the day before the test and arrived at the test centre pale and trembling. It was muggy with light rain and grey smears on the windscreen.

'You can always cancel and try again in a few weeks,' I said, and she shook her head.

'Best to fail now and get it over and done with.'

'You're not going to fail. You're going to pass. Be positive.'

'I'm not the eternal optimist like you.'

'The worst thing you can do is worry about it. In the end, it doesn't matter.'

Her voice dropped. 'Oh, but it does,' she said.

The examiner was a short tubby man in a flat cap and glasses as thick at the bottoms of champagne bottles. He rubbed some warmth into his small hands, then sneezed and blew his nose. I watched them climb into the car. The engine fired. The indicator flashed and Kelly drew into the stream of traffic.

I had forty minutes to kill. I went to Starbucks and flicked through the photos of the kids on my iPhone, the boys playing football, Claire chasing a little brown dog. If I got to jog around the lake once a week these days it was a miracle. I sipped my coffee and scrolled down the list of contacts. I stopped at Rudy Johnson. I had been planning to call him for a long time. I wasn't exactly sure what I was going to say, even when I pressed the call button.

'Ben Foster. My man. How's it going?'

'As good as it gets, I guess...'

'I've been expecting you to call. When do you want to meet?' he said and I laughed. He was two steps ahead of me.

We settled on the Picasso, a café in the Kings Road, at four that afternoon, and I sat back relieved that Rudy had made it so easy to set up a meeting. I remembered that time when I entered the Great Hall after giving Rufus a massage and saw Rudy studying the oil-painted generals on the wall, his wide smile, the way he dominated the space.

I sipped my coffee and enjoyed sitting there doing nothing.

Starbucks was full of young mums with push chairs. Toddlers high on the smell of caffeine ran in circles between the tables, knocking their heads and crying. I read in the *Daily Mail* that Westminster Council planned to scrap all its parking meters so people could use mobile phones to pay for parking. More jobs down the drain. Still, it least it would make life easier for Vivienne.

The rain had stopped and steam was rising from the pavement as I strolled back to the test centre. I arrived just as Kelly left the building and my heart dropped. Tears streamed down her red cheeks. I hurried towards her.

'Jelly Baby, I'm so sorry...'

She sniffed back her tears. She could barely speak. 'I did it,' she gasped. 'I passed.'

'Then what are you crying for? I knew you'd do it.'

'I've never passed anything before.' She held up the certificate. 'This is a first.'

'And it won't be the last. You can do anything you put your mind to.'

She dried her eyes and stared back at me. 'You know something, Ben, I think I can.'

The sky had cleared. Her hair had broken free of the clips and was tossed about in the breeze. The stress and strain had gone. I'd never seen her look so beautiful.

'I'm so proud of you,' I said, and we kissed.

On Sunday, George turned five and Kelly drove us to Lowestoft to visit my mum. I sat beside her with Claire kicking my seat.

'Sweetheart, stop keep kicking the back of my seat.'

'No. No. No.'

'Oh, no, she hasn't started that again,' I said and everyone burst out laughing.

Rudy was waiting with a white wine spritzer at one of the tables outside the Picasso. His flat was down the road. He loved Chelsea and had started buying a season ticket for the football club in 2003 when Roman Abramovich bought the team and made it glamorous.

'Black on the outside, blue all the way through,' he said.

I shook my head. 'Norwich City, man and boy,' I replied. 'Chelsea's all money over passion.'

'That's what makes football sexy.'

'Sexy,' I said. 'I didn't take you for a football fan.'

'Never miss a home match.' His white teeth gleamed as he smiled. 'That's where I do most of my business.'

He called for two more spritzers. He was wearing a grey suit, blue shirt, loafers without socks, smart but casual, hard to place, like his accent, his tenor voice that was a pleasure to listen to. He reminded people he was black, not that he was. He was mixed race and had got the best of both worlds with small solid features and coffee-coloured skin.

Foreign tourists filled the Kings Road with its noisy traffic and damp diesel air. A man went by riding a penny farthing. Only in Chelsea, I thought. A bus stopped, the side sprayed up with an advertisement for *Les Misérables*. Rudy pointed.

'Have you seen it?'

'No, is it good?'

'I came out dancing and weeping at the same time.'

The drinks came. We clinked glasses and got down to what we were there for. I had saved £40,000. I had been following property prices and every month they went up. There was a new build behind Twickenham Park House with flats going for £265,000. Would I have a problem getting a mortgage – bearing in mind I lived in a council house and had not declared the money to the tax man?

'The only problem you have between you and reaching your goal,' he observed, 'is believing there is a problem.'

'Sounds about right.'

'I'll remind you of something else, Ben. A goal is a dream with a deadline.' He pointed at the watch on his wrist. 'The time on the clock is now.'

He explained that the Government turned a blind eye to the property market. Hidden cash from offshore trusts, drug money and dirty money was pouring into London from all over the world. Banks were bursting with cash. The economy had never been stronger. Every free space was being 'monetised,' a new word to me. Buildings were shooting up. I'd seen it with my own eyes. Everyone was getting rich.

'If you're a crooked politician with your hands in the till in Africa or Jamaica,' he said, switching to a Jamaican accent. 'If you're selling publicly owned land and skimming off a percentage in Asia, or robbing the oil and gas money in Russia, what are you going to do with it?'

'Invest in property?'

'You get a bolt hole in London so you've got somewhere to run to when they come looking for you.' He leaned forward. 'There are mansion blocks in Kensington filled with old African generals and old mafia bosses. I've seen it with my own eyes. They sit around in the same bars talking about the good old days when they were throwing their enemies out of helicopters. And what do Revenue and Customs do about it? We've got their jewels in our safety deposit boxes; we've got their money in our bricks and mortar. What do they do? They have another gin and tonic and look the other way.'

Rudy made it sound so intriguing, the group of older guys with thinning hair and nice accents at the next table had shut up to listen. He pulled an imaginary cord in the sky.

'Toot! Toot!,' he hooted. 'The gravy train's coming. If you don't get on board, it's leaving without you.'

He took a slug of wine and glanced through the property brochure I'd brought along to show him. I visualised the smoke from the gravy train slipping into the distance. My pulse was racing.

'Not bad,' he said. 'We could make it work.'

'You reckon 40K's enough?'

'To get a mortgage?' Again he tugged at the air above us. 'I just have to pull a few strings.'

'That's amazing,' I said. 'I've been meaning to call you for ages. I didn't want to, you know, waste your time ...'

He lifted his mobile from the table and held it in his palm. 'We're all connected now, Ben. I do something for you. You do something for the next person. They do something for someone else. Karma in action.' He swallowed the last of his drink and mimed tapping the digits on his phone. 'I'll be in touch.'

As we were leaving, one of the guys at the next table asked Rudy for his card. In the old days, when 'Them' and 'Us' was more clearly defined, a gentleman wasn't in business and didn't carry a business card. It wasn't the old days any more.

Rudy drove out to Southley when he had completed his research. I knew from that time when I gave free massages at the gym that he was a raging heterosexual and arranged a freebie with Dee-Dee. Was this karma in action? She had learned how to monetise her assets and was also saving for a deposit to buy her own flat.

We met after the session in the café for lunch. He had good news. He would be able to arrange a mortgage and had come up with an alternative plan he believed would suit me better. By going out a little further from London, to Guildford, I would be able to buy, not one, but two one-bedroomed flats at £195,000 each with a ten per cent deposit – the £40,000 I had saved. As Rudy put it, if you are going to get on the property ladder, it made sense to climb two rungs rather than one.

The building was on the point of being completed. More than half of the eighty flats had been sold off plan, four of them to Rudy's clients. He had a relationship with the developers. They guaranteed the mortgage through the Royal Bank of Scotland 'the safest bank in the world.' To arrange it all, his fee was £4,000, which I didn't have, and I could pay at £1,000 a month for four months interest free.

He counted on his fingers. 'No papers. No contract. Just a handshake,' he said. 'And one more thing, Ben, I wouldn't do that for everyone.'

He gave me a brochure with photographs of the building, the flats with wide balconies, white walls and built-in appliances, landscaped gardens, underground garage spaces.

'Looks fantastic,' I said.

'It's a great development. Good architect. Nicely finished. You have a good think. Talk it over with you wife.'

'I don't need to. The time will never be *just right*. Let's do it.'

'There's my man.'

We high fived, slapping palms. We ate quiche with green salad and toasted with sparkling water. I walked him out to his car. As he was about to get in, he tapped his head and reached into his inside pocket.

'Almost forgot,' he said, and handed me two tickets for *Les Misérables*.

In six weeks, I was a property owner with two flats, both let out through an agent in Guildford with the rents covering the mortgage. I had my wages and tips from the spa for maintenance and shortfalls between renters. To say I had a new spring in my step would be an understatement.

Rufus had bought another buy-to-rent flat, not in Guildford, in Knightsbridge, but now we were both men of property, his superiority complex was less pronounced. We occasionally had lunch and played tennis at his club. I was fast. I had developed a powerful serve. But he had been playing since he was a child and it pleased him that he always won.

On a whim, Rufus had ordered a new silver Range Rover Sport with a walnut dash and pale grey upholstery. I went with him to the dealership so I could drive his old car back to the house. It was the first time I had been behind the wheel of a Range Rover and appreciated the acceleration, the feeling of owning the road.

Annabel and Kate had been riding when we left the house. When we got back, the groom had taken charge of the horses and they came out to greet us.

'What are you going to do with the old one?' Kate asked her son. I had met a few billionaires and they tended to be practical people.

'I don't know. It's a spare.'

'You already have the old green one parked in the stables. There isn't room for any more. You're turning the place into a junk yard.'

'Then I'll sell the damn thing.'

'If you do, I'll make you an offer,' I said.

'Oh, really! And how much are you going to offer?'

As he looked back at me with a sour expression, Annabel took my arm and pulled close. It was odd, like we were a couple.

'Rufus, you sound like a cad.'

'Cad,' he repeated. 'No one says that anymore.'

'It just happens to be the right word. Whatever the opposite is, that's how you should behave.'

'What, give the thing away?'

'I can't see why not. Ben does so much. It's the least you can do.'

'That's a super idea,' added Lady Catherine.

'Hang on, wait a moment,' I said. 'I did say I'd like to make an offer.'

'An offer I can't refuse?' said Rufus. 'I don't want to end up with a dead horse in my bed.'

We laughed. Even Kate laughed. And she never laughed. Rufus appreciated that and threw up his hands.

'Free massages for a year,' he suggested.

'It's a deal,' said Annabel on my behalf.

'No, no, I can't...'

'Oh, but you can, my dear,' said Kate, and no one says no to a billionaire.

* * *

I had planned to ask Ahmed, my taxi driver mate on the estate, to take me out to Kempton to collect the Range Rover from Rufus. Then I had stroke of genius. I asked Kelly instead. Carly looked after the kids and we drove first to Southley so I could show her where I worked.

Bethany was expecting us. She played the role of Mother Superior at a convent and Kelly would never have guessed that she was the Madame in the biggest brothel in the Home Counties. Denny was his charming self and Anastasia actually smiled.

The trees were in full leaf. People in towelling robes drove golf carts along the curving paths. We went to see the parrots in their tropical enclosure.

'Now I know why you spend more time here than you do at home,' Kelly said.

If she was impressed by Southley, I am not sure what the word is to describe her reaction to Lady Catherine's story book castle. She clamped her hand over her mouth as we entered the gates and her eyes almost popped out of their sockets. Horses in the meadow stopped to watch as we approached over the gravel drive, the countryside stretching out around us unchanged for a thousand of years.

'I thought we were doing well, Ben. The way these people live…'

The liveried servant at the open door lowered his shoulders in a bow as if he was appearing in a documentary and led us through to the Great Hall where Kate was waiting with Rufus, Annabel, Maggs and James Chipping, the Labour Minister in his trademark white suit. We were expected but I had not been expecting a welcoming committee.

Girls in pink gingham served tea with miniature cupcakes. The sun fell through the leaded windows lighting the threads in the carpet and the portraits on the wall. Kelly was wide-eyed, especially coming face to face with Annabel Lee Hartley. It is an odd sensation meeting someone you think you know because you have seen them on TV. It must be even odder for famous people having strangers imagine they know them, something I would witness several times in the months ahead.

The conversation tinkled like the tea cups. Maggs admired Kelly's white summer dress. It was simple, unadorned. It made her appear young and ingenuous, which she was. Kelly was prompted to talk about herself and our children. When it's your first time amongst the rich and famous you can't help but feel inadequate. Kelly sat stiffly as if at an interview, knees together, back straight, jaw stiff from her being uncertain when and whether to smile. It seems as if the things they find amusing you find anything but funny.

Kelly's eyebrows shot up when Rufus plunged his cigarette butt into a half-eaten cup cake and exchanged a glance with Lady Catherine, one mother to another. Kelly didn't pretend to be anything other than what she was. I was proud of her and pleased to have given my wife a glimpse into this other world.

Lord Aberstone made a cameo appearance, his cane tapping as he approached across the ancient floorboards. Kelly lowered one leg in a curtsy as they shook hands.

'It is such a pleasure to meet you, my dear. I do hope they are looking after you?'

'Yes, they are. Everyone's so kind.'

'And how is the tea?'

'It's really lovely.'

'I'm so pleased. It's jolly annoying if it isn't.' He took her hand again. 'What a pleasure.'

He looked vague and lost as he made his way slowly past his painted ancestors into another room and the tall door closed behind him.

There was a maze at the back of the house that I had never seen. We went for a tour and Maggs made sure she and I were lost for a few minutes.

'She's perfectly lovely,' she said.

'Thank you.'

'What a shame you won't be able to bring her to the City of Light.'

'Where?'

She smiled. 'We're going for a junket. Make sure your passport is up to date.'

That day when I had arrived home in the new Golf, it had not been easy to convince Kelly that it was a tax fiddle, that the car hadn't really cost anyone anything. Now we had become a 'two car' family, she took it in her stride.

Passing her driving test had been more important to Kelly than I could have imagined. She had started to believe in her right to make the most of herself – a right working people often don't realise they have. As well as facing the constant grind of making ends meet, she had been held back by a lack imagination as well as confidence. Finally, she had found her wings and was learning to fly.

Kelly had gone monochrome, greys and blacks, simple lines, solid colours. Her name as well as mine was on the deeds for our two flats in Guildford. She had quit her job at the laundry and signed up for a photography course at Richmond College. After spending the best part of two hours in the camera shop in the High Street, she had settled on a new Olympus, the same model Flippo had used to take our passport photos. Her shots of the kids were zany, odd angles, offbeat. She had an Apple laptop and was learning how to use Photoshop. Her goal was to build her own website and set herself up as a children's photographer.

It was no big deal going to a West End show, thousands of people did it every day. But when we jostled along with the crowd entering the Queen's Theatre to see *Les Misérables,* it was a first for us. They were good seats in the tenth row. Kelly wore a new Armani suit with a pleated skirt and a fitted jacket with wide shoulders and one big button, something Vivienne could have chosen. Rudy was right, we came out crying and dancing all the way to Romilly Street where, at his advice, I had booked a table at Kettner's for dinner. A pianist played jazz and, driving home in the Range Rover, it felt as if we had moved up the board on life's game of snakes and ladders.

Kelly wasn't unique on the estate. A lot of our neighbours were starting small businesses. The streets of London were paved in gold. Everyone was staking their claim. Well, not everyone. When Pete Taylor saw me step out of the Range Rover one morning he said in his dour way that the whole world was living on credit and we were heading for the biggest crash of all time.

'Better enjoy it while it lasts,' I said.

'Thing is, son, it won't.'

I nodded, although I didn't agree. I liked Pete, but he was living in the past. He was old Labour. Tony Blair had promised that *Things Can Only Get Better* and it was true. The evidence was all around us. My flats were worth another fifty grand. London's financial services sector had become the biggest in the world. In the previous four years, the Stock Exchange had grown faster and reached the highest levels in history. I read that in the *Daily Mail.*

The Iraq War still dominated the headlines, but the end was in sight. President Bush had ordered what they called a 'surge' with an extra 20,000 troops. The Taliban were scuttling back to the mountains and the American civil authority was establishing a democracy. I had always been against the war. But in 2007, it looked as if Bush and Blair were right after all. By getting rid of Saddam Hussein, they would bring peace to the Middle East and more security from terrorists at home.

23
IT GIRLS

Being a property owner wasn't as straightforward as I'd thought. If a tenant moved out and it was a month before someone new moved in, I still had to find the money for the mortgage. The flats were going up in value. But I was working more hours than ever and Kelly no longer had an income from the laundry. She had done some photo shoots with families on the estate. To launch the business, she charged barely enough to cover the costs, but she was becoming more confident in herself and her ability. That was the upside. It made me happy for her.

The downside was that I was losing sight of the core principles of massage. All through those years when I didn't have any money, I wasn't obsessed by it. We struggled, we went hungry, we got by. Now, I had plenty of money but always needed more. I had thought of myself as a healer when I started work at the spa. I had turned into a total slut. I played every client until they let go of their inhibitions and submitted to their secret fantasies. Ladies who left the massage suite after an unexpected orgasm dug deep into their purses. They helped pay the bills. Vivienne once said every time you sleep with someone all your partners are in bed with you. If that were true, I would have needed a bed the size of Crane Park.

When I wasn't at Southley, I was driving out to the Great Hall to escort Kate to discreet dinners. I rarely missed a week at Frowley, where Maggs had introduced a new kink to our couplings: James Chipping watched the massage, then followed us up the creaking staircase to observe us testing the joints on the old four-poster bed where Oliver Cromwell had dreamed of a chaste and Puritan England. The first time it happened, I felt like a performing chimp. But in all matters carnal, it is surprising how quickly the novel becomes normal. I had never been keen on the Four-Hands Massage. Now, it was just another source of income.

Was I more blasé? More cynical? Had I forgotten how lucky I was and how far I had come? Absolutely. But it is easier to see how we were when we look back; not so easy while we are living the moment. I was surrounded by rich people growing richer as the value of their investments went up even beyond their overheated imaginations. The BIG topic of conversation in 2007 was house prices. I was part of that conversation. A rising tide lifts all boats and I was a Lowestoft trawlerman riding the wave.

Annabel was in pre-production with her movie in Paris. We often met when she was back to London. She could have jumped into bed with her acclaimed co-stars, the film director, every good-looking set designer and cameraman. But she was too canny to get into casual entanglements and feed the tabloid press. Sex for Annabel was less passionate than physical. I could have prided myself on being an Olympic champion between the bedsheets, the greatest fuck on the planet. But it was more likely that she called me for the same reason as men call escorts. I would arrive smiling and in a good mood, sometimes faked, usually not. We'd make love, sprinting to a noisy finish, then rush out for pizza or pasta in one of the restaurants close to her flat off the Earls Court Road. She disguised herself behind dark glasses, but people recognised her and came up, some asking for autographs, most just to blurt out stupid things like – 'Hey, I know who you are.' Annabel had a tic in her neck. It vibrated every time a fan loomed over the table, but she remained courteous no matter how crass and inane the public.

When I was with Annabel, it was hard to believe Angela Hartley was her mother. They shared the same genes, but their early lives had been set on different planets. Annabel's father was an Old Etonian who did something in the City. She had grown up with a French nanny, attended the best schools and started acting with the Footlights in Cambridge. Annabel, Vivienne, Maddy, Zara Swift and their friends were the It Girls of the new millennium, chic, beautiful, highly sexualised while appearing naïve, innocent, virginal.

By contrast, Angela's dad had been a plumber in Maidstone, her mum a nurse; good people, I imagine, the sort Angela despised. She had gone to a grammar school and got a scholarship to Oxford. She had come up the hard way and become more snobby and condescending than those like Annabel, for whom every door was open. Angela was strident, narcissistic, anti-NHS. Like Maggie Thatcher, she believed there was no such thing as 'society,' and had that distorted conviction: If I can do it, anyone can, which is patently absurd. There was room for only one Angela Hartley in the Shadow Cabinet and she occupied that place.

It was inevitable that Angela and I would come to blows. I must have given her a dozen massages – I had the scars on my back to prove it – and there was always some reason why she didn't pay me. I had let this go because the other women in her circle were so generous and, the truth is I was afraid that if I crossed her she would stab me in the back.

It all came to a head when I drove one evening to see her after I had worked nine hours with barely a break at Southley. I arrived with my table as she was about to leave. Her car was waiting outside the building in Lambeth with her driver standing beside the back passenger door.

'Something's come up, we'll have to reschedule,' she said.

'Why didn't you call me, or send a text?'

'Are you telling me what to do?'

'I have driven an hour to get here and spent half an hour finding somewhere to park. You have to pay me.'

'You want to discuss money in the street?'

'I can't afford to keep wasting my time ...'

'So you think your time is more valuable than my time?'

'I didn't say that, Angela ...'

'How dare you ...'

She gritted her teeth. She was shaking. Her driver was facing me. I could see by his expression how happy he was to witness the exchange.

'I have heard you on television talking about fairness. You're not being fair,' I said.

'You people are all the same. Only out for what you can get.'

'I'd say it's the absolute opposite.'

I was the first time I had ever raised my voice. She responded by poking me on the chest.

'Get out of my way.'

I stood aside. I was pleased I had stood up for myself. The driver opened the car door and we exchanged quick glances. I could see he felt sorry for me and I felt sorry for him.

It wasn't unusual when I had a booking with Angela that I would get a call from Vivienne. It happened that day. She asked me to come as quickly as possible in a voice that sounded as if she was at the bottom of a well. I was glad to go. I was as tense as a clenched fist and couldn't face going straight home.

When I arrived, the door was open. The studio was silent. Shadows climbed the walls and the photographs seemed more ominous in the evening light. There was a new addition to the sculpture display: Big Ben on a white pedestal cast in bronze. I had seen it before, Annabel had one, so did Maggs and Maddy Page, but it was still weird.

I went through to the bedroom and called.

'Vivienne. Vivienne. I'm here.'

I heard a muffled sound from the wardrobe. I slid the door open. She was coiled up like a foetus behind her clothes, knees against her chest, her hair covering her face. I tried to urge her to come out and she persuaded me to climb in beside her. She slid the door back in place and I held her in my arms while she cried.

'What's wrong?' I said.

'I don't know.'

'What are you doing in the wardrobe?'

'Hiding.'

I didn't ask why. I knew why. People with everything get depressed the same as everyone else.

'You slipped off the highwire,' I said and her sniffles had a different tone. 'What do you want to do?'

'Just stay here with you.'

'We can't stay here forever.'

'No,' she said. 'There's no happy ever after for people like us.'

We were quiet, just holding each other. Then she unzipped my fly. In the cramped space, she took me into her mouth. Her movements were slow, methodical, as if she were drawing out my energy, refilling her own. I ejaculated. Then we kissed.

'Who are you, Ben Foster? What are you doing in my closet?'

'It's a mystery to me.'

'You're the cuckoo's egg in the nest of the phoenix.'

'That sounds hot.'

'Let's go somewhere.'

We stepped out of the wardrobe. We hugged for a moment. She seemed small, fragile. Her features were drawn. She was clutching her stomach.

'Are you all right?'

She nodded. 'I'm better now.'

I watched her dress in a tartan skirt, white blouse, green blazer, black stockings with suspenders and flat shoes. She pinned up her hair and added a straw hat with a plaid ribbon that trailed over the back of the brim. She turned from the mirror smiling, then tensed up again.

'I have to eat something.'

I followed her into the kitchen. The refrigerator was empty except for bottles of sauces and champagne, a carton of soya milk. There were two bananas going black. She mashed them in a bowl and added a splash of soya. She ate quickly and looked like a schoolgirl with a milky moustache.

'A snack's like a kiss before orgasm,' she said.

'Or after, in this case,' I replied.

She laughed. She wiped the milk from her top lip, then raised both arms as if she were about to execute a dive.

'To infinity and beyond,' she cried.

We chased down six flights of stairs to the street and climbed into the yellow Ferrari. The hood was down. She drove as if on the wall of death, the road unwinding with surreal logic to the gates of Southley. Aurélie, the French girl at reception, studied Vivienne with arched eyebrows as she booked the suite in the old building.

'Do you have any luggage?' she asked, knowing we didn't.

'We only have each other,' Vivienne replied, and took my arm, a scrap of gossip for Aurélie to share with the spa.

The suite occupied the entire top floor. The windows were like portholes on a ship and looked out in all four directions. The night was clear and clean, full of stars to guide us. I remembered that boy on a fishing boat at night, the lap of the waves, the steady boom of the engine. Vivienne was *starving*. While she ordered from room service, I closed the door to the bedroom and called Kelly to say I was still at work.

'I'll probably stay over,' I said.

'People want massages in the middle of the night?'

'There's a reception. It's going to go on late. I have to be back early…' We fell silent. 'How was your class today?'

'It was all about perspective.'

'Keeping it?'

'Maintaining it,' she replied. She paused. 'Take care. Love you.'

'Me, too.'

Kelly must have known all along that it wasn't massage alone that propelled money into our bank account. Subconsciously, she had stopped thinking about the means, and was concerned solely with the bottom line. We were a partnership. It was all about asset building, cash flow. I had spoken often about rich people being confident because they went to private schools. It had influenced Kelly to want that for our children. Now that Ollie was almost seven, she had brought home brochures from Willington, a prep school close to where we lived with fees of £3,000 a year. He would be mixing with boys whose parents would appreciate her unconventional photography. Could we afford it? Could we afford not to?

I looked at the photo of my kids on the screen-saver and buried the phone in my pocket.

Vivienne studied me as I approached across the suite. I sat beside her on the sofa.

'How is she?'

'She's… actually, she's happy.'

'I envy her. It's not easy being happy.'

'It depends where you're starting from. Kelly was working in a laundry washing other people's dirty clothes. Now she's learning to be a photographer.'

'Thanks to you.'

She turned to look at me. I had never told her anything like that before and regretted that I had.

'Not really...'

'You're one of the good guys, Ben. There aren't many.'

'Course there are. You just have to know where to look.'

'What do you think I was doing in my closet,' she said and the mood changed as we laughed.

We ate omelettes and fries. We drank a bottle of wine. Vivienne was always full of energy. But, that night, she was exhausted and fell asleep as we snuggled up on the sofa in front of the TV. I turned it off and gazed out at the dark night. I could hear birds on the roof. The moon was rising, pale and gaunt. I stroked her hair. I wasn't sure what we were doing in Southley. It meant something. It always meant something. I was persistently unfaithful to Kelly. I was unfaithful to her every single day. But I never felt disloyal. With Vivienne, it was different. I was more than just a gigolo. Rescuing her from the wardrobe had created a sense of conspiracy. We shared a secret.

The following morning, we swam and made love under the power shower. We had breakfast and watched as Bethany entered the dining room, all in black, fiercely efficient. Vivienne gave her an enthusiastic wave and asked her to join us. She took a photograph of Bethany and me. She asked me to take a picture of Bethany and her, then flicked through her collection showing Bethany shots of herself falling from a horse. I had no idea why Vivienne was doing this, but when she left Southley that morning, Bethany was unusually pleasant for the rest of the day.

Having set the precedent of staying away for the night, it was easier to justify my absences on the two occasions that came up before the rich crowd migrated for the summer.

The first occasion was a week later. I met Vivienne at the studio, a car drove us to Heathrow and we flew first class to Amsterdam. A hotel courtesy car was waiting to take us to the *Waldorf Astoria*, an imposing 17th-century palace a short walk from Dam Square. Southley was upmarket. The *Waldorf Astoria* was old-fashioned luxury.

Our suite was below the eaves with views over the rooftops. We slept late in a bed big enough to hide in and had breakfast at noon with fizzing mimosas. We made love on the white sofa, then stood naked like a sculpture gazing at our reflections multiplied around the bathroom.

'In an invisible mirror you see your invisible self,' she said.

'It would hide all your faults.'

'If you have any.' She turned. 'Don't let's shower. I want to smell you on me all day.'

The sky was streaked in cloud. We walked arm in arm along the edge of the canals without a need for talking. I loved being a foreigner in a foreign place. It was like escaping from yourself. The hands on the clock had stilled. I couldn't read the advertising hoardings or understand what anyone was saying.

We smoked marijuana in a coffee house. We went to the marijuana museum, the sex museum, sex shops with dildos in every colour, shape and size. She bought a nun's habit with scarlet underwear, a black monk's costume for me; a whip. We rode bicycles and visited the house where the diarist Anne Frank hid from the Nazis. We ambled through the national Rijksmuseum and, across the square, the museum showing the work of Vincent Van Gogh.

'He was poor all his life,' she said. 'Now his paintings sell for millions.'

'Isn't that what they call irony?'

'All life is irony. It would be unbearable if it wasn't.'

It was late afternoon, not so crowded. It was possible to be alone for a moment and study the paintings. I had never understood art. I had thought you had to know about the painters and their times. I realised that day that you didn't need to know anything at all. Art either grabs you, or it doesn't. I stared at the thick furious swirls of oil paint giving life to flowers in vases, the stormy night sky bursting with stars. I could see myself in Van Gogh's self-portrait. He was suffering a terrible pain he couldn't rationalise or understand. Perhaps just the pain of living. I would never be able to explain it. But I felt it. Vivienne stood beside me.

'You're crying,' she said. She pulled on my lapels and licked away my tears. 'I wanted to tell you something. I'm clean.'

'Clean?'

'I've kicked coke. I'm so happy.'

She led the way to the men's toilets where we made love against the wall in one of the cubicles. We could hear water flushing, the sound of men peeing against the urinals, the main door opening and closing. Her voice rose in a stifled cry as she climaxed. Everything was suddenly clear, her hiding that day in the wardrobe, the stomach cramps, the mood swings, Amsterdam.

We wandered among the crowds through the narrow alleyways of De Wallen, the red light district, where the prostitutes display themselves from behind glass windows. We stopped and she pointed at a transvestite.

'Do you fancy her?'

'With a tranny, I wonder who puts what into whom.'

She laughed. We walked on. We stopped at another window, a girl of about twenty with moon white skin and green eyes.

'I do envy them,' Vivienne said.

'You envy the idea, not the reality.'

'You're getting so clever. Why don't you kiss me?'

We kissed. Then she looked into my eyes.

'There in an innate pleasure in falling from grace,' she said. 'The feeling that you are doing wrong. Working girls are wise women. They know things.'

She could have been talking about me. Not that I was wise, or the girls in glass cages were wise. They fucked for money. The same as me. I didn't know if Vivienne was blind to this, or if it was all part of some complex game. The first time I went to her apartment, she gave me a cheque for £500. When I told her it was too much, she said: Not for a work of art in progress.

Anyone who had seen her lick away my tears in the Van Gogh museum would have seen two people in love. But Vivienne didn't believe in love. That was her problem.

24
CITY OF LOVE

Vivienne tapped the face of her watch as she observed me approach, out of breath and jogging at a steady pace. She was standing outside her building where a driver was loading a pair of Louis Vuitton suitcases into the back of a vehicle.

'You are a very naughty boy. I was about to leave without you,' she said. 'Did you remember your passport?'

'Oh my God, I don't think I did,' I replied. I ran through my pockets. 'No, hang on, here it is.'

'That's not funny.' She touched a fingertip to her cheek. 'You may kiss me.'

The second I did so, she moved away. I threw my gym bag in with the cases and we took off for London City Airport, a twelve mile journey that took an hour. When we arrived, we found Maggs and James Chipping in the lounge gathering up the free newspapers and magazines. On the floor, gripped between the Minister's polished brogues, was an official red box. He handed it to me.

'Take this, there's a good chap,' he said.

We walked through the security formalities to the loading bay and climbed the steps into an 8-seater Learjet. The engine was already running.

The Minister hooked wire-framed glasses over his ears and read from folders in his ministerial box. Vivienne and Maggs flicked through magazines and gossiped. I stretched out in the big pale cream leather seat. I was going up in the world. I had flown economy to the Canaries, first class to Amsterdam, but you can't beat a private jet. We buckled up for take-off. I gazed down at the slate grey English Channel until the plane climbed into the clouds and a male steward served coffee.

We were whisked through passport control at Paris Le Bourget. A porter with a full beard and white robes pushed the luggage on a trolley out to a waiting car and the wide roads took us into the city centre in forty minutes. Adjoining suites had been reserved at the *Hotel Meurice*. We went to our rooms to 'freshen up,' and dashed off to have lunch at *Les Deux Magots* where, according to Vivienne, Ernest Hemingway always hogged the stove in winter while he wrote his short stories.

'Writers have such cold souls,' Maggs said. 'Except you.'

'I'm just a dilettante,' Vivienne replied.

'Aren't we all,' added the Minister.

This was funny for some reason and they laughed.

Vivienne caught the eye of the waiter and pointed to the empty wine bottle. He touched his hand to his chest, gave a theatrical bow, and hurried off to fetch another.

Vivienne was all in white, a sheer blouse, narrow, calf-length pants, thick-soled trainers, a loose jacket. She was always chic. Now she was French chic with the addition of a red beret and round sunglasses. Heads turned. The way men smiled at her had less of a sexual connotation, more an appreciation of her beauty. She acknowledged the flattery by returning the smile and I understood why the City of Light was also the City of Love.

While Maggs and the Minister went to the Louvre, Vivienne and I raced off to the Latin Quarter to see The Panthéon, the resting place of Victor Hugo, the man who wrote *Les Misérables*.

'Critics always tell us this book and that book will change our lives,' she said. 'Only *Les Misérables* changed my life.'

'Mine, too,' I replied, and she looked back at me with a surprised expression.

'I changed from a socialite to a socialist.'

'You are being ironical?'

'No, I am not, actually. You always underestimate me.'

'That's not true. I think you're amazing.'

'No you don't.'

'I do. But you're hardly a revolutionary, Vivienne. I've seen a photograph of you with the Queen.'

'She's a sweetie.' She tapped the side of her head. 'I'm a revolutionary up here. Where it matters. You haven't kissed me since we arrived.'

'I thought I was in your bad books.'

'Are you?'

We kissed for the tourists.

We hailed a cab and the vehicle wriggled like an eel through the narrow streets to the Eiffel Tower. We chased up the first two floors then took the elevator to the top where Paris encircled us, the most beautiful city I had ever seen, not that I had seen that many. The driver had waited, doors open, moustache twitching. He kissed Vivienne's hand when she gave him €100 and he took off for our next destination as if his very life depended on it.

The launch waiting for us on the banks of the Seine was nothing like a fishing trawler. It was long, low, white and narrow with brass trim, wide windows and a crew in sparkling white uniforms. It even smelt good. Maggs and James were with several buttoned up couples, men in blazers, women with a disdainful air. Everyone knew everyone and everyone spoke French. I had no idea what they were talking about, but it sounded romantic.

We set off at a leisurely pace. A pair of seagulls stood on the stern rail watching to see what the propellers threw up to the surface. The sun caught the spray so that it shimmered like silver coins and the air had a distinctly French aroma, cologne, coffee and croissants. I was surprised to see so much activity on the river banks, cafés, stalls with paintings and antiques, booksellers.

A woman in a straw hat with a large brim who had seen me standing alone on deck left the salon and came to join me. She pointed at a church with a large dome and said something I didn't understand.

'I'm sorry, I don't speak French,' I said, and she looked mystified.

'Then you should learn,' she replied, and walked off again.

We arrived back at the *Meurice* at nine, leaving barely enough time for a quickie in the round bath before changing for dinner.

Vivienne wore a black leather pencil skirt with a zip up the front, a top consisting of leather straps and zips like a harness. In stilettos and dark glasses, she looked like an advert for BDSM. I wore a black suit and a thin black tie like a character from *Reservoir Dogs*. James Chipping was his debonair self in his white suit. Maggs was ultra-glam in a pink gown with her breasts exposed to full effect and an emerald necklace that matched her eyes.

Our table for six was in the back corner of the restaurant. J-J and Annabel rushed in with two security guards who sat at another table watching for paparazzi and public nuisances. J-J hated all that shit, but it was in the contract. After all the kissing and complimenting, he talked about his twin pit bulls – Mark and Bark – that he missed, his kids who were a pain in the ass, and his best friend who had run off with his wife.

James leaned across the table.

'When your best friend steals your wife, the best revenge is to let him keep her.'

'Yeah, fuck 'em.'

We laughed and drank wine.

J-J wasn't only shorter, he was ten year older than he appeared when he was on screen, but dressed young in ragged jeans, Converse All-Stars, a tee-shirt with the words 'I'm With Stupid,' and a black suit jacket with badges and stains. There was a smart-casual dress code, but it doesn't apply beyond a certain level of fame. You didn't notice J-J's clothes, you just recognised J-J. He had small perfect features, sparkling teeth, brown eyes with long lashes. He was a capable actor, but still it was hard to know why he had been picked out from the seven billion people on the planet to be a living god.

I gazed around the table. Annabel looked like a virgin sacrifice in a white dress with bare arms, legs and shoulders. Vivienne was erotica incarnate. Maggs had an air of excess and debauchery with her red hair shining beneath the chandeliers. Others dining at the *Meurice* that night must have gone to bed with sore necks from trying to peek at our table.

After wine at lunch, wine on the river and wine with dinner, I would have been happy to climb the stairs and call it a night. But that's the thing with the rich club, they have an energy gene. They never know when to stop. The plan had been to go on to the popular *Les Chandelles* in the Palais-Royal Quarter, but James insisted that it had become 'too popular with the plebs.' He had discovered a new venue beside the Bastille.

Everyone nodded in agreement. They hated repetition.

'I'm just going to powder my nose,' Annabel said, and the women laughed as they ran off to the loo.

'I think I'll do the same,' J-J said, and glanced at me.

'I'm all right,' I told him.

James sniffed the back of his hand as he looked at me across the table. 'You don't?'

'Rarely.'

'Good for you.'

'And you?'

'Aren't we obliged to try everything life has to offer?'

'Not everything,' I said, and he smiled. 'Do you mind if I ask you something, those papers you were reading on the plane, are they, like, government secrets?'

'You know you shouldn't ask,' he replied.

'I'm sorry…'

'The secret is there are no secrets. Only confusion.'

As the clock struck twelve, we climbed with the body-guards into a stretch limo that slid like a black moth through the darkened streets to a place where men with restless eyes and near naked girls stood in a line behind the velvet ropes that led to a door guarded by two gorillas in monkey suits. We were expected. James slipped money into each of their hands as we were ushered in.

He turned to me. 'Always be liberal with doormen, cabbies and head waiters,' he said, and smiled as he put his arm around my shoulder. He cast his eyes forward to J-J's retreating back and lowered his voice. 'He talks about wives and women, but he's rather partial to tall dark handsome men. As am I.'

'Not me,' I said.

'Oh, but I know that. I always know.'

We were led along an arched tunnel to an alcove shaped like an egg with a curved seat around a low table. I sat on the end, Vivienne at my side. Her eyes were coke bright. She had been clean for a week but couldn't resist temptation. She held my hand and seemed excited like a child at the circus. It was a circus.

Below us was an improvised stage where a skinny girl stripped from an elaborate gown and underwear with lots of straps and bows. She had tassels of crystal beads clamped to her flat chest that she jiggled about, the beads catching the light. Finally, she removed her knickers to reveal a penis that I had not been expecting and drew some applause from the audience hidden in dark eggs like our own.

We watched a woman with pendulous breasts beat a plump naked man with a pink feather boa. A girl balanced on her shoulders for a man to drink champagne from the cup of her open vagina. A man in a matelot shirt and naked from the waist down appeared on a unicycle carrying a large sign that read *Sourire* – smile. Three double-jointed girls in impish masks with red-painted skin presented oral sex in endless tortuous positions. Another girl appeared with a bowl of ping-pong balls that she inserted one at a time into her cleft before shooting them out into the darkness.

Some of the girls, I thought, were probably employed by the club and performed whatever sex acts were expected of them. The rest were members of the public who got their kicks being part-time performers. It was compelling but tiresome, less erotic than monotonous.

A waiter in a hood wearing nothing but a leather case around his genitals arrived with a dusty bottle that he cleaned then opened. He poured red wine from the bottle into a carafe and left us with six glasses. James removed his spectacles from a silver case, read the label, then placed the bottle back on the table. As J-J went to pour the wine from the carafe, James reached for his hand and stopped him.

'It is a 1947 Saint-Emilion,' he said. 'The wine has waited for us. Now we should wait for the wine. Let it breathe.'

'Hey, I like that.' J-J glanced at Annabel. 'We should try and get that in the script.'

'That will upset the applecart.'

She was sitting next to Vivienne, black and white, like yin and yang. Vivienne took Annabel's hand and pinned J-J with one of her forceful stares.

'Do you know who upset the applecart?' she asked and he shrugged.

'Search me, hon?'

'It was Eve.'

'Like in Adam and Eve?'

'It wasn't an apple she plucked in the Garden of Eden. Eve didn't limit herself to one desire, she had an entire basket of desires. It wasn't Adam that she wanted...'

'What did she want?' asked J-J, and Vivienne's eyes grew bigger as she stared back at him.

'Everything,' she replied.

The girls giggled and touched cheeks. They squirmed in their seats as if they couldn't sit still. They were coked up, happy to be with each other. The world about them was irrelevant and they disappeared together before James poured the wine.

'They have missed a treat,' he said, and Maggs shook her head.

'They have other treats in mind,' she told him.

We touched glasses. I tasted the wine and it streamed through me like a magic potion. Before I saw the paintings of Van Gogh, I didn't have a clue about art. I did not appreciate the subtlety of wine until that night below the cobblestone streets of Bastille when we drank Saint-Emilion bottled before I was born.

'Well?' asked James.

'Shit, man, it's something else,' J-J replied, and James looked at me.

'It's too good to describe,' I said.

'It is the taste of lust,' Maggs suggested, and James nodded in agreement.

'With an added hint of taboo.' He took another sip from his glass. 'Two centuries before Christ, the Romans worshipped Bacchus and created wines that freed them from all modesty and restraint. They stripped naked and took part in wild orgies.' He glanced at me again. 'The masters sampled the serving girls while the manservants sampled their wives.'

'You know something, there's a movie in this.'

'If you need a consultant, J-J, I would be happy to oblige.' James raised his glass. 'Drink up, life is too short for anything but the best.'

At that moment, two naked girls appeared to offer relief massage. James took the hand of one of them. He spoke like a schoolteacher.

'Why are they here? Why are we here? What was the purpose of the Bacchanal? Being dressed is civilized. Being naked is a challenge to civilisation. The purpose of the orgy is to break down traditional attitudes in order to open the mind and live life free of limitations and rules.'

'I'll drink to that,' said Maggs.

'You always do, my dear.'

We finished the bottle and left the table. Maggs and James went one way, I went the other with J-J. He stayed close by my side, whispering comments about the other clubbers, the film, his fucking lawyer who was killing him. He was one of the most famous people in the world and acted as if we were best mates. It made me feel special. People recognised him, but the etiquette was for patrons to leave celebrities in peace, and there were security men to deal with any who might forget.

We passed below a row of three arches. Standing on plinths before each one was a naked girl in a blindfold, legs spread, arms stretched and chained to the wall. The girls were positioned at a height where you could lick their shaved clefts as you passed. That's what we did, and I thought how pleased they would have been had they known J-J that night had appraised their juices.

We paused at a chamber occupied by men in leather with instruments of punishment and pleasure. In another, we watched a scrum of skinny girls with perfect figures being pierced by men with grotesque bodies. It's odd, but when you see them all thrown together they stop appearing gross and incongruous. It was humanity doing what was human. We observed couples and groups engaged in recreating every position in the Kama Sutra. Witnessing others getting off was tedious to me and I had a feeling it held little interest to J-J. He was there because he was there, doing what big stars are expected to do. They buy islands, adopt African babies and want to save the planet.

We moved on to a high-ceilinged arena where girls in feathered costumes like birds of paradise flew through the air between trapezes. Occasionally, a girl dropped from the trapeze into the arms of one of the men gazing up from below and he would carry her off.

J-J glanced back, then took my arm as he whispered. 'I fucking hate those two guys, they're killing me.'

The bodyguards with their contractual obligations were behind us, enjoying the perks of their profession. I was glad it was J-J they were watching not me.

We moved on. There were surprises around every corner. Pleasure was the drug of choice. We believed things could only get better and nothing mattered more than getting rich and getting off. James had talked about the Roman love of orgies. Two thousand years later, we had turned full circle and I had a feeling that night that our society would go the same way and collapse in ruins.

We went down a flight of stairs and entered a round room with a domed roof. The light was golden. Classical music played. At the centre, there was a shallow, circular pool surrounded by a wide bench covered in what appeared to be white fur. In the pool, naked girls swam, kissed, made love. There were a few men sitting on the edge displaying their erections, their legs dangling in the water. Girls paused to give them a lick and swam on. There were alcoves for copulating couples you could watch from the gallery above where you sat at tables with drinks and snacks.

Maggs and James were at one of the tables. Vivienne and Annabel sat on the edge of one of the niches. I wasn't sure if they had seen us, but a moment after we appeared, Vivienne dropped her clothes and descended a ramp to the pool. Annabel came towards us.

As we climbed the stairs to the gallery, J-J said to her that they should bring the film director to the club to open his mind.

'Reptiles never change their minds,' she replied.

He looked back at me. 'I fucking love you English, you always say weird stuff.'

They continued the film talk as we joined Maggs and James. I watched Vivienne. She ignored the erections being proffered and swam back and forth in slow strokes like a beautiful fish. We ordered a bottle of wine and crêpes suzette. The wine was still sleeping in the carafe when J-J left the table and went back downstairs.

The crêpes came. James poured the wine.

'How are you enjoying Paris?' Maggs asked.

'It's special.'

'It is. We must do this more often.'

Vivienne must have left the pool. I didn't see her and expected her to join us at any moment. That moment didn't come. We finished the food and wine. I led the way down from the gallery. As I turned the corner of the stairs, I saw Vivienne in the alcove immediately below where we had been sitting. She was in her favourite position, naked on all fours. J-J was ramming into her from behind, his frayed jeans about his ankles.

25
GLOBAL WORLD

It was autumn. Leaves were falling from the trees. The Ladies were back from the Mediterranean for a new round of cocktail parties, receptions, art shows, auctions, black tie dinners, where I played the extra man, the walker.

Vivienne had stayed in Paris with Annabel. Several weeks went by, then I received a text saying: Why haven't you called me? I called immediately.

'Vivienne.'

'Ben.'

'I got your text.'

'Do you love me?'

'Probably.'

'Now I'm sad,' she said. 'Do you know what love means?'

'No, I don't think I do.'

'Nobody does, except the honey bees when they smell pollen.' She laughed. 'Love smells of moonlight and old photographs. Love is the sound of your name being called by your lover.'

'Vivienne,' I called.

'Now I'm happy,' she said. 'I missed you. Are you at Southley?'

'Yes, till five.'

'That is so perfect. Come after.'

When I arrived at the studio, the monk's costume she had bought in Amsterdam was hanging on the open door with the word 'Change' on a slip of paper pinned to the cloth. A chair had been placed beside the door where I left my clothes. I stepped into the habit, pulled the hood over my head and tied the rope about my waist.

There was no light except the dying day through the tall windows. She appeared at the far end of the studio, a holy sister in black, her face framed in white, as pretty as sin. When I approached, she darted between the marble sculptures. I chased her, flicking at her fleeing back with the rope belt. She wanted to be beaten. I was happy to oblige. Flogging Vivienne as a nun with a rope or beating her dressed as an angel with the flat of my hand ended the same way – between the sheets. Sex had become the most tedious aspect of my life, but I never tired of making love with Vivienne.

We showered. She was chatty, content. She had fallen in love with the southern coast of Turkey. It was like Greece before the tourists. The people weren't money grubbers. The food was better. The wine was darling. She blow dried, then secured her hair with a black velvet band. I loved watching her. It was like a ballet the way she bent to slip into her panties, her arms coiling to snap into her bra. Every gesture was precise, calculated. I zipped her into a black gown. From a drawer, she took a pale blue leather case containing a diamond necklace and earrings. I hooked the necklace in place.

'You look wonderful.'

'It's just a mask,' she said.

'No, it's you.'

'Is it?'

I drove to Groucho's. Annabel and J-J were at a table next to the bar. Their film was being edited in London and that night they were appearing together on a TV chat show. J-J poured champagne. He put his hand on mine as I reached for the glass. He spoke with a polished English accent.

'Be patient. The drink has waited for you, now you must wait for the drink.'

We laughed. We all had different memories from that night together in Paris.

We had only been at Groucho's for ten minutes when a messenger came for Vivienne. A car was waiting.

'Life is just one thing after another,' she said, addressing Annabel. 'The American Embassy. I promised daddy.'

Every man watched as she left the bar. The women, too. I didn't know why she hadn't told me she had another engagement. Then, why should she? I had no idea why in Paris she'd had sex with J-J for me and the whole world to see. Girls were fucking in every corner, under every spotlight. But why Vivienne? Why on all fours like a dog in the park? The scene had stuck in my head like a picture on the wall. I was envious, resentful, and had no right nor reason to be so. I told myself I didn't care about her and was angry with myself because I did.

I finished my drink and drove home. Kelly cooked linguine with scallops, brown butter and peas. I opened a bottle of Chablis Fourchaume. Life is too short to drink bad wine. Ollie had started at Willington and Kelly was eager to promote her 'candid' family photography.

'I don't want to be too forward and appear pushy, and I don't want to hold back and let the chance go.'

'Use your intuition. Wait till it feels right.'

'What if it never feels right?'

'When your desires are strong enough, you'll know when it's right.'

She sipped her wine. I had lit candles. She smiled and, at that moment, it could have been Vivienne sitting across the table from me.

I put the dishes in the dishwasher and turned on the TV in time to watch J-J and Annabel talking up their film. J-J told the chat show host that he had picked up the phone the moment he finished reading the screenplay to call his agent. He told him not to look at any other projects. He had found the role he was born to play.

Annabel dabbed at her eyes and nodded in agreement. The film was more than just a standard rom-com, it had heart, a message. It was a film for today. She said how lucky she had been to work with two of the 'greatest talents' in Hollywood, and how they had helped her in the challenging role of falling in love with them both. She was funny, witty, adorable, self-effacing. The normally caustic host wiped away a tear. The audience clapped.

'We'll have to see that one,' Kelly said.

'You know, I know both of them?'

'Is there anyone you don't know?' she replied.

I continued to provide my services to Caroline, Maggs and other Committee Ladies. I didn't see Angela Hartley, except on the news. She had got into the habit of waving her finger at rival politicians to make her points. One of the newspapers had dubbed her Lady Finger in a headline, and the moniker had stuck. I had been afraid there was going to be some fallout after our spat, but I kept touching wood and my luck seemed to be holding.

A week before Christmas, Rufus invited me to White's, a gentlemen's club in St James's, where I saw Prince Charles having lunch with a man with a loud voice and lots of white hair. I was at a table with Rufus and two of his polo playing chums, Sebastian – Bash – and Carlos de la Cueva. They had all invested in property and couldn't make up their minds whether it was a good time to buy or time to sell.

'In a property deal, the seller always loses,' said Carlos, and it seemed oddly prophetic.

We ordered the dish of the day, Yorkshire grouse with parsnip and bread sauce. Bash complained that the meat was tough, to which Carlos de la Cueva said game birds only taste well when flavoured with the oil from your own gun.

We raised our glasses to toast this claim.

The grouse had a strong, smoky taste, and it was the first time I had eaten roast potatoes as good as those my Gran used to make. I glanced at the royal guest across the dining hall and it struck me that in Gran's worldview there was a glaring contradiction. She was a rebel, dyed in the wool Labour, anti-establishment, but in the family photograph album I had inherited there was a picture of Charles and Lady Diana.

Next time I had a free moment, I went to the crematorium to leave a bunch of flowers on the grassy knoll where Gran's ashes were supposed to have been buried, the first time I had done that since she'd died.

At Christmas, I visited The Lodge with some new books and board games. We spent the holidays with mum in Lowestoft, then took the kids back to the Canary Islands, which I had promised but could ill-afford. The children deserved a treat, I had seen so little of them, and I needed a rest.

The closing months of 2007 had been a struggle. Josh, one of my tenants, an IT graduate who had been working as a security analyst in a software start-up, lost his job and scarpered back to Liverpool leaving two months' rent unpaid. It was another two months before the agent found a new tenant, a Nigerian girl studying to be a beauty therapist at Guildford College. It was short term, but she paid in advance to the end of her course in July.

I had worked most rest days to cover our costs and, with Dee-Dee, battled with Christian and Anastasia for a share of the Four-Hands treatment. Denny Doyle had left Southley to work in

Dubai and had not been replaced. We were still busy, but change was in the air and Dee-Dee needed those tips, the same as me. Thanks to Rudy Johnson, she had got a mortgage on her own flat and had learned how to turn every massage into a seduction. We were living the working-class dream. We may have sold our souls to the sex trade, but we were on the property ladder.

It was at the beginning of 2008, when I learned that the world had become 'global.' I heard the word on the BBC news used to describe corporations, banking, finance, the housing market. In the United States, mortgage defaults began to rise as property prices started to fall. Lenders had allowed people with insufficient assets to take out what they called subprime mortgages. When they couldn't keep up the payments, the banks put in claims that drove insurance companies into bankruptcy, pushing down stock market prices in Wall Street and London. It wasn't a tidal wave, but Josh, my tenant, had lost his job when the ripples reached Guildford.

When I asked Rudy if the same could happen here, he just laughed. He was as buoyant as ever, his smile gleaming after a session with Dee-Dee. Business goes through natural adjustments. Foreign investors were flocking to London, Russians, Malaysians, Chinese. The housing market had become 'over-heated,' but it would settle down and continue its 'upward trajectory.'

'Every adversity, every failure, every heartache carries with it the seed of an equal or greater benefit,' he said, quoting Napoleon Hill. 'If there's a dip in house prices, that's the time to buy.'

Rudy was like cocaine. I felt a lift when I saw him, but drug highs never last. I was grateful that my flats were occupied and I carried on like the rest of the global world in an impassive daze. I played Pink Floyd on the stereo and gunned the black Range Rover down the outside lane at stupid speeds. I manipulated every woman who entered the massage suite and, when the treatment ended in a moment of ecstasy, left her with the impression that it had never happened before. Then I went through spells of hating myself for being a user. I'd try playing it straight, only to watch my tips decline like the stock market.

I told myself I wasn't trapped, but I was. I had grown used to providing my family with a certain standard of living. George would be following Ollie into Willington in the autumn. When Claire started taking ballet lessons, Vivienne sent her two outfits in pink and white from Harrods. Of course, they didn't cost anything. They were on someone's account. But now Claire had found where she belonged: on stage, the prima ballerina. The lessons meant another weekly bill.

Vivienne had bought a rundown Ottoman mansion on the Turkish Mediterranean. I managed to get three free days by working double-shifts and told Kelly I was going to treat a patient with a slipped disc. One more lie hardly mattered. I flew alone on a private plane to Antalya. Vivienne was waiting at the airport. She was all in white, a kaftan, harem pants, her hair wrapped in a turban, a turquoise necklace to match her eyes.

We drove through country lanes between fruit fields to a house with a walled courtyard where workmen were painting, cleaning, putting new beams on the roof. The site manager was a middle-aged man with sharp brown eyes and a cigar stuck in the corner of his mouth like an old gangster. When Vivienne stepped from the car, he bowed low, not in a humble way, but an old-fashioned way that showed respect. She had learned a few words of Turkish. Whatever it was she said made him laugh and he bowed again.

When she introduced us, he looked deep into my eyes as if he were her father and crushed my fingers as we shook hands.

One of the workmen carried my bag upstairs to a room with faded wall hangings, heavy furniture and yellowing photographs of soldiers on horseback with fezzes and long rifles. Vivienne's apartment in London was white, clean, minimalist. The house with its view of the sea and Greek islands dotted along the horizon was the opposite. Everything needed to be cleaned and restored, but she was content, more herself outside England with its invisible pressure, of things you do and don't do. In Turkey, we weren't upper-class and working-class. We were just two more foreigners.

In the bazaar in Bodrum, we drank hot sweet tea from small glasses – burning our fingertips. She bought brass candlesticks and slippers with curled up toes. We made love in an old bed that creaked with the moon watching through the open window. We drove to small villages and sat at rickety tables beneath giant fig trees. We drank cold beer and visited the Sanctuary of Apollo. It was mid-July, hot and dusty.

'Roman travellers came here to see the oracle and divine the future.'

'Like us?' I said.

'But we don't have to worry about the Persians.'

She took my hand and we ran up the temple steps. The marble columns were warm to the touch and golden in the sunset. We stood close but didn't kiss. She was mindful of the customs. I could smell wood smoke and roasting meat.

'I'm starving,' I said.

'You eat like a fisherman.'

'What do fishermen eat?'

'The wind,' she replied.

We drove into Bodrum and ate lamb with grape sauce. We walked around the harbour looking at the boats. She pulled close and held me tightly. It felt like the first time we met, magical, intense, confusing. Vivienne knew everything about me, who I was, what I did. But I was just a single thread in the tapestry of her life. I knew almost nothing about her. I would search the internet and discover obscure articles she had written for Sunday magazines, the death of the honey bee, English teeth, the

Dragon's Blood trees on the lost island of Socotra with herself in Arabic dress pictured beneath those rare trees found nowhere else on earth.

The following morning, we rented a boat and sailed to the island of Kos to see the ruins of Neratzia, a Knights Templar fortress. We stood on the battlements and stared back across the sea to Turkey. I read the brochure, but the history meant nothing to me. I didn't know the before and after, the connections. I had thought it clever to avoid the lessons at school and regretted it. I didn't want my children to make the same mistake.

26
EVERYONE WEARS A MASK

I flew back alone to London and didn't see Vivienne again until the end of July. I had been invited to a masked ball at an estate in Scotland and we met at City Airport. We took off in the Learjet with Maggs, James Chipping, Maddy Page, Zara Swift and two men I had never met before. One was a French politician, loud and opinionated. The other was a Queen's Counsel, softly spoken, extremely polite and famous for taking on human rights cases.

We arrived in the early evening at a castle that looked as if it had been built in the time of King Arthur. It was huge with square towers, a moat and a drawbridge. There must have been fifty bedrooms, but there were many more guests and our party shared a room overlooking dense pine woods rising into irregular mountains.

We changed into costumes. Vivienne was in ballerina mode, a black swan with a black feather mask. Maggs was the perfect Marie Antoinette with a big dress, big hair, an elaborate mask, her bust like a cake straight from the oven. Maddy Page and Zara Swift were limber and feline in animal heads and body-paint. The French politician dressed as the musketeer d'Artagnan with a floppy hat and sword. The lawyer was a graceful Harlequin and James Chipping an unlikely Superman.

Vivienne never travelled light and had brought in a large trunk a costume for me consisting of a white tailed suit, white shirt, white shoes and a white tie. She painted my face white and I looked out through the slits of a white mask she buckled at the back of my head. On top of my head, she placed a white top hat.

'Why the white suit?' I asked her.

'Because it's you,' she said. 'You don't wear a mask to hide yourself, but to reveal who you really are.'

'And you're a black swan?'

'Sometimes I'm a white swan.'

As the sun went down, we trooped down the stairs and crossed the drawbridge. Yellow lanterns hung in the trees and nude girls in fox masks and foxtail butt-plugs streaked through the shadows. They were hunted by packs of men who ravished them, then sent them on their way to be caught and ravaged again. It was rapid, exhilarating. There were whoops and whistles. The French politician joined the pack and a man in a scarlet jacket blew a brass horn every time a girl was caught and spread out on her back.

'Don't you want to join in?' Vivienne asked.

'No. Do you?' I said.

'Do you want me to?'

'No.'

She lifted her mask. 'We are here at the same time. It is not the same as being here together.'

'I know that.'

She wandered off with Maddy and Zara. Superman appeared at my side as they vanished from view.

'Powerful men need a woman as a sign of their power,' he said. 'Strong women don't need a man. She either wants him or she doesn't.'

'Meaning?' I asked.

'There is never one meaning to anything, Ben.'

We watched as the foxes were caught and the hounds gave them what they had been paid to provide – £5,000 each for the night, according to James. The girls were Russian, he said, new on the scene, blondes with perfect figures and white skin covered in mud and bruises. We cheered as they skipped, tails bobbing, back across the drawbridge into the castle.

The scene was something you might see in a film set in the past or the future. The masks had freed us from normal conventions and turned the crowd into a noisy mob. Men swaggered around with swords, courtiers and cavaliers from various ages. Others were relaxed in leather and chains. There were vampires, the Phantom of the Opera, a Chinese man in a red sarong, a man in a George Bush mask, perhaps it was George Bush? There jesters and clowns, a hangman and an Inquisitor, both in hoods. The women were more exotic, a flock of angels, French maids, courtesans, birds of paradise, the Queen of Hearts. Some of the guests had gone all out with costumes that were stunning and extravagant. Others, girls mostly, were more eye-catching in nothing but their masks.

The moon was rising. We went back into the castle. Musicians in black wearing masks from the new film *V for Vendetta* played and guests danced beneath ancient candelabra in the baronial hall with armour decorating the walls. The air smelled of candle-wax and marijuana. Young men and women in erotic costume sidled through the masquerade with trays of drinks and hors d'oeuvres. A midget in the robes of a bishop moved through the hall with lines of cocaine in neat rows on a white mortarboard hat balanced cautiously on his head. In his hand he held a goblet containing short white straws.

We stopped to watch the George Bush look alike ramming into a girl dressed as an Arabic princess.

'How very apt,' James said.

I had been introduced once as a highwire walker, so it came as no surprise when James presented me as an MI6 agent to a

Russian woman dressed as a princess and holding a mask on a stick. She asked me if I had any new information on Aleksandr Litvinenko, the former Russian security officer who had died from radioactive poisoning – murdered, it was thought, by the Russian secret service.

'Not at present,' I said.

'Insider knowledge is like insider trading,' James added, 'and best not spoken of.'

'The hypocrisy of you English!' she snapped, before swirling off in her ball gown.

'The Russians aren't coming,' he whispered. 'They're here, and they're here to stay.'

We moved on. I listened as a red devil in a long cape and horns said the war in Iraq was going so poorly, Labour would soon be out on their ears. His companion, the hangman, raised his glass and his voice thundered through his hood. 'We'll be able to get rid of the damned health service when we're back, dumb the thing down and sell it off piecemeal.'

They clinked glasses and I wondered if Vivienne was right, that their costumes revealed who they really were.

Apart from the tall Russian girls, there were oligarchs, cabinet ministers, MPs, members of the House of Lords, the titled, and those who could be described as celebrities were at the ball in their private capacity as members of the elite. We spoke to two American bankers, new to London, who had paid £10,000 to be invited. They had not come for the sex, it was optional, but to make contacts. What everyone had in common was the knowledge that networks which begin at private schools continue at masked balls where you can deny you were ever there.

Why was I there? I wasn't accompanying Vivienne or Maggs. I was a bit player, an extra. I was a trusted gigolo, trusted to perform, trusted to keep my mouth shut, trusted to have had regular checks for HIV and sexually transmitted diseases. Which I did. I was trusted to take the cash, live the life, lie to my family. I was a male prostitute adding a little balance to the legion of young girls drafted in to open their legs for the rich and famous.

The hall slowly emptied. People wandered upstairs. In every room I saw mating couples, threesomes, moresomes. I saw a girl on all fours giving head to a flabby old guy in a mask with a long nose while another flabby old guy dressed as the Marquis de Sade was giving it to her from behind. Similar scenes were repeated in one room after the after. I saw Vivienne whipping a woman in red. When she caught my eye, it occurred to me how easy I was to spot, the tall man in white in the gloom of the orgy.

I recognised Angela Hartley by the seven moles that formed the shape of the Big Dipper on her upper thigh. In saw Maddy and Zara like a pair of cats lapping at the genitals of Viking in a horned metal mask. The midget with the head tray continued to circle and I wasn't surprised to see Flippo – Filippo Borghese Pecci – dressed as a razor blade.

'Is that you?' he said. 'You look so classy.'

'It's only a mask,' I replied.

He laughed and gazed around the room. 'This is what it must have been like in the last days of Rome.'

He took the hand of the Queen of Hearts and they wandered off. If I was there to entertain, I wasn't very entertaining. When sex is your living, an orgy is overkill. I drank a lot. I descended the long flight of stairs and crossed the drawbridge into the quiet of the trees. Nothing stirred. There were no birds. Perhaps they had shot them all.

The silence was broken as a car started and I watched two cones of light move through the woods and vanish into the distance. It was a clear starry night like you get sometimes when you are out at sea laying nets and life for a few moments is in prefect harmony. After my dad died, I often went down to the harbour with his old pair of binoculars to study the boats moving across the horizon. I knew he had drowned. I went to the funeral. I shook hands with the fishermen who had tried to save him. But I had got it into my mind it could have been a mistake, that somebody else was in the coffin, and my dad was on board one of those boats finally coming home.

When I returned to the castle, a lot of people were sleeping, drugged, drunk, sated. In some rooms, they carried on eking out vague pleasures from the dead hours after the musicians stopped playing. Vivienne was wearing her black strap-on which she had inserted into Superman while he bent over the groin of the Harlequin.

She waved her fingers for me to come closer. She slipped her tongue into my mouth through the slit in the mask, then whispered in my ear.

'I love you.'

It was the saddest thing anyone had ever said to me.

The orgy went on all night. The costumes lost their elegance in the light of day and most people had abandoned their masks. Tables were erected in the baronial hall where a traditional English breakfast was served.

We were due to fly back to London at four that afternoon, allowing me to get home and back to Southley the following day. When we arrived at the airport, we learned that the pilot, a man of my age, had suffered a heart attack and had been rushed to the nearest hospital. Another pilot was on the way to Edinburgh by train, and we would leave as soon as he arrived.

This was an amusing turn of events for the rest of the group. They enjoyed the unexpected. But it meant I would be away for an extra day. I called Kelly first, then Bethany to explain what had happened.

'I'll see you when you deign to appear,' Bethany said, and put the phone down.

I arrived back at work a day late, the first time it had happened, and Bethany behaved as if I had molested one of the clients.

'Tell me again what happened, I don't think I heard you properly?' she said.

'I was at a party in Scotland. The pilot had a heart attack...'

'The pilot? I suppose you were with your posh friends?'

'It's not like that.'

'You really ought to get over yourself. You aren't even qualified.'

'I've been qualified enough for the last two years. Nobody has more repeat bookings than me.'

'You obviously haven't noticed that Christian is catching up. He's become very popular.' She took a long breath through her nose. 'Your bookings are down...'

'Bookings at the hotel are down...'

'Every week they go down.'

'They are going down for everyone. It's the economy, stupid.'

She went red and wobbled on her heels. 'How dare you,' she shot back. 'Get your things and get out. You're fired.'

It was all so sudden, unexpected. I felt relieved as if a giant burden had been lifted from my shoulders. We stood staring at each other. I could have apologised. I didn't mean what I'd said. It was just a phrase I'd heard. But I didn't apologise. I was fed up with being in competition with Christian, the Viking, fed up with the health checks, fed up with selling myself to old women so they would give me money. It was soul destroying. I drove out of the gates at Southley that morning and felt happy for the first time in ages.

The feeling only lasted two days. The Nigerian student who had rented the flat had finished her course and left Guildford. The property remained empty and the agent said there was little chance of finding another tenant during the summer. 'Problem is,' he said, 'they've flung up so many new flats there's no one to fill them.'

My regular clients left for the Mediterranean immediately after the ball. When they got back after the summer, I planned to give them more attention and felt optimistic about building up my private practise.

I gave Pete Taylor a foot massage and told him I'd lost my job. He shook his head.

'Not the best of times to do that, mate. Unemployment's going go through the roof.'

'All the time you've been predicting a crash, the economy's just gone up and up.'

'That's right, son. The higher you go, the further you fall.'

I started jogging again in Crane Park. I had more time for the children. But the lines came back to the corners of Kelly's eyes as our savings went into paying the mortgage on an empty flat. She couldn't comprehend why I had given up my job a month before George was about to join Ollie at Willington. I tried to explain, but never found the right words. There was nothing to be gained by making a confession – Maggs had said once it was just a form of boasting – and, anyway, the truth wasn't just sleazy, it was unbelievable.

In the previous two years, I had had sex with more than two thousand women. I didn't want to do that anymore. I told Kelly I had left Southley – I never admitted I was sacked – because I couldn't stand being at the beck and call of spoiled hotel guests when there were a lot of ordinary working people in need of my skills.

While I built up my private business, I intended to return to St Mary's University, retrain as a physiotherapist, then work in the NHS. When I went to the office, I was shocked to discover that in the last three years the entire system had changed. You now needed A-levels to apply for courses, sports therapy as well as physiotherapy. I did not have A-levels and it would take two years to get them, that's if I passed.

That wasn't the only blow to come in September. I already had one empty flat when Stephanie, the social worker who had been in the other flat since it first went on the market, got married to a widower with two teenaged children and moved in with him. I sold the Range Rover to keep up the payments.

The previous year, in September 2007, my regular clients had called me when they returned after the summer. In September 2008, I had to call them. Maggs was busy. Rufus had gone to live in Los Angeles with Annabel. I had never understood their relationship and probably never would. Kate had taken Lord Aberstone to a cancer clinic in Australia. Caroline and her husband were building a hotel in Agadir. Vivienne was still in Turkey. Finally, I called her.

'Ben. How are you? Did you have a lovely summer?'

'Not exactly. I'm not at Southley anymore.'

'So I hear. That's wonderful. When you burn bridges it lights the way ahead.'

'That's one way to put it.'

'It's the only way, Ben.' She paused. Her tone changed. 'I spoke to Angela the other day, your remember her?'

'Of course.'

'By all accounts that Norwegian boy, what's his name, Christian, has become her new pet.'

'Pet?'

'You know Angela. She's always so amusing.'

'I'm sure he's doing a good job.'

'But it will never be quite the same, though, will it? It's like losing a tooth.'

I wasn't sure what she meant and didn't ask. I remembered when I had first met the Ladies of the Committee. It had felt as if I was being interviewed to replace someone. Now I was being replaced. I heard someone calling her, a man with an American accent.

'I'd better go,' I said. 'I hope to see you when you get back.'

'Of course you will.'

The line went dead.

Every night, the BBC reported an unending succession of downturns and disasters. Debts were being measured in trillions of dollars and I never could work out who had loaned those trillions or how they could ever be paid back. On 15 September, the investment bank Lehman Brothers filed for bankruptcy. It was the result of the subprime mortgage crisis in the United States and shockwaves reverberated across the world. The 'global' banks that were too big to fail had failed. Millionaires lost everything and killed themselves.

Pete was right. More than one million people in the United Kingdom were soon to be unemployed. I was one of them.

Vivienne called me about a week later. It was a Saturday afternoon. Kelly had taken the children to a birthday party and I heard the roar of Vivienne's Ferrari as she spoke.

'I'll be with you in a couple of minutes. I have to see you,' she said.

She was walking down the path a few minutes later. I opened the door and we gazed at each other across the threshold. She was wearing an A-line white dress, her hair thrown back by the wind.

'Are you going to invite me in?'

She stepped inside. We kissed. Her lips were dry. She took my hand and led me straight upstairs to the bedroom.

'My shoulders are so tense,' she said.

'Vivienne, Kelly will be back any minute.'

She removed her dress. She was deeply tanned and wasn't wearing underwear. She stood across the room in the light from the window, outrageous, irresistible. I was stupid. I was a bastard. Two years of sex on a daily basis had ended in a long barren summer while Kelly adjusted to our new situation. I was like a junkie with my drug of choice. I was drawn to Vivienne by some sort of madness. She pulled off my clothes. We fell across the bed. She dug her nails in my back.

'Ouch...'

'A little pain, you know you want it.'

We didn't hear the door open downstairs. Kelly had forgotten something and must have seen the Ferrari outside the house when she returned to get it. She came quietly up the stairs into the bedroom. I am not sure how long we continued making love before we noticed her standing there.

'It's only sex, Kelly,' Vivienne said.

'You fucking bitch. Get out of my house.'

'There's no need to be rude.'

Vivienne stepped from the bed and stood there for several seconds. Then she slipped into her dress. She looked from Kelly back at me.

'I have something for you. It's in the car.'

There was confusion and hatred in Kelly's eyes. She was trembling.

'I'm sorry,' I said.

I followed Vivienne downstairs and up the path.

'I'm never going to see you again, am I?' I said.

'Probably not, no,' she replied.

'You said you loved me.'

She smiled. 'You shouldn't take those things literally. Words are only words.'

She reached into the car and gave me a white box. She then folded into the driving seat, the engine roared like an aeroplane and she took off, gaining speed and vanishing around the first corner.

I opened the box. Inside, wrapped in bubble paper, was the cast of my cock. I put it back in the box and dropped it in the bin.

Kelly didn't speak to me for several weeks. I apologised and kept apologising. There was no question of my moving out. I had nowhere to go. Neither did she. We had three children. I followed in the wake of Lehman Brothers and filed for bankruptcy when I fell behind with the payments on our two flats. It was a relief to lose them.

A week or so before Christmas, I was in Twickenham reading ads in the window at the newsagents when I heard a voice out of the past.

'Hello, mate, haven't seen you since last Christmas.'

It was Vinnie Castro. We gave each other a man hug.

'Good to see you, Vinnie, what's up?'

'You know, same old, same old.'

I laughed. 'How's Marley these days?'

'Living the dream. His mum in Jamaica died. He moved over there. He's got a little juice bar on the beach.'

'I'm pleased for him. That's what he always wanted.'

'How about you, Ben, still coining it in?'

'I wish. I'm looking for a job.'

'You serious?'

'True as I stand here.'

'We need someone at The Lodge, if you're up for it.'

'I'm up for it.'

He smiled. We shook hands.

'I'll see you Monday,' he said.

91291366R00177

Made in the USA
Middletown, DE
29 September 2018